Capable Citizens and Improvident Democrats

The Scottish Electoral System 1884–1929

Michael Dyer

SCOTTISH CULTURAL PRESS

Also published by Scottish Cultural Press:

Men of Property and Intelligence: The Scottish Electoral System prior to 1884, Michael Dyer (1 898218 22 6)

Jacobite Risings in Britain: 1689–1746, Bruce Lenman (1 898218 20 X)

Jacobite Clans of the Great Glen: 1650–1784, Bruce Lenman (1 898218 19 6)

Parish Life in Eighteenth-Century Scotland: A Review of the Old Statistical Account, Maisie Steven (1 898218 28 5)

Scottish Lifestyle 300 Years Ago, Helen & Keith Kelsall (1 898218 06 4)

Scottish Burgh Surveys, Historic Scotland [for full details contact SCP]

First published 1996
Scottish Cultural Press
PO Box 106, Aberdeen AB11 7ZE
Tel: 01224 583777
Fax: 01224 575337

British Library Cataloguing in Publication Data
A catalogue record for this book is available from the British Library

ISBN: 1 898218 23 4

Printed and bound by BPC-AUP Aberdeen Ltd

Contents

List of Tables

Acknowledgements

The author wishes to thank Pamela Strang, Dr Lawrence McLean, Dept of Geography, Aberdeen University, and Ronald Anderson of *The Herald* for their help in the production of this book.

The author also acknowledges with thanks the financial assistance received from the Carnegie Trust for the Universities of Scotland.

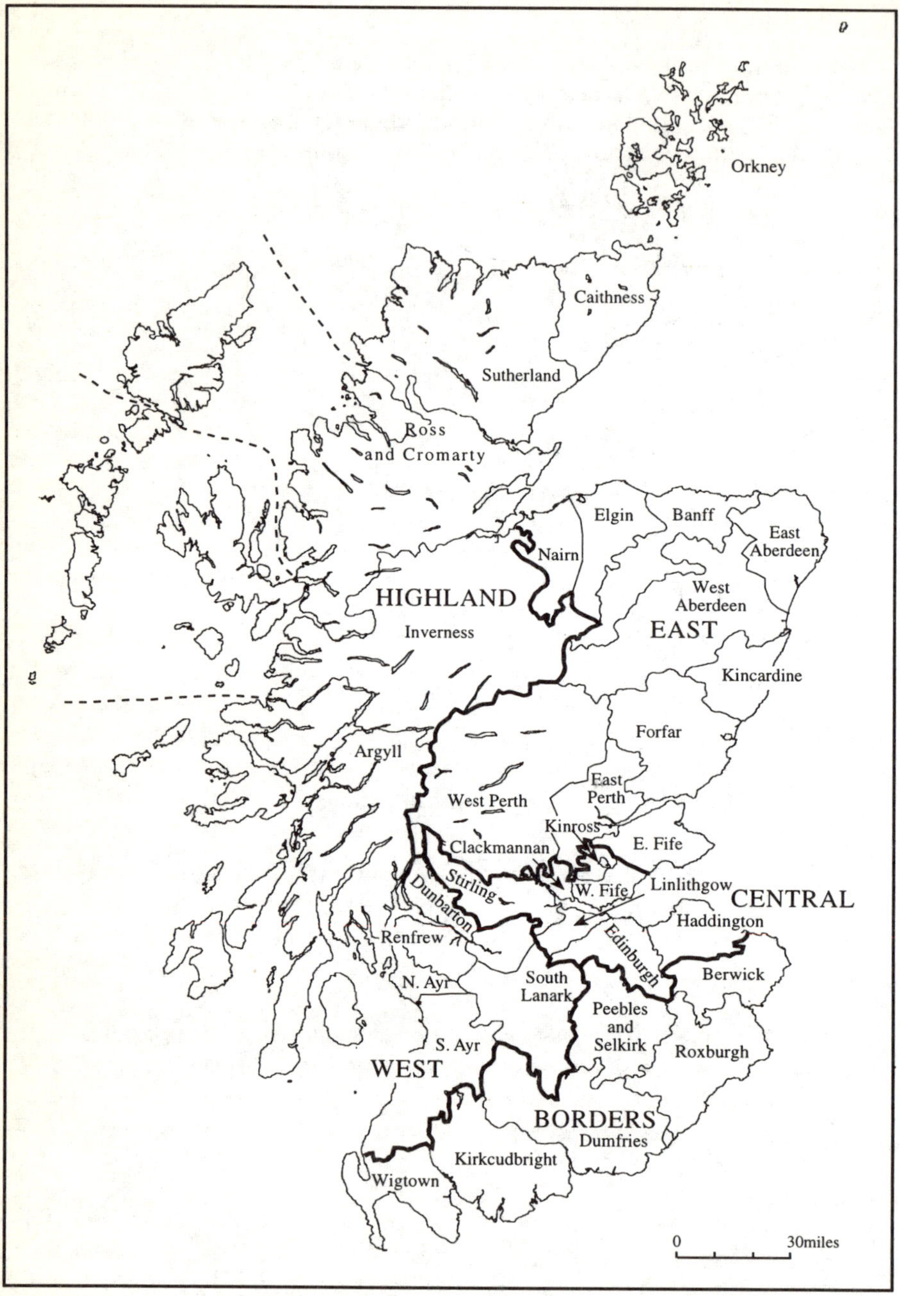

Scottish County Constituencies 1885–1918

Definition of Regions

Any system of geo-political regionalisation is likely to produce a disputed classification on both geographical and political grounds, and this scheme is no exception. The task is particularly difficult when searching for a system sufficiently robust to cover a lengthy period, because economic and political change suggest different classificatory schemes at different times. As far as possible, for comparative purposes, I have sustained the framework adopted in *Men of Property and Intelligence*, though in analysing voting behaviour I have removed Ayrshire and Bute from Central and placed them together with the inner Clydeside counties in a new group called West. The reason for this somewhat confusing manoeuvre is that while Ayrshire and Bute share with Lanarkshire, Dunbartonshire and Renfrewshire the political consequences of the home rule crisis, they are isolated from the impact an expanding Glasgow had on changes to the electoral system.

A second problem is that some burgh districts, 1885–1918, have their constituent parts in different regions. In Chapter 2, where they are so dispersed, I have divided their influence proportionate to their share of their respective District's electorate in each region. In Chapter 4, however, where such fine adjustments are not possible, Districts of Burghs have been allocated to those regions in which a majority of their electors resided.

Briefly the rationale behind the system is as follows:

The four major cities merit isolation because they are different in character from their surrounding areas, and Leith is included with Edinburgh because it is part of the same metropolitan complex; the Highlands and Islands covers the Crofting Counties; the East includes the mostly rural counties between the Moray Firth and the Firth of Tay, plus East Fife. From 1885–1918, the Borders include those counties bordering on England plus Peebles and Selkirk, but with Peebles and Berwickshire becoming the lesser portions of joint constituencies with South Midlothian and Haddington, respectively, they are excluded from Borders after 1918. Clydeside is restricted to those counties bordering directly on Glasgow, and the West includes those counties plus Ayrshire and Bute. Central, in Chapters 2 and 6 includes all the remaining constituencies in the central belt from Ayrshire to Fife, but in Chapters 4 and 7 excludes Ayrshire and Bute.

Regions 1885–1918

Aberdeen	(2)
Dundee	(2)
Edinburgh/Leith	(5)
Glasgow	(7)

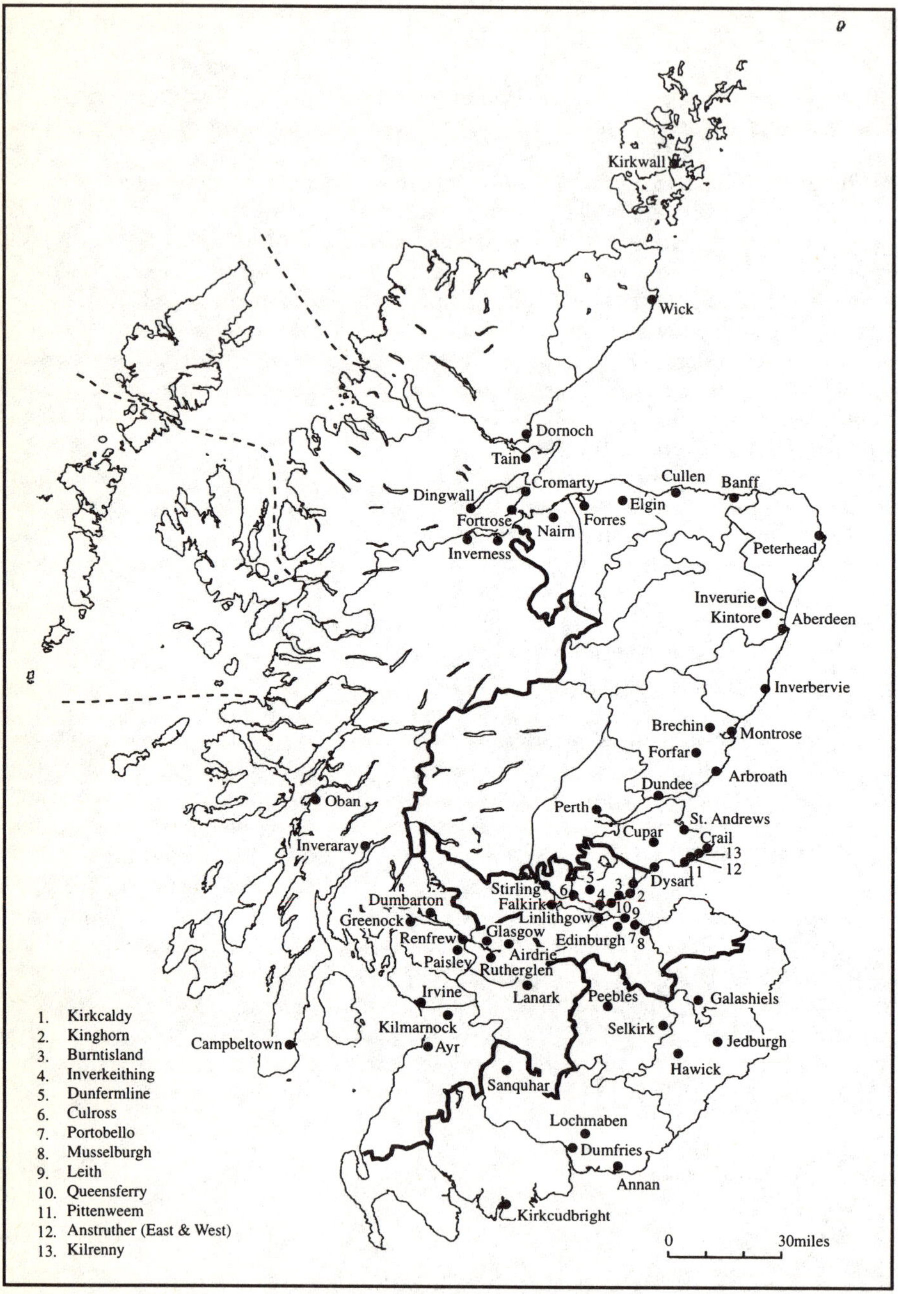

Scottish Burgh Constituencies 1885–1918

Scottish County Constituencies 1918–1950

Highlands and Islands – Orkney & Shetland, Caithness, Sutherland, Ross & Cromarty, Inverness-shire, Argyll, Wick Burghs, Inverness Burghs (greater part).

East – Elgin & Nairn, Banffshire, Aberdeenshire (2), Kincardineshire, Forfarshire, Perthshire (2), East Fife, Perth, Elgin Burghs, Montrose Burghs, St Andrews Burghs, Inverness Burghs (lesser part).

Central – West Fife, Clackmannan & Kinross, Stirlingshire, Linlithgow, Edinburghshire (Midlothian), Haddingtonshire, Bute (Chapter 2), Ayrshire (2) (Chapter 2), Kirkcaldy Burghs, Falkirk Burghs (lesser part), Kilmarnock Burghs (greater part) (Chapter 2), Ayr Burghs (greater part) (Chapter 2).

Clydeside (Chapter 2) – Dunbartonshire, Renfrewshire (2), Lanarkshire (6), Greenock, Paisley, Falkirk Burghs (greater part), Kilmarnock Burghs (lesser part).

Borders – Berwickshire, Roxburgh, Peebles & Selkirk, Dumfriesshire, Kirkcudbrightshire, Wigtownshire, Dumfries Burghs, Hawick Burghs.

West (Chapter 4) – Clydeside + Ayrshire and Bute (counties & burghs).

Regions 1918–1950

Aberdeen	(2)
Dundee	(2)
Edinburgh/Leith	(6)
Glasgow	(15)

Highland – Orkney & Shetland, Western Isles, Caithness & Sutherland. Ross & Cromarty, Inverness, Argyll.

East – Moray & Nairn, Banff, Aberdeen & Kincardine (3), Forfar, Perth & Kinross (2), East Fife, Montrose Burghs.

Central – West Fife, Berwick & Haddington, Midlothian & Peebles (2), Linlithgow, Stirling & Clackmannan (2), Ayrshire & Bute (3) (Chapter 6), Stirling & Falkirk Burghs, Dunfermline Burghs, Kirkcaldy Burghs, Ayr Burghs (Chapter 6).

Clydeside (Chapter 6) – Dunbartonshire, Renfrewshire (2), Lanarkshire (7), Dumbarton Burghs, Greenock, Paisley.

Borders – Roxburgh & Selkirk, Dumfries, Galloway.

West (Chapter 7) – Clydeside + Ayrshire & Bute (counties and burgh).

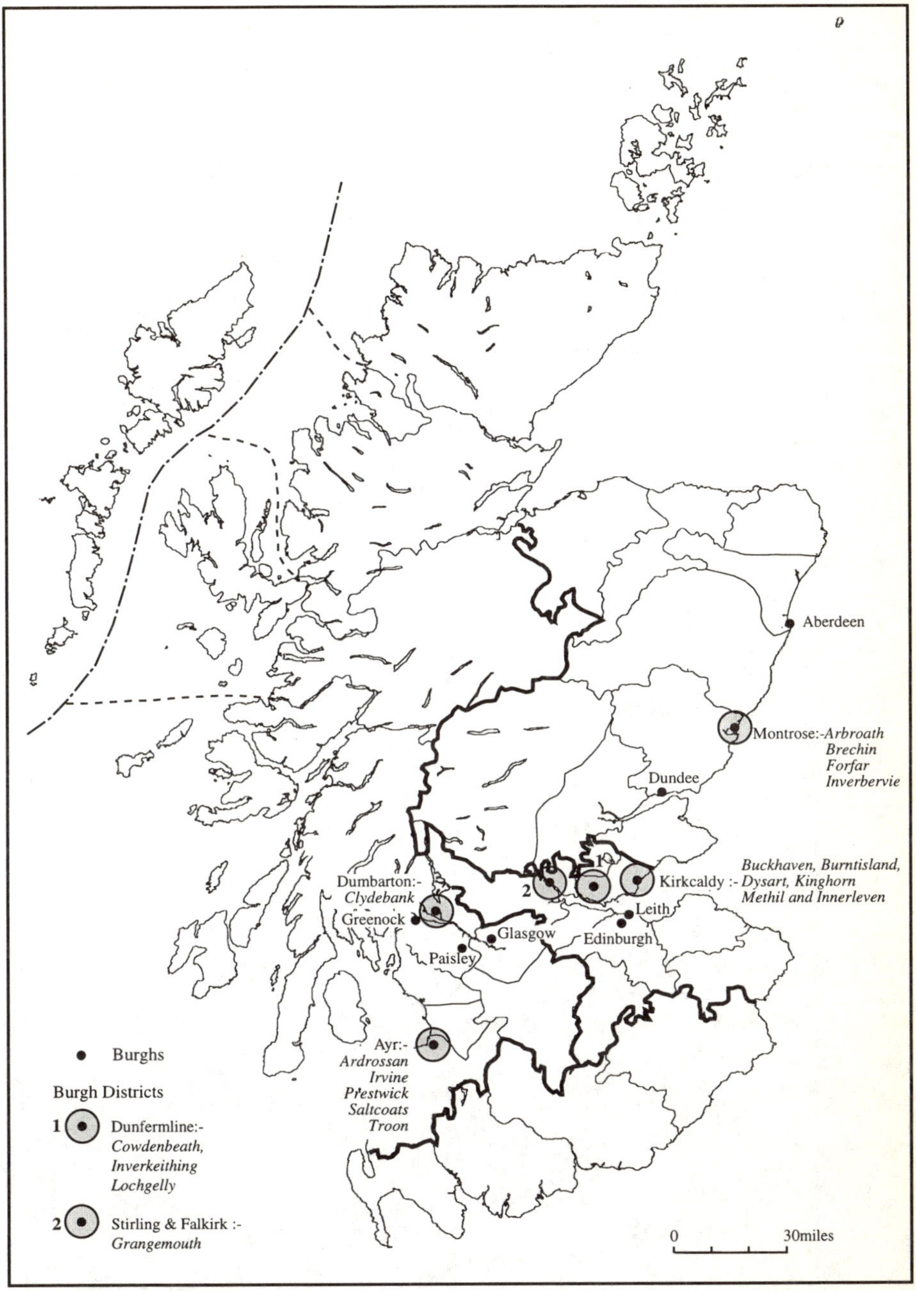

Scottish Burgh Constituencies 1918–1950

GLASGOW 1885

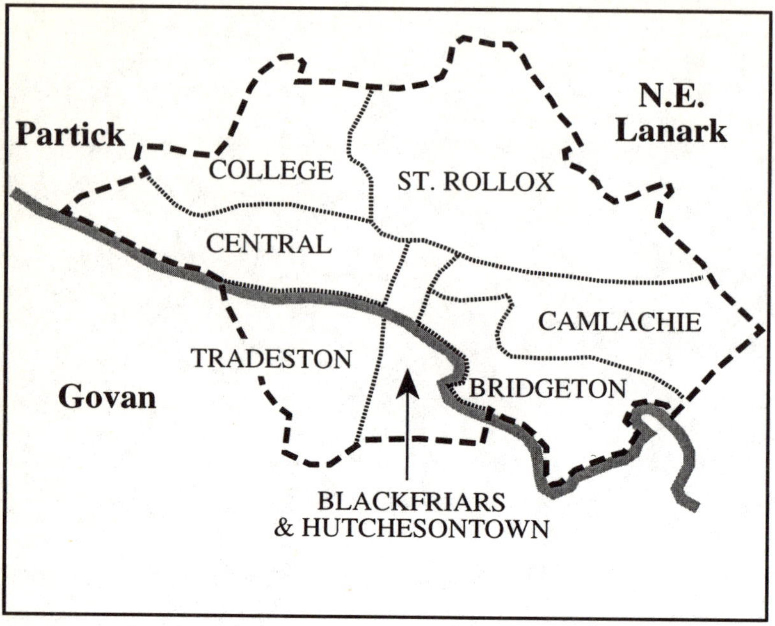

GLASGOW 1918

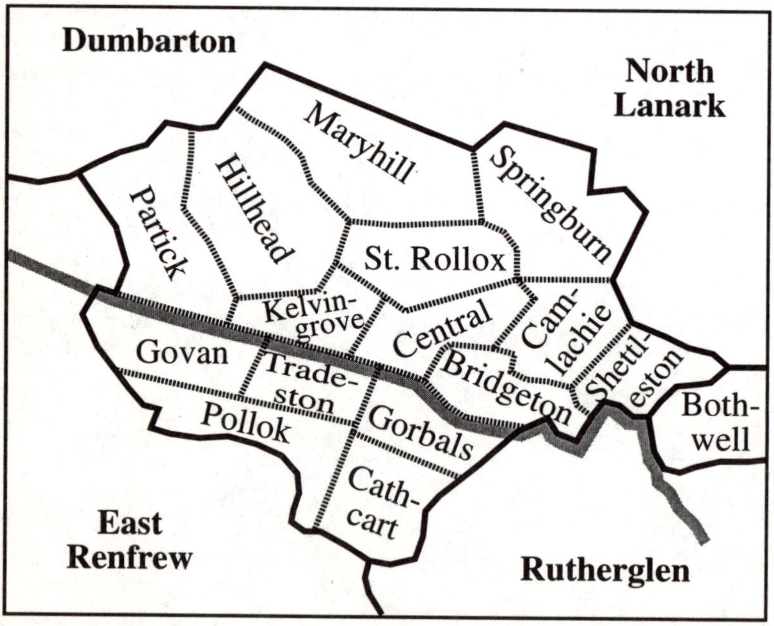

Glasgow Burgh Divisions 1885–1918 and 1918–1950

1 *Introduction*

According to Rokkan: 'The histories of Western European politics since the French Revolution have a number of traits in common: all extended the right of political participation to wider and wider circles of their citizens and finally, with few exceptions, introduced universal and equal suffrage for women as well as men; all developed – some of them quite early, others more slowly and erratically – nationwide party organisations based on mass memberships; and have all experienced, largely as a result of the universalisation of suffrage and the growth of mass parties, a decline in strictly territorial politics and an increasing emphasis on functional cleavages cutting across the traditional divisions into localities and provinces' (Rokkan: 226). From his study of Norway, he identified four important features contributing to the process of national integration: 'the formal *incorporation* of strata and categories of residents kept out of the system under the original criteria; the *mobilization* of these enfranchised citizens in electoral contests; their *activation* into direct participation in public life; the breakdown of traditional systems of local rule through the entry of nationally organized parties into municipal elections, what we call the process of *politicization*' (Rokkan: 227). This schema was intended to provide a framework for comparative electoral studies, and is one which commends itself to an analysis of the evolution of the Scottish electoral system and the incorporation of its citizens into the political process.

Within that context of increasing national integration the development of the Scottish electoral system can be usefully divided into five phases: (1) Traditional (pre-1832); (2) Transitional (1832–1884); (3) Standardisation (1884–1918); (4) Democratisation (1918–1929); and (5) Post Democratisation (1929 to the present). *Men of Property and Intelligence: The Scottish Electoral System prior to 1884* covered the period before 1884, whilst this volume focuses on the period from 1884 to the general election of 1929, the first held under universal adult suffrage.

Employing Rokkan's categories, developments prior to the Third Reform Acts might be summarised as follows:–

Formal Incorporation. Before 1832, the electorate was confined to representatives of the self-appointing corporations in the Royal Burghs and barely 3,000 landowners in the countryside. In 1832, following the First Reform Act, 64,447 Scotsmen, (around three per cent of the population outside the Highlands), were registered to vote, rising to 231,376 (seven per cent of the population) in 1868, following the Second Reform Act. A sharp distinction was drawn between the burgh and county franchises. From 1832–1868 the £10 burgh qualification enfranchised most middle class male householders, and from 1868 the householder franchise incorporated a large number of respectable working class male electors. In the counties, however, the franchise was largely confined to landowners and larger tenant farmers – more of the middling sort from 1868 – and a class of faggot voters created by landowners manipulating tenancy agreements. Consequently, while in 1873, 12.7 per cent of the burgh population was enfranchised, the privilege was enjoyed by only 4.4 per cent in the counties. The county electorate remained significantly smaller than in England, and the 'Celtic Fringe' – the Highland counties – was hardly affected at all by the 1832 and 1868 reforms.

Mobilisation. Prior to 1832 most seats were uncontested, though the nature of the system meant that when they were disputed a very high proportion of the registered electorate voted – virtually 100 per cent in the burghs. Between 1832 and 1865 the mobilisation of voters was particularly low, tending to decline over the period as a whole. Only half the seats in the burghs and only a third in the counties were contested in general elections, with turnout in the burghs averaging only 69 per cent as against 74 per cent in the counties. Fewer than 8,000 Scots cast a ballot in 1859, as against more than 40,000 in 1832. The low level of participation in the burghs reflected their one-party (Liberal) character, which inhibited the establishment of organised political parties, even on a local level, so that elections were not routinely contested. The high incidence of inter-Liberal contests also discouraged the emergence of the strong partisanship on which high levels of mobilisation are mostly based. In rural areas the small number of contested returns arose from a mixture of nomination, the effective determination of county representation by the registration courts, and a declining interest of Conservative landowners in the electoral battle. The higher turnout in county seats, however, indicated the persistence of a traditional Whig– Tory confrontation, and the high level of control exercised by the landowning elites over a largely compliant electorate.

Although there was a significant increase in participation, 1868–1880, 30 per cent of burgh seats and 39 per cent of county constituencies were uncontested. Even in 1880, five of the 22 burgh and seven of the 32 county MPs were returned unopposed. On the other hand, turnout averaged 78 per cent in the burghs and 83 per cent in the counties, and around 200,000 voted in 1880 – 57,767 in the counties, 54,555 in single member burghs, and the rest in Glasgow, Dundee and Edinburgh.[1] Lower turnouts continued to be associated with the major cities, and participation remained at its highest in the small burgh districts and the Borders.

Activation is connected with mobilisation: 'How far had they been organizationally mobilised before they were given the right to vote? How long did it take to mobilize them for electoral participation once they had the vote?; and how quickly were citizens from these lately underprivileged strata recruited into organisational work in the political parties, into candidacies and public office?' (Rokkan: 227).

Before the 1880s autonomous modern political parties did not exist. Only in Edinburgh and Glasgow did locally-based factions operate on a semi-permanent basis. In most burghs, 1832–1868, the main stimulus to periodic political mobilisation arose from religious identification, which formed the permanent bases of the political tendencies. The festering conflict within the kirk ensured that the burgh £10ers were eager to exercise the franchise as early as 1832, but as the intensity of the religious conflict declined after the Disruption so too did electoral participation down to 1865. With four fifths of the burgh electorate participating in elections, 1868–1880, however, there is every indication that the new working class householders had anticipated their enfranchisement well in advance. This development was assisted by a diminution of unopposed returns, an increasing number of two-party confrontations, and early moves towards the establishment of local party organisations. In the counties, where politics largely remained the preserve of interested landed families, the tenant electors, 1832–1868, played a passive role until called upon to vote by their landlords, but from 1874 the ballot, associated with the establishment of farmer associations, enabled the tenantry to establish a degree of political independence.

The wider political emancipation enjoyed by the new classes of electors varied considerably. From 1832, the previously unenfranchised upper middle class in the larger burghs immediately assumed political leadership, providing personnel for the reformed structure of municipal government, parliamentary election committees, and MPs from within their own ranks. Their power, however, was dependent on securing the support of independent lower middle class £10ers, who were active as members of election committees, expressed their opinions forcefully in public meetings (which on important municipal issues assumed the proportions of direct democracy), and generally constituted a 'shopocracy'. In the smaller burghs, where there were no large-scale businessmen, the £10 electorate exercised a more passive role, ceding responsibility for organising parliamentary elections to nearby landed elites, who provided candidates from within their own number. The new £10ers, however, played an important active part in burgh administration. The 1868 householder franchise was not associated with the emergence of working class councillors or MPs, although in the larger cities trade unionists were active in Radical Associations.

In the rural areas, the political rights of the parliamentary electorate as a whole remained highly circumscribed. Indeed, the political system established in the counties, 1832–1884, had been designed to minimise change. For most of the period local parties were largely indistinguishable from the personal property of politically active landed proprietors, and county government, based on the direct representation of big landowners (the commissioners of supply), remained unreformed until 1889.

Politicization. The intrusion of national parties into local politics was non-existent.

Despite the reforms of 1832 and 1868, the Scottish electoral system 1832–1884, though very different from its predecessor, retained most features of a pre-modern system. Even in the burghs the franchise formally incorporated fewer than half the adult male population, and open voting prior to 1874 consolidated the control of landlords in the counties. The absence of political parties attested to the weakness of functional cleavages transcending locally-based social configurations of power, whilst the reforms curtailed the ability of national politicians to manipulate electoral outcomes. Consequently, the territorial features of the system were enhanced rather than diminished after 1832. The base of territorialism, however, was the individual constituency, so that regional and Scottish-based centres of power failed to develop.[2] Despite the importance of locality, representation never became parochial, because MPs continued to be drawn principally from landowners, who through education, marriage, and the acquisition of property across Britain and Ireland formed a highly integrated

UK-wide ruling class, and representatives of the bourgeoisie who tended to be closely connected with the City, the Inns of Court, and global commercial interests. Consequently, while the electoral system was fragmented at its base, it failed to undermine the integrated character of the parliamentary elite.

Capable Citizens and Improvident Democrats considers the transformation and modernisation of this system under the impact of two major changes; firstly, the impact of the equalisation of the franchise between the counties and burghs and the extension of the franchise to three fifths of adult males, in 1884; and secondly, the realisation of adult manhood suffrage in 1918 and the completion of female adult suffrage in 1928. Attention is focused on the attitudes and impact of Scottish politicians on the reform process – considerably less than in earlier periods – mostly as expressed in House of Commons debates. Analysis of the electoral system makes reference to various Parliamentary Papers. In making use of a variety of secondary material, I am particularly indebted to FWS Craig's compilation of electoral statistics; *The Electoral System in Britain Since 1918* (DE Butler); *The Age of Alignment* (C Cook); the mine of information in *A Political History of Scotland* (IGC Hutchison); *The Politics of Reform 1884* (A Jones); *Scottish Labour Leaders, 1918–39* (W Knox); *Social Geography of British Elections, 1885–1910* (H Pelling); *Electoral Reform in War and Peace, 1906–18* (M Pugh); *Who's Who of British Members of Parliament* (M Stenton & S Lees); as well as the scholarship of N Blewett and J Kellas.

Notes

1. 155,397 votes were cast in Dundee, Edinburgh and Glasgow, where each elector had two votes each.
2. Apart from the largely personal bailiwick established by the Duke of Buccleuch in the eastern Borders (Brash).

References

Brash, JI, *Papers on Scottish Electoral Politics, 1832-1854*, Edinburgh, 1974.

Dyer, M, *Men of Property and Intelligence: The Scottish Electoral System prior to 1884*, Aberdeen, 1996.

Rokkan, S, *Citizens, Elections, Parties*, Oslo, 1970.

2 *The Reforms of 1884–5*

The fundamental flaw in the Second Reform Act was that by avoiding a significant revision of the county franchise and a credible redistribution scheme, even by nineteenth century standards it failed to constitute a satisfactory settlement. The broadened distinction between the county and burgh franchises was a nonsense, for the pretence of regarding county and burgh societies and interests as fundamentally different in character, with the counties considered as purely rural communities and commercial/industrial activities as the exclusive province of burghs, was even less grounded on reality than in 1832. By 1884, the absurdity was illustrated by Gladstone in reference to Clydeside, where Glaswegian artisans lost their votes as they followed their work down river (*Hansard*, 285: 110), and by Broadhurst, who read out a letter in parliament from the secretary of the Clyde Shipwrights' Association, indicating that whereas 19,442 held a local government franchise in Partick and Govan, (municipalities in Lanarkshire), a mere 3,462 were registered to vote in parliamentary elections (Jones: 1). The case for the equalisation of the burgh and county franchises, therefore, was overwhelming.

Whereas previous reform legislation had distinguished between the various nations of the United Kingdom, the franchise and redistribution bills of 1884/5 treated them as a territorial whole. Although this novel approach was principally the product of parliamentary tactics and designed to obfuscate the continuing over-representation of Ireland (Jones: 1), it also symbolised the increasing uniformity of the various national electoral systems, especially with respect to the franchise. Standardisation was particularly welcomed by the Scots because it strengthened their case for additional seats.

Gladstone's approach to reform to 1884 concentrated on the franchise, and he introduced a franchise bill before displaying his intentions on redistribution. He couched his proposals in characteristically conservative terms, declaring the principle behind the bill to be the extension of the franchise to 'capable citizens' (*Hansard,* 285: 110) in the counties, including 'the minor tradesmen of the country and skilled labourers and artisans... especially in connection with our great mining industry,' and the 'peasant [who is] not in the highest sense, but in a very real sense, a "skilled labourer", even though the peasant has a "defect" in being too ready, perhaps, to work with and accept the influence of his superiors' (*Hansard*, 285: 108-9). Gladstone's imputation that the peasantry would vote with their lairds was somewhat disingenuous, but was clearly designed to dampen the fears of Whig and Tory lairds (Jones: 21; *Hansard*, 285: 175).

The franchise proposals, however, did not simply equalise the franchise by extending the 1867/8 burgh qualifications to the counties, they also liberalised the existing burgh franchise. In the first place, they removed the stipulation that a householder should be rated for the relief of the poor. Secondly, they removed the limitation which denied the vote to householders whose homes were tied to their jobs. The latter amendment was particularly important, for while it had little impact in the burghs, the old dispensation would have excluded a large number of rural 'service voters', as this group of electors were known. Additionally, the £14 rating qualification in the counties was replaced by a £10 clear annual value franchise, and minor amendments were introduced to restrict faggot voting. The overall impact was almost to double the total Scottish electorate, as the numbers enrolled in the burghs grew by a fifth and by two and a half times in the counties.

Whatever misgivings the Conservatives may have had regarding the introduction of household suffrage to the counties, which drew from Randolph Churchill the observation that agricultural labourers were more likely to be enthused by a chapter read to them from the Greek New Testament than a discussion of political questions (*Hansard*, 285:175), their divided leadership, heavily influenced by Lord Salisbury, opted not to oppose the franchise proposals (Jones: 79-82). Instead, they refused to support a franchise bill until the government had outlined its redistribution amendments, for there was a real danger that if a dissolution followed on the passing of the franchise bill the Conservatives would be heavily defeated in the existing English county constituencies. As Sir Stafford Northcote observed, 'It is upon the redistribution of seats that power, and the characteristics of our legislation, are to be founded' (*Hansard*, 285: 459).

With the Whigs supporting the ministry and the Chamberlainites content to sustain the existing boundaries *sine die* (Jones: 28), the Liberal majority remained remarkably united in support of the franchise bill, and the Conservatives were unable to exploit the reform issue as effectively as in 1866. Consequently, the process of enactment in the Commons went smoothly, and no amendments were accepted by the government, including one from John McLaren (Edinburgh) to restrict further faggot votes, as they railroaded the measure through the committee stage (Jones: 226). It was a measure of Liberal discipline that not only was a first reading amendment to increase the number of Scottish members – moved by two Tories, Admiral Sir John Hay (Wigtownshire) and Robert Cochran-Patrick (North Ayrshire) – defeated, but it found no practical support even from Scottish Radical members, the most vociferous critics of Scotland's under-representation. Advanced Liberals were further embarrassed by having to vote against a Conservative amendment proposing to include women in the franchise. Amongst Scottish Liberals, only Cameron (Glasgow), Fraser Mackintosh, the unpredictable member for Inverness Burghs, and the Caithness baronet, Sir John Sinclair, voted with the opposition. Along with ten other Scottish Liberals, John McLaren, whose stepmother (the daughter of Bright) was president of the Edinburgh Society for Women's Suffrage, was absent from the division[1], but 35 of his colleagues, including the Radicals Baxter and Peddie, trooped into the 'no' lobby. Four Scottish Tories backed the proposal, Charles Dalrymple (Bute) voted against, and three, including Lord Elcho, abstained (*Hansard*, 289: 204-7).

Predictably, the Lords rejected the bill, creating a minor crisis, but in reality opening the way to a political fix between the party leaders: Gladstone, Dilke and Salisbury as the principals, with a supporting cast of Hartington, Granville (temporarily), and Northcote (Jones: Chapter 7). In return for a deal over redistribution, Salisbury indicated his willingness to support the reintroduction of the franchise bill. The advantage to both sets of party leaders of a consensual approach was that it enabled them to maintain control over their backbenchers, and meant that the terms of the redistribution bill did not have to be defended on the basis of principle but as a compromise measure worthy of bi-partisan backing. Consequently, Gladstone was able to secure his objectives on the franchise, and to isolate minorities within the Liberal party (such as those demanding proportional representation), from the official opposition, with whom they might otherwise have combined to defeat the bill for a variety of conflicting reasons, as had happened in 1866.

The basis of agreement between the party leaders was that all boroughs and groups of boroughs with populations under 15,000 were to be 'liberated' (suppressed), and their seats reallocated. Although the Liberals would have preferred to extinguish boroughs below 25,000 in population, no fewer than 79 English and Welsh boroughs, together with 22 in Ireland, fell under the more generous rule, and under a similar guideline, 36 English and Irish two-member boroughs each lost a member. Thus, while the 1885 Redistribution Act still deferred to ancient rights of representation, it also genuflected to the principle of equal electoral districts.

In Scotland the problem of balancing the clamour for more members in areas of substantial population growth with the reaction of entrenched interests was not so acute as elsewhere. With Scotland receiving an extra twelve seats, and each burgh grouping considered as an aggregate of all its individual components for the purposes of suppression, no constituency was marked for liberation apart from the Haddington and Wigtown Districts, while areas of gross under-representation were appeased. Consequently, as in 1832 and 1868, Scotland avoided severe reapportionment.

Although all but two Scottish burgh districts were to survive under the agreed rubric, it appeared that the cabal of party leaders had left open the question as to whether those remaining might be reorganised. For a number of years the distribution of burghs within the groups had seemed too antiquarian and irrational even to mid-nineteenth century politicians, and in 1866 they had commissioned a parliamentary paper on the subject (*PP,* Session 1866, LVII). Illustrating the problem, the report indicated the average distance between the two widest-apart burghs in each grouping to be 60 miles and the median 40 miles. At the greatest extreme was the Wick District, where Dingwall in Cromarty was a 158-mile journey by steamer, road, and rail from Kirkwall in Orkney, closely followed by the Ayr Burghs, in which Ayr and Oban in northern Argyll were divided by a 157-mile trip by steamer and rail. The most proximate burghs were in the Leith District (created in 1832), where only six miles separated the head burgh from Musselburgh, and Kirkcaldy Burghs in which Kirkcaldy was a mere eight miles from Burntisland. It was generally agreed that the burgh district system needed reform, or at least some degree of rationalisation, but there was no consensus as to what that should be.

The fairest solution would have been to throw the burgh districts into their counties to create more county divisions, extra seats for Glasgow, and a single burgh constituency of Leith. Such an approach, however, commanded little support outside Glasgow, and few agreed with Buchanan (Edinburgh), that the population standard of 15,000 should be applied to each of the contributory burghs within a district rather than to the group as a whole (*Hansard*, 295: 826). Most Liberals, however, were disinclined to remove a class of constituency that ever since 1832 had been almost exclusively their own, returning between a quarter and a third of all Liberal members, and there was no desire to offend either Liberal MPs or Liberal notables who dominated the politics of the various burgh districts. At the same time, Conservatives were reluctant to have Liberal voters dumped on the counties. Liberal MPs, therefore, tended to favour a reform which would rationalise the system by regrouping burghs to make them geographically more proximate, and supported the ejection of a few minnows into the counties, though not at the expense of reducing the number of burgh districts. The Conservatives favoured rationalisation as a means of increasing the number of burghs in groups and reducing the number of groups. Both these approaches were bogus as reforms, because the Liberals would have proportionately reduced the number of voters in burgh districts, which were already over-represented, and the Conservatives would have further reduced the number of electors in the smaller counties. The instincts of the party leaders were to leave the burgh groupings as they were, lest all the problems that had bedevilled Scottish redistribution 1867/8 be revived to no great purpose. Backbench pressure on both sides of the House, however, was such that the matter could not be ignored.

The provisions relating to Scotland, as outlined in the redistribution bill of December 1884, were modest in conception and cautious in approach. With fourteen seats at his disposal, Gladstone proposed to increase the representation of Glasgow and Lanarkshire by four seats each, Edinburgh by two, and the counties of Fife, Perth, and Renfrew, plus the burgh of Aberdeen, by one each. The only other proposed changes were extensions to the parliamentary burghs of Edinburgh, Glasgow, Galashiels, Greenock, Hamilton, Kilmarnock, Port Glasgow, Renfrew and Kirkcaldy, incorporating those parts of their municipalities which hitherto had been located in surrounding county constituencies. Significantly, there were no proposals to amalgamate any of the smaller counties, and there was to be no tinkering with the burgh districts, apart from the removal of the Haddington and Wigtown Burghs. In terms of management, it was the optimum solution because it recognised new social forces without challenging traditional interests, and was in accord with the principles that had emerged in 1832 and 1868. The essentially conservative character of the scheme was further underlined by Gladstone's willingness in power to concede to Conservative sensibilities two points he had denied them in opposition: firstly, that the increase in the number of Scottish MPs should arise from an expansion of the House rather than suppression in England, and secondly, that the multi-member cities of Aberdeen, Edinburgh and Glasgow should be divided into single-member constituencies.

The Scottish Liberal members were not impressed by the scheme. They resented not receiving extra seats at the expense of England: they saw in the division of the larger burghs a ruse to enhance Conservative representation – a hurt compounded by the absence of any proposal to amalgamate the smaller counties; and were particularly annoyed that no amendments were proposed to the burgh district system. Consequently, the government were thrown onto the defensive, and before the second reading, in answer to a question regarding the burgh districts from Cameron (Glasgow), Dilke conceded that the matter 'ought to be threshed out before the whole House' and, 'if the Scotch members could agree amongst themselves in advance, that would greatly facilitate the matter'

(*Hansard*, 294: 655). Other critics included the English Conservative, Raikes (York), who on the second reading referred to the 'utter enormity of the present system of Scotch burghs,' as, 'it is impossible to point to anything more absolutely indefensible, on any ground whatever' (*Hansard*, 294: 655). It was, therefore, arranged that between the second reading and the committee stage the lord advocate, James Balfour, would meet the Scottish MPs to hear their views and devise a set of redistribution amendments in accordance with them.

Table 2.1: Lord Advocate's Proposals for the Rearrangement of Burgh Districts in Central Scotland *

Existing Burghs	**Proposed New Structure**
1. *Ayr Burghs*	1. *Ayr Burghs*
Ayr	Ayr
Oban	Irvine
Inveraray	Kilmarnock
Campbeltown	
2. *Kilmarnock Burghs*	2. *Renfrew Burghs*
Kilmarnock	
Dumbarton	Dumbarton
Port Glasgow	Port Glasgow
Renfrew	Renfrew
Rutherglen	
3. *Falkirk Burghs*	3. *Lanark Burghs*
Falkirk	
Airdrie	Airdrie
Hamilton	Hamilton
Lanark	Lanark
Linlithgow	Rutherglen
4. *Stirling Burghs*	4. *Stirling Burghs*
Stirling	Stirling
Culross	Falkirk
Dunfermline	
Inverkeithing	
Queensferry South	
5. *Kirkcaldy Burghs*	5. *Kirkcaldy Burghs*
Kirkcaldy	Kirkcaldy
Burntisland	Burntisland
Dysart	Dysart
Kinghorn	Kinghorn
	Dunfermline
6. *Leith Burghs*	
Leith	
Musselburgh	
Portobello	

*As published in the *Scotsman*, 4th February, 1885

Following his meeting in January 1885 with the Scottish members (all but eight of whom were Liberals), Balfour produced a series of amendments that went beyond the somewhat narrow remit implied by Dilke, and seemed to challenge the understanding between the front benches that had dictated the parameters of the initial scheme. Firstly, Balfour recommended the removal from their groups of burghs under 1,000 in population: Inverbervie from Montrose Burghs into Kincardine; Kintore from Elgin Burghs into West Aberdeenshire; Fortrose from Inverness Burghs into Ross and Cromarty; and Dornoch from the Wick District into Sutherland. Secondly, to make Leith an independent parliamentary burgh, its satellites – Portobello and Musselburgh – were to fall into Edinburgh or Midlothian. (Most Scottish members also felt that a consequently enlarged Midlothian should then be divided, but only if Scotland were granted an extra seat.) Thirdly, Campbeltown, Inveraray and Oban were to be thrown into Argyll in an attempt to rationalise the Ayr District. Fourthly, there was to be a regrouping of burghs in central Scotland (Table 2.1), that would involve Linlithgow and South Queensferry dropping into Linlithgowshire, Culross into Kinross and Clackmannan, and Inverkeithing into West Fife. Fifthly, and most controversially, Balfour agreed to the union of Bute with Argyll, in order to form a constituency of North Argyll, centred on Oban, and a Bute and South Argyll division including the Cowal and Kintyre Districts of Argyll. Sixthly, he recommended the fusion of Caithness and Sutherland to provide a constituency of Western Isles, carved out of parts of Ross and Cromarty and Inverness. This latter proposal reflected the fears of Munro Ferguson of Novar, MP for Ross and Cromarty, who had earlier prevailed upon the Duke ofArgyll to alert Gladstone that unless the Hebrides were isolated, their crofting electorate would produce a Scottish Parnellite party with five members in the House of Commons (Savage: 125-6).

The lord advocate's plan was so biased towards Liberal intersts that it was a direct challenge to an overall redistribution package designed to mollify Conservative fears. The Tory position in Bute was directly threatened by its proposed amalgamation with Cowal and Kintyre, and the intention to liberate even the smallest burghs contravened the agreement to treat burgh districts as a whole. The rationalisation of the burgh districts in central Scotland was an attempt to off-load surplus burgh Liberal majorities onto the more marginal shires, and while thirteen parliamentary burghs were thrown into the counties, there was no parallel proposal to reduce the number of burgh districts, Leith apart, from those identified in the original bill. Additionally, Whig interests in Caithness and Sutherland were unsympathetic (unwisely so), to the Hebridean proposal.

Support for Balfour's scheme, however, met strong Liberal resistance, for while it advanced his party's interests in general, it frequently failed to do so in the particular. The approval of Oban Council for their exclusion from the Ayr Burghs because their town was to become the focal point of North Argyll, and the favourable reaction of Rothesay Council to the union of Bute, Cowal and Kintyre, were exceptional (*Scotsman*, 11.2.1885). More typical were the irreconcilable cross-pressures faced by Campbell-Bannerman (Stirling Burghs). Although Stirling Burgh Council were content to loose their old associates and become linked to Falkirk (*Scotsman*, 17.2.1885), a public meeting in Dunfermline, rejecting a transfer to Kirkcaldy, resolved to lobby their member to remain with Stirling (*Scotsman*, 10.2.1885). Falkirk Liberal Association, however, while accepting the burgh's loss of status as a head burgh, welcomed the marriage with Stirling on the understanding that its divorce from Dunfermline stood (*Scotsman*, 17.2.1885). In Ayr, the burgh council supported exclusion of the Argyll burghs from their district, but expressed opposition to the inclusion of Kilmarnock (*Scotsman*, 10.2.1885). Kilmarnock Burgh Council was predictably offended at their town's demotion as a returning burgh and considered they merited a member all of their own (*Scotsman*, 10.2.1885). In the Highlands, Fortrose felt slighted at its loss of parliamentary status (*Scotsman*, 10.2.1885), the provost of Thurso organised strong opposition to the union of Caithness and Sutherland (*Scotsman*, 19.2.1885), and in Sutherland a public meeting sent letters of protest to the lord advocate and the Marquis of Stafford on the same matter (*Scotsman*, 19.2.1885). So strong was the feeling in Kintore, Aberdeenshire, that a petition opposing their ejection from the Elgin District was signed by virtually all the adult inhabitants (*Scotsman*, 12.2.1885).

Tory pressures were generally hostile to the revised scheme, and particularly to the reorganisation of the Highland counties. The Rothesay Conservatives, for example, petitioned the Marquis of Bute against the proposal (*Scotsman*, 12.2.1885); and given that the political context of reform was one in which 'the government may propose...[and] Lord Salisbury...dispose,' the lord advocate was forced to abandon 'most of what was valuable and what was worth fighting for' (*Scotsman*, 7.3.1885). The amendments finally presented to parliament, therefore, bore 'melancholy testimony to the way in which the work of the one high officer in Scotland is set aside' (*Scotsman*, 11.3.1885). All that remained from Balfour's original plan were the proposals to remove Oban, Inveraray, Linlithgow, South Queensferry, Fortrose, Dornoch, Inverbervie and Kintore from their districts, and a rearrangement of the groups in central Scotland. Even so, Peddie (Kilmarnock Burghs) succeeded in dissuading Balfour from his original intention of placing Kilmarnock within a reorganised Ayr District.

The Conservative veto on the more substantive aspects of the lord advocate's scheme had dealt Balfour's plan a mortal blow, while the concession to Kilmarnock discredited what remained. One by one his critics closed for the kill (see committee stage debate, *Hansard*, 295). Sir George Campbell (Kirkcaldy Burghs) opposed the regrouping of his district, Fraser Mackintosh (Inverness Burghs) and Munro Ferguson (Ross and Cromarty) defended Fortrose, and Asher (Elgin Burghs), the solicitor general, while formally supporting the expulsion of Kintore from his constituency, made his disagreement with the policy abundantly clear.

When Sir Stafford Northcote administered the *coup de grâce* by intimating that the liberation of individual burghs with fewer than 1,000 inhabitants was not in accordance with the general principles agreed between the front benches, the government cut its losses, abandoned all further amendments, arranged to withdraw those already passed, dropped all thoughts of regrouping, and retreated behind the plan presented at first reading.

If the Liberals were balked in their aim of reorganising the burgh districts, Conservative backbenchers were thwarted in their perennial attempts to extend their composition. General Alexander (South Ayrshire) gained insufficient support for the inclusion of Old Cumnock and Galston in the Ayr Burghs; Sir John Hay (Wigtown Burghs) failed to add Stranraer, Dalbeattie, Castle Douglas,

Moffat and Lockerbie to the Dumfries Burghs; Charles Dalrymple (Bute) made little progress with his suggestion that Jedburgh, doomed as a member of the Haddington group, be linked to the Hawick Burghs; and Orr-Ewing, fearful for his position in Dunbartonshire, failed to find significant backing for a Dumbarton District based on the rising industrial burghs north of the Clyde. The House of Lords passed an amendment moved by the Marquis of Lothian that Jedburgh be added to the Hawick Burghs, but with Lord Salisbury indicating the Lords would not insist on their amendments, the lower house returned it to Roxburgh (Jones: 10).

Thus, the 1885 redistribution scheme emerged from committee and entered into legislation in the form it had been presented to the Commons the previous December (*P.G.Stat.*, 1884-5, ch.23).[2] Its shape was decided less by principle than by the exigencies of political management. To that extent it was firmly in the tradition of 1832 and 1868, when the reformers had sacrificed redistribution to the franchise. Summarising the process, the *Scotsman* concluded:

> The simple fact is...short of the division of the country into equal electoral districts, no scheme of redistribution could possibly be devised which would not present anomalies. Everyone knows that the present Redistribution bill is a compromise and that unless there had been a compromise it would have been impossible to deal with the question at all (21.3.1885).

Although the issue of Scottish redistribution had once again been ducked, the allocation of fourteen new seats to the major cities and mainly industrial counties tipped the balance of representation away from rural/small town constituencies for the first time. Thus, while malapportionment remained an important feature of the electoral system after 1885, there was at last a grudging recognition that Scotland had ceased to be a predominantly agricultural society.

The System

The Franchise (*P.G.Stat.*, 1884-5, ch.3)

The Reform Act of 1884 both liberalised existing voting qualifications and equalised the franchise between county and burgh. Under the new regime, the franchise could be most conveniently classified under four main headings (after Nicolson): (a) the householder franchise, (b) the service franchise, (c) the lodger franchise and (d) the occupation franchise. Additionally, the new legislation tightened restrictions designed to limit the creation of fictitious votes.

(a) The Householder Franchise

The major component of the new system was the householder franchise based on twelve months' inhabitant occupation, which from 1868–1884 had been peculiar to the burghs, but was now made universally applicable. Furthermore, whereas in 1868 an inhabitant occupier had been defined as the occupant of a dwelling house 'separately rated for the relief of the poor' in burghs where such rates were levied, the 1884 Act dropped the rating stipulation, extending the vote to all adult male householders. Thus, a male who only occupied a single room, sharing the premises in which he lived, was a potential elector. Even a change of tenancy did not disqualify, provided it was continuous and within the same parliamentary burgh or county division; and following a court ruling of 1875, a change in status from owner to tenant within the same calendar year was no disability (Nicolson: 10).

In divided burghs, a claimant moving from one division to another within the qualifying period was regarded as having been continuously resident in his new constituency for the purposes of registration; but a voter moving from one county division to another, even in the same county, had to be twelve months' resident in his new location before qualifying for the vote. A burgh voter, however, could only vote in one burgh division in any burgh, whereas a county elector could vote in as many county divisions in which he held the necessary qualifications in the same county. The distinction between divided burghs and divided counties rested on the treatment of divided burghs as parts of a single constituency, whereas divided counties were regarded as so many distinct entities.

Rated electors continued to lose their entitlement to the franchise if they failed to meet their assessment either through official exemption or non-payment by a specific date; and any householder who received parochial relief within any year preceding the end of July was also excluded from the register. As before, however, it was no impediment to receive charity from private sources.

(b) The Service Franchise

The service franchise was part of the householder franchise, and as such was subject to the same privileges and limitations.

Under the terms of the 1868 Act, as it applied to the burghs, the franchise had been denied to householders who lived in property from which they were liable to be removed if they resigned or were dismissed from their current employment. Some schoolteachers, for example, suffered under those restrictions until the Education (Scotland) Act, 1878, specifically exempted them from such disabilities (Nicolson: 5, *n.* 1). Although only a small number of burgh citizens were thought to have been denied the vote under this clause, it was clear that an extension of the principle to the countryside would adversely affect the claims of many tenant farmers. Consequently, the 1884 Act ruled that where a tied tenancy did not involve accommodation shared with the employer, the householder would qualify for the vote. Thus, a caretaker occupying a basement office, and a servant eating and sleeping in a separate apartment of his own, were both deemed to constitute 'households' under the terms of the new legislation. It was further stipulated that in the counties where such 'service voters' names did not appear on the valuation rolls, they were henceforth to be included, although not for the purposes of rating. As householders, 'service electors' were still required to occupy separate dwellings, so that while tenant farmers could claim a vote, farm servants living in bothies, and servants sleeping in their masters' houses and eating in their kitchens, remained disfranchised.

(c) The Lodger Franchise

The £10 lodger franchise remained basically as it had been in 1832 and 1868, but it was now extended to the counties. It was also ruled that for the first time joint lodgers in Scotland could claim the vote, provided the value of the property unfurnished when divided by the number of lodgers was not less that £10 per annum. Unlike householders, a lodger, somewhat prejudicially, lost his residential qualification as he moved from one division to another in the same burgh, but successive occupancy in the same parliamentary constituency, in the case of burgh districts, was regarded as continuous residence.

(d) The Occupation Franchise

The terms of the occupation franchise in the counties remained the same as in 1868, except that the qualifying annual value of property was reduced from £14 to £10, while that in the burghs remained as it had been in 1832. The importance of this franchise was that it enabled businessmen living within seven miles of a burgh to cast a vote with respect to the occupancy of commercial premises valued at £10 or more per annum.

£10 burgh owners and £5 county owners continued to enjoy the franchise, but with restrictions. After 1832, the owners of sufficiently large feu duties could claim the vote as proprietors, but in 1884 the act terminated the right to the franchise 'in respect of the ownership of feu-duties or ground-annuals, or in respect of an annuity out of land as distinguished from a liferent' (Nicolson: 21). This removed the criticism of the reformed franchise by such men as Cay (1850) that the 1832 Act had failed in its intention of severing the link between mere superiority and the vote.

A more important problem tackled in 1884 was the question of joint ownership and joint tenancy of the same lands and heritages as the basis for multiple claims. In 1868, a maximum of two votes had been permitted except (i) where the shares had come by inheritance, marriage, marriage settlement, or *mortis causa* conveyancing, and (ii) where the joint owners or tenants were bona fide partners carrying out a business. Under the new legislation, only one person could claim on a joint ownership or tenancy; and although the earlier exceptions remained, it was explicitly detailed that if more than one vote was to derive from the property, the total value of the 'land or tenement' divided equally between all the owners/tenants had to be sufficient to render each a vote. Where the owners/tenants claimed unequal shares, the onus was on them to prove it. Clearly, this provision was designed to limit the manufacture of fictitious votes.

Other minor changes, such as the elimination of the 1832 £50 tenant occupants and those paying £300 grassum, were less prejudicial than a recognition that the new household franchise had rendered such franchises redundant, and no elector currently registered on a terminated qualification lost his vote.

Registration (*P.G.Stat.*, 1884-5, ch 16)

The work of registration continued to rest heavily on the rating assessors appointed by the town councils in the burghs and commissioners of supply in the counties, with the valuation roll, modified to include non-rated service voters, forming the basis of the electoral register. A major development in the counties was the requirement not only that the register be corrected each year – as under the County Voters Act of 1861 – but also that a new register be prepared annually, in conformity with burgh practice since the Burgh Registration Act, 1856.

The construction of the roll began with the assessor arranging for a list of inhabitant occupiers to be completed before the end of May each year. A month later he received from the collector of the poor rate a list of persons who had been exempted from the poor rate or were in arrears of payment, and of those who in the previous year had been in receipt of parochial relief. He would then add to the list of eligible inhabitant occupiers any other accepted claims – e.g. from lodgers – and publish a provisional register by 15 September, which was then open to inspection. Particular care had to be taken with respect to divided burghs to ensure that no elector was registered in more than one division. Ten days later, through the town clerk or sheriff clerk, the assessor submitted the draft register, together with notices of objection and claims for inclusion, to the sheriff for adjudication in the registration courts. By the end of October, final appeals would have been heard and the new register come into force.

The system of registration in Scotland has been considered more efficient and comprehensive than the registration process adopted elsewhere in the British Isles, so that in December 1910, for example, in contrast to Ireland, England and Wales, the general election in Scotland was fought on a new register (Blewett: 38*n*). It was also observed that there were substantially fewer objections to the draft register in Scotland than elsewhere; and the lodger franchise, which had to be individually claimed each year, expanded more in Scotland than in the rest of Britain.

The Electorate, circa 1900[3]

By 1900 there were 661,748 registered electors in Scotland (373,465 in the counties and 288,283 in the burghs), 57 per cent of the adult male population, adjusting for plural electors. Just over 85 per cent of the electorate were registered as tenants or occupiers – i.e. as householders – 12 per cent as owners or life-renters, and only 2.3 per cent as lodgers. Rather more than three per cent of the roll was composed of electors living outwith the constituency in which they held a ballot.

Although the franchise was formally equalised between the burghs and counties in 1884, the proportion of adult males with the vote continued to vary quite widely between constituencies due to the 'poverty' exclusions, and the bias of the system against the more mobile members of the community and working class lodgers. Consequently, with the notable exception of Highland, there was a greater degree of enfranchisement in rural areas (in both burghs and counties), than in the large urban settlements, apart from Aberdeen; and due to the low level of enfranchisement in Dundee, Edinburgh/Leith and Glasgow, the counties emerged with a more popular constituency than the burghs for the first time since before 1832. In 1900, for example, whereas an estimated 58 per cent on average of males in a county constituency held the ballot, only 56 per cent did so in the burghs (Table 2.2).

Regionally, possession of the vote was at its greatest in the Borders and East, where almost two thirds of adult males were enrolled. Forfar and Wigtown, in which 69 per cent had the vote, recorded the highest proportionate enrolment of all county constituencies, and the Montrose District (72 per cent), Hawick Burghs (71 per cent), and Dumfries Burghs (69 per cent), were the most heavily enfranchised of all burghs. Even in Aberdeen, 66 per cent of adult males were enfranchised in both parliamentary divisions (despite their highly contrasting social composition), the same as in neighbouring counties; and only in Dundee

(50 per cent), where the roll was more limited than in Glasgow, was the regional pattern broken.

Table 2.2: Proportion of Adult Males Enfranchised and Disfranchised for Non-Payment of Rates and Receipt of Parochial Relief, circa 1900

	Proportion of Adult Males Enfranchised		Proportion of Adult Males Excluded from the Franchise for Non-Payment of Rates or Receipt of Parochial Relief	
	Counties %	**Burghs %**	**Counties %**	**Burghs %**
Aberdeen		66		1
Dundee		50		19
Edinburgh/Leith		55		4
Glasgow		51		9
Highland	52	57	7	18
East	65	65	3	17
Central	59	58	3	6
Clydeside	53	53	3	12
Borders	65	70	2	9
All	**58**	**56**	**3**	**8**

The Highlanders remained the least enfranchised of the rural population despite a substantial increase in their registration. Across the crofting constituencies only 52 per cent of men were entitled to vote, ranging from 58 per cent in Argyll to 47 per cent in Ross and Cromarty (which included the bulk of the Outer Hebrides), and 44 per cent in Sutherland, the least franchised of all Scottish counties. The burgh district of Inverness, with 53 per cent enrolled, recorded one of the lowest proportions in burgh constituencies, but Wick Burghs (64 per cent) was above the average.

It was, however, in industrial areas that the limitations of the 1884 Act were most evident, and particularly so on Clydeside. In Glasgow Blackfriars and Hutchesontown, Bridgeton, Camlachie, and Tradeston, and in Lanarkshire Govan, North East and North West, under half the adult male population was registered to vote in 1900; while in Greenock, which had the smallest proportionate franchise in Scotland, it was a mere 41 per cent. Out of 20 constituencies on Clydeside, only Renfrew East (66 per cent) and Lanarkshire South (59 per cent), a part rural division, were above the national average. Throughout the remainder of the central belt from Bute and Ayrshire to West Fife, the Lothians and Edinburgh, some three-fifths of adult males were eligible to vote, ranging from 68 per cent in the mining constituency of Clackmannan and Kinross to 53 per cent in the adjacent county of Linlithgow, and 43 per cent in Central Edinburgh. With five out of nine county constituencies in the Central region possessing an adult male franchise of 60 per cent or more, as against two out of eight burgh seats (including Edinburgh/Leith), the bias against the urban industrial centres observed on Clydeside was also replicated there.

The disparity between the degree of enfranchisement in county and burghal constituencies is largely explained by the operation of those clauses which denied the ballot to recipients of parochial relief and non-payers of their rates. But for those provisions there would have been just over 18,000 additional county voters (the equivalent of five per cent of registered county electors), and just under 39,000 more electors in the burghs (13.5 per cent of the burgh enrolment) in 1898. Around three quarters of all such exclusions arose from non-payment of rates, 17 per cent from official exemption from rate payment, and the rest for receipt of parochial relief. For all three categories the common denominator was poverty. Fishermen were the archetypal case in that a poorly rewarded occupation led them to defer paying their rates until the end of the summer fishing season in September, and as a result lost their entitlement to the ballot. Projecting the 1898 exclusions onto the roll of 1900, it is probable that without the poverty exclusions the total adult male enrolment would have been increased by five points to 62 per cent: 61 per cent in the counties and 64 per cent in the burghs.

In the counties, the impact of rating and parochial relief penalties was at its severest in Highland, which accounted for 37 per cent of all county 'poverty' exclusions. Had the 1,041 adult males removed from the register on account of their poverty in Sutherland been enfranchised, the proportion of adult males enrolled would have risen from 43 per cent to 62 per cent, and from 46 per cent to 62 per cent in Ross and Cromarty but for the exclusion of 2,688 otherwise qualified voters. Elsewhere the impact was more marginal. In Lanarkshire, for example, the 2,666 caught by the poverty clauses were a mere 1.7 per cent of all adult males. The only significant local concentrations outside Highland were in the parish of Wemyss in West Fife, where 562 men fell foul of the poverty disqualifications, and amongst the inshore fishing villages stretching along the Moray coast from Lossiemouth down to Fraserburgh and the environs of Peterhead, which reduced the proportion of men registered in Elgin and Nairn by three per cent and by seven per cent in both Banffshire and East Aberdeenshire. Similarly, of the 280 denied the vote for similar reasons in Berwickshire, 180 came from the fishing community of Eyemouth. In the Borders as a whole, however, the poverty clauses disfranchised less than two per cent of all adult males, which in a small measure helps to explain the high level of enfranchisement in this region.

Undoubtedly the biggest impact of the poverty clauses on the franchise was in the burgh constituencies of the east coast from Wick down to Dundee and St Andrews. Significantly, most of these seats (Dundee excepted), were strongly associated with inshore fishing. But for the poverty exclusions, the proportion of adult males with the ballot in the Wick District would have been 87 per cent rather than 64 per cent; 86 per cent as against 62 per cent in the Elgin Burghs – where in Peterhead the number of voters would have increased by more than half – 88 per cent rather than 72 per cent in the already highly enfranchised Montrose District; and 80 per cent as against 67 per cent in St Andrews Burghs. The reinstatement of the poor in Perth would have increased the proportion of men with the ballot from a modest 58 per cent to 71 per cent of adult men. In

Dundee, an extra 6,877 voters would have enfranchised 69 per cent of adult males as against the prevailing 50 per cent, surpassing Aberdeen, where, with fewer than 400 in both constituencies removed for non-compliance with the rating and parochial relief clauses, the pattern of high burgh exclusion was broken.

In other regions the burgh picture was more patchy. On Clydeside, for example, the removal of poverty clauses would have raised the proportion of men with the vote in Greenock from 41 per cent to 67 per cent, but by only five and six per cent respectively in Paisley (to 62 per cent) and Kilmarnock District (to 60 per cent). An advance of nine per cent in Glasgow would still have left two-fifths of men without the ballot, and in Edinburgh/Leith, the proportion of men enfranchised would only have risen to a very modest 59 per cent.

Even with the removal of poverty penalties, fully 38 per cent of adult Scotsmen would have still remained without the vote in 1900. In part this was due to the limitations placed on the lodger franchise, which by 1911 was extended to only seven per cent of the electorate: 29,000 in the burghs and 28,000 in the counties. Sixty-eight per cent of all burgh lodgers were located in Glasgow and Edinburgh, where they constituted around one in seven of the electorate, while the same proportion of all county lodgers were concentrated in the Clydeside counties of Dunbartonshire, Renfrewshire and Lanarkshire, comprising one in nine of their electors. Elsewhere lodgers were few and of no electoral importance. The inadmissibility to the register of lodgers paying less than £10 annual rent for unfurnished accommodation was particularly prejudicial to the enfranchisement of working class lodgers. Before 1914, the average rent paid by a Scottish miner as an occupier was seldom above £9 per annum, and the occupier of a two-roomed Glasgow tenement was only charged £11 per annum. In such property, therefore, it would have been surprising to find a lodger meeting the £10 rental requirement. Furthermore, working class lodgers were less likely to enjoy a room to the exclusion of others, a further condition of the lodger franchise. Enrolled lodgers, therefore, are thought to have constituted a relatively well-off section of the electorate – e.g. sons of wealthy occupiers living in a big house (Blewett: 40).

Unfortunately, it is impossible to indicate precisely the proportion of males who might have been added to the register had all lodgers been included. There is, however, circumstantial evidence to suggest the prevailing regulations bore heavily on industrial areas, where there was extensive overcrowding. It was estimated that in the decade before 1914 some 20 per cent of the one million inhabitants of Glasgow lived in accommodation in excess of three persons to a room (the definition of overcrowding), as did 28 per cent in Paisley, where 'new houses are said to be too expensive for the poorest class of the population, who are poor either because of small earnings, irregular employment, sickness, careless living and improvidence, drink, or a combination of all or any of these' (*Housing Report*, 1917–18, para 756), and around 26 per cent in Greenock, where 'four families of sixteen persons were recently found occupying a one-roomed house' (*Housing Report*, 1917–1918: para. 759). Similarly, in Dundee, where 'the standard of family life is lower than in Edinburgh and Aberdeen, but not quite so low as in Glasgow' (*Housing Report*, 1917–18: para. 736), overcrowding involved almost a quarter of the population. Outside the cities, the situation in the industrial burghs and counties was often worse due to the absence of middle class suburbs. In the Lanarkshire burghs of Airdrie, Coatbridge, Hamilton, Motherwell and Wishaw, overcrowding affected more than 40 per cent of the population, rising to more than half in Armadale, a mining town in Linlithgow. The counties of Ayr, Stirling, Dunbarton, Mid-lothian and Fife had more than a fifth of their inhabitants overcrowded, increasing to 36 per cent in Linlithgow and 40 per cent in Lanarkshire.

All the places cited above were characterised by low levels of enfranchisement. The connection between overcrowding and the vote can be illustrated by one or two examples. It was reported in Wishaw that there were six one-roomed houses in which lived a total of fourteen adult males, plus ten females. Of these men, only three, occupiers, provided they had fulfilled the residential and rating requirements, could have been considered eligible for registration. Similarly, in Dunfermline, a two-roomed house was cited where a tenant occupied the kitchen with his two adult brothers and mother, while the other room was inhabited by the occupier, his wife and family of four children, so that only one out of four adult males could have expected to find himself enrolled. Although these examples may be considered somewhat extreme, there is little doubt that overcrowding was a problem, having significant political as well as other social consequences. By contrast, in the agricultural counties of Aberdeen, Berwick, and Wigtown, where the proportion of the population overcrowded was 4.6 per cent, 10.9 per cent and 8.4 per cent respectively, the proportion of males enfranchised in each case was well above the national average.

Perhaps even more important than the restrictions on the lodger franchise was the impact of the year's residential qualification required of both occupiers and lodgers. It has been estimated that 20-30 per cent of the electorate in burgh constituencies moved each year, as against only five per cent in the counties (Blewett: 40). A more precise distinction in Scotland, however, was between rural/small town areas and regions of rapid economic growth. Low levels of enfranchisement, for example, are found in both the counties and burghs of Clydeside and the rest of industrial Scotland, where industrial expansion and urbanisation stimulated mobility, whereas higher levels of registration are discovered in the East and Borders, including a number of the burgh districts, where the population was generally static or in marginal decline.

Plural voting was not a prominent feature of the Scottish franchise. In 1900 there were around 13,000 non-resident electors in the counties (3.5 per cent of the total), and 7,000 in the burghs (2.4 per cent of the total). The largest concentrations were in Bute and the business division of Glasgow Central, where such electors respectively comprised one in six and one in five of the enrolment. Additionally, nine per cent of the register in Edinburgh West and Peebles and Selkirk were non-resident, and eight per cent in Kirkcudbright. It is unlikely that the business vote was decisive in any constituency in more than the odd election, with the possible exception of Glasgow Central and Edinburgh West, where Unionism was stronger than in adjacent seats.

Miners and Roman Catholics

Although not constituting classes of electors as defined by the reform legislation, there were two groups of voters, most of whom were newly enfranchised in

1884 – miners and electors of Irish Roman Catholic extraction – who comprised important minorities in the electoral system from 1885, so it is perhaps appropriate that their distribution and impact is briefly considered here.

By 1910 twelve of the 83 British constituencies in which miners constituted ten per cent or more of the electorate were located in Scotland, where West Fife, whose colliers were 50-60 per cent of the enrolment, was ranked amongst the dozen most mining seats (Gregory: 12-13). Miners were also 30-40 per cent of the register in Linlithgow and North East and Mid Lanarkshire; 20-30 per cent in South Lanarkshire, Midlothian, Stirlingshire, Falkirk Burghs and South Ayrshire; and 10-20 per cent in North West Lanarkshire, Haddington and North Ayrshire. North East and Mid Lanark, and the three Lothian constituencies were represented by Liberals from 1885 to 1918, as was West Fife until it went Labour in December 1910. Stirlingshire was Liberal in six general elections, but the Falkirk Burghs, South Ayrshire and North West Lanark returned Unionists three times each. South Ayrshire was equally shared between the parties, and North Ayrshire was mostly Unionist.

Table 2.3: The Estimated Irish Nationalist Vote as a Percentage of the Electorate in January, 1910*

(Figures in brackets denote the times the seat was carried by a Unionist in General Elections, 1885–1910)

20-25 % Nationalist		**10-15 % Nationalist**		**5-10 % Nationalist**	
West Fife	(0)	Glas. Blackfriars & Hutchesontown	(1)	Glas. College	(2)
				Stirling B.	(0)
		Dunbartonshire	(4)	Glas. Tradeston	(5)
15-20 % Nationalist		Greenock	(4)	Stirlingshire	(2)
		Leith B.	(0)	Glas. St Rollox	(5)
Kilmarnock B.	(3)	E Central	(0)	Glas. Camlachie	(6)
Falkirk B.	(3)	Mid Lanark	(0)	Glas. Central	(6)
		NE Lanark	(0)	Dumfriesshire	(3)
		Glas. Bridgeton	(1)	Paisley	(0)
		West Lothian	(0)	Ed. East	(0)
		NW Lanark	(3)	East Lothian	(0)
		Dundee (2 seats)	(0)	South Lanark	(2)
				Ayr B.	(6)
				Bute	(7)

There were eighteen seats where the Irish Nationalists were between one per cent and five per cent of the electorate: West Renfrew (5), Ed. South (2), Hawick B. (0), Perth (1), Wigtownshire (8), East Renfrew (6), Roxburgh (3), Midlothian (0), Lanark Partick (2), South Ayrshire (3), West Perth (6), Kirkcaldy B. (0), Ed. West (7), Clackmannan & Kinross (0), Kirkcudbright (6), Lanark Govan (3), North Ayrshire (5), and Argyll (3).

* The seats are ranked by size of the Irish Nationalist vote.

Source: *Scotsman* 18.1.1910.

Clearly there were numerous factors – religion, for example – affecting the outcome of elections in mining constituencies, but the capacity of the Liberals to carry the heavily mining seats of Mid and North East Lanark consistently in a region where the Orange influence was strong would seem to support the contention that miners were more inclined than other sections of the working class to vote for the Liberal Party.

It was estimated in January 1910 that some 46 constituencies possessed an Irish Nationalist vote, ranging from one per cent in Argyll to 24 per cent in West Fife (Table 2.3). Nearly all this group of electors were working class and resident in the industrial central belt, a substantial proportion being involved in mining. In most electoral contests their leaders instructed them to support Liberal candidates and not to divide the home rule constituency by voting for socialists. Such influence was supplemented by Nationalist activity within trade unions and trades councils to discourage the adoption of socialist candidates. By and large the Irish Catholics maintained their discipline, although by the end of the period the attraction of Labour, which appealed to both their class and ethnic identity, was considerable, and the three seats Labour won – West Fife, Dundee (1), and Glasgow Blackfriars and Hutchesontown – included significant Nationalist constituencies. The benefit of the Irish Nationalist vote to the Liberals is not easy to calculate, as Table 2.3 suggests. In general terms, however, the Nationalists assisted the Liberals in containing the left, but opposition to their demand for home rule produced a reaction that laid the foundation for a revitalised right with the emergence of Unionism.

Seats and Electors

The addition of twelve extra seats in 1885 and the equalisation of the franchise substantially reduced the difference in electoral size between Scottish constituencies, as the coefficient of variation between them fell from 0.90 in 1880 to 0.35 (see Table 2.4). The movement to greater overall equality was also evident within both burgh and county constituencies, where the degree of variation halved in both cases.

Table 2.4: Coefficients of Variation between the Distribution of Seats and Electors, 1832–December 1910

	Counties	Burghs	Single and Divided Burghs	Burgh Districts	All
1832	.75	.71	.47	.45	.74
1865	.76	.94	.62	.44	.91
1868	.52	.75	.48	.53	.90
1880	.65	.73	.48	.56	.90
1885	.33	.37	.23	.49	.35
Dec. 1910	.51	.45	.34	.56	.49

In the single (and now divided) burghs, the variation was reduced from 0.48 in 1880 to an impressive 0.23 in 1885; but in the burgh districts, where the number of electors ranged from more than 10,000 in the Kilmarnock and Leith groups to less than 3,000 in St Andrews Burghs and barely 2,000 in the Wick District, the variation (0.49) still remained greater than it had been between 1832 and 1865, despite the loss of the Wigtown and Haddington Districts. The improved variation in the counties reflected both the new divisions and the semblance of a popular franchise in the Highlands for the first time.

By 1910, demographic trends had vitiated some of the gains evident in 1885, so that while the overall relationship between the distribution of electors and seats remained better than previously, due to the equalisation of the franchise, the relationship within the counties was no better than in 1868, and in the burgh districts was as poor as in 1880.

There were just over twice as many electors enrolled in 1885 than in 1868, and each constituency had an average of just over 8,000 electors (Table 2.5). Due to the depressing influence of the burgh districts,[4] there were on average almost 800 more voters in each county seat than in the mean burgh constituency, and the gap had more than doubled by December 1910.

Table 2.5: Distribution of the Electorate in 1885 and December 1910 by type of Constituency

	Seats	Average Electors per Seat, 1885	Average Electors per Seat, Dec.1910
20 Largest Counties	20	10,506	16,696
19 Smaller Counties	19	6,093	6,728
All Counties	39	8,356	11,840
Burgh Districts*	13	5,256	7,365
Single and Divided Burghs**	18	9,267	12,173
All Burghs	31	7,585	10,156
All	70	8,015	11,094

* Minus Leith Burgh, plus Perth

** Minus Perth, plus Leith Burghs

The largest county constituency in 1885, with 15,109 electors, was Ayrshire South, and the smallest, Bute, with an enrolment of only 2,943. Although there was a tendency for the larger county seats to be found in industrial areas, Ross and Cromarty, Argyll and Inverness were amongst the 20 largest counties – the two former, in 1885, having more voters than five of the six Lanarkshire divisions – and the mining constituencies of Haddington and Linlithgow each had fewer than 7,000 electors. Between 1885 and December 1910, as the coefficients of variation demonstrate, the disparities of size between county constituencies increased. Whereas the number of electors in the twenty largest county seats expanded on average by 6,000, they grew by only 700 in the 19 smallest. Consequently, while in 1885 the 20 largest shire seats were on average 72 per cent greater than the smaller ones, the difference by the end of 1910 had more than doubled to 148 per cent. Predictably, the biggest change was on Clydeside, where the electors in 1910 were twice as numerous as in 1885, with the proportion of all county electors claimed by the Dunbartonshire, Lanarkshire and Renfrewshire advancing from 25 per cent to 37 per cent over the period. By contrast, the number of electors in Roxburgh between 1885 and December 1910 decreased by a third, in Ross and Cromarty by a fifth, and by smaller proportions in Caithness, Orkney and Shetland, Elgin and Nairn, and Wigtown. Dumfries, Inverness, and Ross and Cromarty, ceased to be counted amongst the larger county constituencies, being replaced by the two Renfrew divisions and Linlithgow.

Despite the suppressions of 1885, the traditional burgh districts were on average only half the size of the larger counties, less than three fifths as big as divisions in the single burghs, and smaller than the more diminutive counties. The Dumfries, Inverness, St Andrews, and Wick burgh districts were less than half the overall national average, and only the Kilmarnock and Montrose Districts (Leith Burghs apart), above it. By contrast, thirteen of the single burgh constituencies were over the national mean, with Paisley (6,794) the smallest, excluding Perth. Inequalities, however, were less quick to develop amongst the burghs than in the counties, largely due to an actual decline in Glasgow's share of all burgh electors from 32 per cent in 1885 to 28 per cent in December 1910, and an increase of just over one per cent in the proportion of burgh electors in the districts, due principally to enhanced rolls in the Ayr, Falkirk, Kilmarnock, Kirkcaldy and Stirling groups. The modest revival in the burgh districts was sufficient by 1910 to make them on average larger than the nineteen smallest counties.

In regional terms, the main beneficiaries of redistribution were Clydeside and Glasgow, whose collective representation increased by nine seats, reducing the gross inequalities of the earlier period (see Table 2.6). Nevertheless, in 1885, Glasgow should have received three more divisions and her adjacent counties two extra in recognition of their population, or three and a half more in respect of their proportionate share of the electorate. Even a relative decline in Glasgow's electorate, and a lower than average level of enfranchisement in Glasgow and Clydeside – which due to the municipal expansion of Glasgow had become completely interwoven – indicated the area might have reasonably claimed an extra seven and a half seats by December 1910.

Less justified in a regional context was the addition of one and a half seats in Eastern Scotland, following the division of Fife and Perthshire, where a loss of two members would have been justified on the criterion of population. The 'problem', of course, was that while the division of the two large counties was quite appropriate, the survival of Perth (elect. 4,369), St Andrews Burghs (2,837), and the Elgin Burghs (4,182) was certainly not. Although a proportionately high level of enfranchisement supported the argument for an extra half member in 1885, even that more favourable measure would have sanctioned a reduction of two seats by 1910.

The extra member for Aberdeen was in accord with natural justice; but three rather then two more seats in Edinburgh/Leith would not have been over-generous, especially as Musselburgh and Portobello remained within the burgh district and Midlothian remained undivided.

The most favoured region was the Borders, for despite its loss of the Wigtown Burghs and its share of the liberated Haddington District, it retained eight seats: two and a half more than was merited on the basis of population or electorate. In Berwickshire, Roxburghshire, and Wigtownshire, the electorate declined between 1885 and December 1910, so that by then the region was approaching twice its deserved representation. Similarly, the Highlands, over-represented by one or two members in 1885, despite a substantially increased electoral roll, faced the possibility of losing three seats in any future equitable redistribution, by December 1910.

Table 2.6: Regional Impact of the 1885 Reform Act

				'Fair' Distribution by:		
		Population		(a)	(b)	(c)
	Electorate 1885	Enfranchised %	Seats	Pop 1885	Elec. 1885	Elec. D.1910
Aberdeen	16,069	15.3	2.0	2.0	2.0	2.2
Dundee	17,412	12.1	2.0	2.8	2.2	1.8
Edinburgh/Leith	44,097	14.2	5.0	6.0	5.5	6.2
Glasgow	75,293	14.7	7.0	10.0	9.4	7.8
Highland	50,644	13.7	8.0	7.1	6.3	4.8
East	99,078	18.6	13.3	10.3	12.4	9.9
Clydeside	107,020	14.6	12.3	14.2	13.4	19.0
Central	105,968	17.0	12.4	12.1	13.2	14.2
Borders	45,451	15.9	8.0	5.5	5.6	4.3
All	**561,040**	**15.4**	**70.0**	**70.0**	**70.0**	**70.2**

Central, perhaps only one or two seats light throughout the period, was more or less given its due in the context of nineteenth century attitudes towards reform. It was, however, a measure of the rough justice of the period that this region included, in 1885, Bute (elect. 2,943), Stirling Burghs (5,228), Kirkcaldy Burghs (5,282), and Ayr Burghs (5,449), on the one hand, and South Ayrshire (15,109), Edinburghshire (12,924), Stirlingshire (12,486), and North Ayrshire (12,465), on the other.

Conclusion

The progress of the Third Reform Bills, an 'episode…of comparative unexcitement in a decade of extraordinary turbulence' (Jones: 236) was less controversial than that of its predecessors of 1832 and 1868: a tribute to the prestige of the party leaders, Gladstone and Salisbury, who fixed a deal which minimised the disruptive influence of Radical backbenchers and Tory backwoodsmen.

The values which informed reform of the franchise, now extended to 'capable citizens', continued to reflect the nineteenth century contention that the ballot was a privilege to be earned rather than a right to be conceded. The householder had to demonstrate his rectitude through the payment of rates and avoidance of parochial relief, lodgers only qualified for the vote in exceptional circumstances, the claims of the peasant were recognised because he was the equivalent of a skilled worker – evidence of self-improvement – and there was no room intended for the likes of the improvident drinkers of Paisley. A franchise that excluded more than 40 per cent of adult males and all females was remote from the democratic spirit of the twentieth century.

Despite the equalisation of the franchise, the degree of enfranchisement varied significantly from one region to another. While the rural areas of the East and Borders, together with their burgh districts, had relatively high proportions of men on the register, in parts of Glasgow, Clydeside and other urban/industrial areas, barely half of adult males were enrolled, and in a few constituencies there were more without the ballot than with it. Consequently, the degree of integration achieved by the 1884 franchise was uneven and particularly biased against the industrial working class.

As in 1832 and 1868, Scotland avoided redistribution through the acquisition of extra seats, and a generosity of approach towards the diminutive burgh districts which was denied to the smaller English boroughs. Consequently, while in 1885 the four big cities and the three counties of Clydeside claimed half the population, they were granted only two fifths of the parliamentary seats, one fewer than the rural regions of Highland, East and Borders and their associated burgh districts, incorporating less than a third of Scotland's inhabitants. Thus, the under-representation of industrial workers was paralleled by an under-representation of industrial regions.

There were, nevertheless, several important developments associated with the 1884/5 reforms. In the first place, the equalisation of the franchise significantly reduced the differences in political culture between burgh and county politics, and for the first time gave the Highlands a measure of reform which had been effectively denied in 1832 and 1868. Secondly, despite the limitations of the 'redistribution' scheme, urban/industrial constituencies outnumbered rural/small town constituencies for the first time by around 38 seats to 32 seats, and single and divided burghs (18 seats) at last outnumbered the archaic burgh districts (13 seats). Thirdly, the division of Glasgow, Edinburgh and Aberdeen introduced a new principle of considerable consequence for the political development, party organisation, and representation of the larger cities.

Perhaps most important of all, the growing social diversity of the greatly expanded electorate was to place considerable strains on the voter/party alignments which had developed between 1832 and 1880, making some realignment of voters and parties almost inevitable. Furthermore, the need to mobilise the new mass electorate was to greatly accelerate the development of the political parties, producing a new class of political activists and further enhancing the status of British party leaders. Thus, the standardisation of the electoral system was to advance the integration of Scottish politics within the wider political system.

Notes

1. His father, Duncan, had supported John Stuart Mill's attempt to introduce female suffrage in 1867, 'I shall vote for it,' said he, 'and I don't see how a man who had a good mother can do otherwise' (Mackie, Vol.II: 102).
2. The provisions relating to Glasgow were modified in 1896 (*P.G.Stat.*, 1896, ch.17).
3. The data in this section are based mainly on, *PP* Session 1895 (389) Vol. LXXXIX, 315; *PP* Session 1895, (389), Vol. LXXXIX, 319; *PP* Session 1898 (376) LXXX, 755; *PP* Session 1901 (85) Vol., LIX. 115; and Craig.
4. For the purpose of this analysis, Leith Burghs is treated as a Single Burgh, which to

all intents and purposes it had been since its creation in 1832; and Perth is placed with the Burgh Districts because it was an anomaly created to appease anti-reform sentiment in 1832.

References

Blewett, N, 'The Franchise of the United Kingdom, 1885-1918', *Past and Present, Vol. 32*, Dec. 1965

Cay, J, *An Analysis of the Scottish Reform Act with the Decisions of the Courts of Appeal*, Edinburgh, 1850.

Craig, FWS, *British Parliamentary Election Results, 1885-1918,* London, 1974

Gregory, R, *The Miners and British Politics, 1906-1914,* London, 1968

Hansard (3rd Series)

Jones, A, *The Politics of Reform, 1884*, Cambridge, 1972.

Mackie, JB, *The Life and Work of Duncan McLaren*, 2 vols, London, 1888.

Nicolson, JB, *Analysis of Recent Statutes Affecting Parliamentary Elections in Scotland,* Edinburgh, 1885.

Parliamentary Paper Session 1866 (314) LVII, 791, *Return showing the distance of each contributing burgh in Scotland from the other contributing burghs in the same district of burghs, &c.*

Parliamentary Paper Session 1895 (389) Vol. LXXXIX, 315, *Return showing with respect to each Parliamentary Burgh, Division of Burgh, and District of Burgh, in Scotland, the number of Parliamentary Electors on the Register for 1895, distinguishing them as to their Qualifications.*

Parliamentary Paper Session 1895, (389), Vol. LXXXIX, 319. Return *showing with respect to each County or Division of County in Scotland, the number of Parliamentary Electors on the Register for 1895, distinguishing them as to their Qualifications.*

Parliamentary Paper Session 1898 (376) LXXX, 755; *Return of the number of Rated Inhabitants in each Parish in Scotland whose names were omitted from the Parliamentary Register in 1898, in respect of Non-Payment of Rates.*

Parliamentary Paper Session 1901 (85) Vol., LIX. 115. *Return showing with regard to each Parliamentary Constituency in the United Kingdom, the Total Number, as far as possible, the Number in each class of Electors on the Register now in force.*

Parliamentary Paper, Session 1917-18, Vol. XIV, cmnd. 8760, 345, *Report on the Housing of the Industrial Population of Scotland, Rural and Urban, 1917-18.*

Public General Statutes, 48 & 49 Victoria, cap. 3, *An Act to Amend the Law relating to the Representation of the People of the United Kingdom.*

Public General Statutes, 48 & 49 Victoria, cap 16, *An Act to amend the Law regulating the Registration of Voters in Scotland.*

Public General Statutes, 59 & 60 Victoria, *Glasgow Parliamentary Divisions Act.*

Savage, C, 'Scottish Politics, 1885-6,' *Scottish Historical Review,* Vol. 40, 1961

Scotsman

3 *The Party System, 1884–1910*

The Third Reform Act was associated with a fundamental change in British electoral culture caused by the creation of a mass electorate, leading to a new alignment of voters, and a decisive shift away from a focus on peculiarly local matters to the appeals of national leaders and party programmes in the determination of parliamentary representation. In Scotland the developments of the late 1880s were more consequential than in England, because they marked the end of Liberal monopoly in the towns, and the creation of a Unionist coalition that in 1900 was to carry a majority of both burgh and county constituencies.

As early as 1868 there had been a threat to the Liberal coalition because the extension of the franchise had increased the diversity of interests to be reconciled, and the further reduction and equalisation of the qualifications in 1885 made the maintenance of Liberal unity even more difficult. In the rural areas the enfranchisement of the smaller farmers inevitably intensified the political conflict between the Whig landlords and their tenants, who wanted legislation to enhance their rights and the introduction of the elective principle to county government. Even before 1885, the Highland crofters had formed their own party because they had never identified with the Liberal landowners, and in 1885 enjoyed their first electoral successes (Crowley; Hunter). Traditional Liberalism was also threatened in the industrial areas by the greater enfranchisement of manual workers, who were potential clients of the various socialist parties that emerged in the late nineteenth century. Clearly the Liberals had to adjust their position to meet the demands of these new forces, even if a shift to the left was to alienate some erstwhile support.

A second set of problems for traditional Liberalism arose from the development of Liberal associations instituted to formalise the nomination of candidates and mobilise the expanding electorate, because it created a layer of political activists whose values were not necessarily functional to the party's electoral success (Kellas: 1964). Hitherto Scottish Liberalism had survived as an amorphous agglomeration of local elites with differing interests and values, which coexisted largely because there was no need for them to co-operate on a national or even regional basis. The Scottish Liberal Association (SLA), created in 1881, and dominated by Whig grandees, the Earls of Elgin and Fife, sought to maintain local independence by restricting the activities of the SLA to the mediation of constituency disputes and the provision of legal information. Policy-making was outside its remit, and membership was based on individual application rather than constituency delegation.[1] In the west, however, the Glasgow Liberal Association, reflecting the perspectives of a membership drawn disproportionately from the voluntaries, was Chamberlainite in organisation and sentiment, and having ensured that six of the seven Liberals adopted for the new Glasgow divisions in 1885 supported disestablishment and disendowment of the Auld Kirk, sought to use the SLA to impose a similar test on all Liberal candidates throughout Scotland. Consequently, there developed a conflict between traditionalists (mostly, though by no means exclusively, Whigs), who disliked the intrusion of party federations into constituency affairs, and the modernisers (generally Radicals), who were skilled in caucus politics, and sought to use the various levels of the developing party structures to impose centrally-determined lines of policy. Churchmen were particularly unpopular with the new constituency activists, so that a significant feature of the 1885 general election was the number of contests in which Independent Liberal Churchmen fought disestablishers nominated by Liberal associations.

In September 1885, the Radicals established a National Liberal Federation (NLF) in Glasgow on the same day that Chamberlain visited the city. Lacking the support of Gladstone and Rosebery, however, the NLF was denied the prestige necessary to become an outright rival of the SLA, choosing, instead, to act as a pressure on it. Nevertheless, at a meeting of the SLA in Perth, on 16 October, NLF supporters dominated the proceedings, and passed a motion 400:7 in favour of disestablishment, which precipitated the resignation of the Earl of Fife, the party president. In early November, however, a third force, Gladstone, who stood between the sectarianism of the Radicals and the oligarchic Whigs, and enjoyed the trust of most Liberal voters, indicated at a meeting in the Free Church Assembly Hall that disestablishment had a low priority and ought not to be a test question in the selection of Liberal candidates. As a result the NLF lost its impetus. Following an election in which neither the SLA nor the NLF played an important part, and central organisation rested heavily on himself and Rosebery, Gladstone sought to reorganise the discredited SLA on the lines of the NLF. Lord Elgin, however, still wanted to retain the separation of organisation from policy-making, but before matters could be brought to a head the home rule crisis intervened.

Principles apart, parliamentary arithmetic dictated that the Liberals would have to make some gesture to Irish nationalism following the enfranchisement of the Catholic peasantry in 1885. In Scottish terms, however, Gladstone's declaration in favour of home rule was little more than counterproductive in its immediate consequences (though not in the medium term), because it provided the catalyst which broke Liberal hegemony in the burghs. Amongst commercial interests home rule was seen as a compromising free trade, and the chambers of commerce in Greenock and Glasgow broke their traditions of political neutrality to oppose the policy. Leading newspapers, including the *Scotsman*, *The Glasgow Herald*, and the *Daily Free Press* in Aberdeen, deserted Gladstonian Liberalism; and Orange influence amongst the working class – with its cry that home rule meant Rome Rule – produced a constituency for Unionism that might otherwise have been favourable to the Liberals (McCaffrey). Significantly, the leaders of Liberal Unionism emerged from the antidisestablishers of 1885, although Free Churchmen were by no means absent from Liberal Unionist ranks. In rural areas, home rule and its association with land reform was the last straw for most of the Whig lairds, who left Gladstone to make common cause with the Conservatives.

The polarisation of 1886 helped to resolve the organisational conflicts within the Liberal Party. The SLA failed to support Gladstone's Irish policy, but the NLF revived to back the prime minister, effecting a reconciliation between itself and the Grand Old Man. Gladstone's accord with the Glaswegians and other Radicals was a logical development, because he needed the activists of the local

Liberal associations, like the members of the NLF, to replace the old élites which were deserting to Unionism, and the new constituency parties needed him to establish their credibility with the electorate.

Throughout 1886 Lord Elgin continued to oppose reform of the SLA, not wishing to adopt a particular line on home rule and seeking to maintain a position of neutrality towards Gladstone. The central importance of the Irish policy and the loss of most Whigs, however, made such a position untenable, and the rank and file forced on the executive a vote of confidence in the prime minister, which paved the way for a merging of the NLF and the SLA in December 1886. Under the new constitution, constituency delegation replaced individual membership as the basis of representation on the council and at the conferences of the SLA, and the majority view of the council constituted the policy of the party. Thus, the organisational values of the Glasgow Radicals informed the revamped SLA, and the ending of individual membership marked the transition of Scottish Liberalism from a confederacy of notables to a modern political party.

The rationalisation of Scottish Liberalism enabled the party to protect itself on the left by incorporating the Crofters, and the adoption of home rule secured the support of the Irish working class, which inhibited the development of the socialist parties. Furthermore, the espousal of social reform, particularly after 1906, enhanced the appeal of the party amongst manual workers. The leftward drift of Scottish Liberalism, however, should not be overstated. Rural radicalism was rooted more in the values of the peasantry than those of landless farm servants, and urban Liberalism continued to enjoy the support of significant sections of the commercial and manufacturing establishment. Thus, while the post-1906 collectivist policies of the British-wide Liberal government proved popular with Scottish working class voters, the local party members 'Had little belief in the 'New Liberalism' of Asquith, Haldane and Lloyd George, which brought collectivism (in the shape of the welfare state) within the party's programme. The Scottish Liberals were individualists...they promoted...Church disestablishment, crofters and tenants rights, and home rule for Scotland. National insurance, pensions and a minimum wage were much too Socialist, and they viewed with alarm these parts of the new Liberal policy' (Kellas 1968: 184). Rosebery described the 1909 budget as 'inquisitorial, tyrannical, and socialistic' (Donnachie et.al.: 8). After 1918 such attitudes were to push the Liberals firmly to the right, but in the meantime their strength continued to rest on their historic position as a centre party representing a broadly-based national consensus.

The revitalisation of the right was clearly a function of dissent within Liberalism as the party reshaped its ideological boundaries. Even before 1886, the capture of the Liberal interest in the west by disestablishers had strengthened the Conservatives, who emerged from the general election of 1885 with a threatening electoral base in both the counties and burghs. The home rule crisis enabled the right to effect a breakthrough in terms of seats in the west; but in the eastern burghs, where Liberalism was more entrenched, Liberal Unionism achieved a more fundamental change by establishing a two-party political culture in place of a near monopolistic Liberalism. As a result, the Unionist coalition extended the influence of the Conservative party rooted in the landed aristocracy – now politically unified by the inclusion of the Whigs – to the middle class in urban and industrial seats. To a certain degree, therefore, the growth of

Unionism indicated the development of social polarisation in urban electoral behaviour. Nevertheless, the religious dimension was also very important because the right could not have made a major impact without the support of many working class Orangemen, who were a critical element in the politics of Glasgow and the West (an area of increasing electoral importance), for more than seventy years after 1886.

The organisational development of the Unionist parties was perhaps less impressive than the growth in their vote. Nevertheless, the number of affiliates to the National Union of Scottish Conservative Associations expanded from 83 in 1883 to 258 in 1894, and at the 1893 annual conference all constituencies (except Orkney and Shetland) were associated with one of six regional divisions (Urwin). The constituencies, however, remained highly autonomous, and activity ranged from that of the largely inert North and East Divisions to the Western Division in which regional officers sought to stimulate the work of the associations, and where 'as early as 1895 the Conservatives in the College Division of Glasgow had been undertaking regular canvasses of the whole constituency' (Urwin: 110). As a result, Conservative registrations increased significantly in Glasgow, and was in part responsible for substantial Unionist gains in the city, culminating in the complete expulsion of the Liberals in 1900 (Hutchison: 197). Working Mens' Conservative Clubs were introduced to Scotland for the first time in the 1890s; and other schemes to attract the newly enfranchised included social events, such as dances and musical evenings, the founding of a flute band in Glasgow Bridgeton, and the formation of a club to politicise the cyclists of Dunbartonshire (Hutchison: 198). The Earl of Hopetoun, however, drew the line at picnics for party workers in the grounds of landowners (Hutchison: 195). It would appear, nevertheless, that most of these organisational advances were heavily concentrated in the urban parts of western Scotland, and even there the progress of the 1890s was vitiated after 1900 (Hutchison: 223-5). By 1911, a report on seats in eastern Scotland described a state of disorganisation and demoralisation not dissimilar from that found in 1876 (Hutchison: 221; Crapster). Energetic attempts by the centre to revitalise moribund associations met with some success, and various propaganda campaigns were undertaken, but with the message against them there was little the activists could hope to achieve.

The Liberal Unionists and the Conservatives remained distinct until 1912, although there was a strong level of co-operation at the national level to ensure they presented common candidates in elections.[2] In some constituencies the relationship between the parties was so close that by 1892 their links had been formalised in Greenock, and by 1900 they had merged into a single organisation in Glasgow St Rollox (Urwin), but more generally co-operation between the parties was more difficult in Scotland than elsewhere (Hutchison: 207). Ideologically, the Conservatives were particularly suspicious of the Radical Unionists' association with disestablishment, temperance and Highland land reform (Hutchison: 208-9), and many Liberal Unionists were temperamentally more Liberal than Tory. There were also, of course, conflicts of interest over the allocation of parliamentary candidatures. Liberal Unionist associations were frequently fictitious, which was resented by Conservatives when Liberal Unionist candidates were imposed on them in such constituencies; while an aggressively independent and well-organised Liberal Unionist Association in the

West was disliked by the local Conservatives, who regarded its activities as a threat to the progress they had already made in 1885 (Hutchison: 211-2). At first, the Conservatives deferred to Liberal Unionist candidates, but as the latter, with their reliance on the generation of 1886, failed to sustain the momentum of the initial disruption, the balance changed. As Liberal Unionist MPs retired or suffered defeat, the Tories, with their stronger grass roots inevitably became the senior partner, replacing Liberal Unionists with their own candidates. The unification of the two parties in 1912, therefore, was less than a marriage of equals, despite brave assertions to the contrary (Hutchison: 226).

The political developments within the major parties brought a greater ideological and organisational coherence to Scottish electoral politics. Change was particularly evident in the burghs where the new two-party system simplified voter choice, and permanent party associations replaced ad hoc electoral committees; and in rural constituencies the traditional rivalry between Whig and Tory proprietors was replaced by parties closely aligned to the socio-economic polarisation between landlord and tenant. Although regional and national party structures could do little to interfere in the activities of local associations, their influence would seem evident in the reduction of inter-party fights – assisted by the increasing probability of seats being lost to opponents in such circumstances – and the virtual elimination of unopposed returns. The general election as national referendum had arrived.

Electoral Competition, Parties and Candidates

Opposed and Unopposed Returns

An important feature of electoral competition, 1868–1880, had been a sharp reduction in the proportion of uncontested elections, which had most characterised returns under the First Reform Act. That trend was continued between 1885 and December 1910 when only six per cent of all returns in both burgh and county constituencies were unopposed.

In the burghs there were fifteen unopposed returns over the eight elections, all but two involving Liberals: four in 1886 and December 1910, three in 1885, two in 1895, one each in 1900 and 1906, and none in 1892 and January 1910. Significantly, all the uncontested Liberal constituencies were in the eastern half of Scotland, away from the centres of Irish immigration, and most were in burgh districts. Elgin Burghs was uncontested in 1885, 1886 and December 1910; and Stirling Burghs returned Campbell-Bannerman without opposition in 1885 and 1906, and Arthur Ponsonby in December 1910. There was no disputed election in the Hawick District in the first and last election of the period; no Unionist surfaced in either of Aberdeen's new divisions or Leith Burghs in 1886; and there were walkovers for Liberal candidates in Edinburgh Central in 1895 and Kirkcaldy Burghs in December 1910. More symbolic of the changed nature of burgh politics, however, were the unopposed returns of an incumbent Liberal Unionist in Edinburgh West (1895), a predominantly middle class constituency, and of a Conservative in Glasgow Central (1900), at the hub of the city's commercial and financial activities.

All county constituencies were contested in 1892, 1906 and January 1910. All but two seats were fought in 1885, when the Liberals were returned unopposed in the new mining division of West Fife and in the adjacent traditional Whig stronghold of Clackmannan and Kinross. In the crisis election of 1886 there were five unopposed returns: Liberals in Midlothian, Fife West and Kincardine, a Liberal Unionist in North Ayrshire, and in Inverness-shire Fraser Mackintosh finessed both the Conservatives and Liberals as a Unionist Crofter. Subsequently, there were Conservative walkovers in East Renfrew and Wigtown in both 1895 and 1900; but it was the election of December 1910 that produced the most unopposed candidates: Liberals in Banff, Kincardine, Elgin and Nairn (which had been Conservative in 1895 and 1900), Orkney and Shetland, Ross and Cromarty, Inverness, and Clackmannan and Kinross, and a Conservative in Wigtown. Although the eight uncontested seats in December 1910 reflected a lack of enthusiasm for two elections in the same year, it was also a consequence of severe Unionist despondency in the Highlands and the East, where in Kincardineshire the Conservatives felt their activities would be better directed towards political education through lantern-slide lectures on tariff reform than in electioneering (Dyer).

Parties and Candidates

The developing party system was dominated by the bi-polarity established after 1886 between the Gladstonian Liberals in alliance with the Crofters, on the one hand, and the Conservative and Liberal Unionist coalition on the other. Additionally, there were the socialists who snapped at the heels of Liberalism in some industrial constituencies, although they failed to match even the modest breakthrough they achieved in England.

(a) *Independent Liberals*. The establishment by the Liberals of a network of constituency associations for the purposes of controlling the nomination of candidates and fighting elections was a novel feature of the 1885 general election. This ran counter to traditional burgh practices, in which various Liberal factions, dominated by local notables, either bargained over the selection of a single nominee, or ran Liberal candidates of equal status against each other. It was only from 1885, therefore, that the concept of official or unofficial (independent) Liberal candidatures had any meaning. The transition was particularly dramatic in Glasgow and Edinburgh, because their division into single member constituencies undermined the city-wide structures and understandings that had enabled the Radical and Whig factions to reconcile their differences through a proportionate distribution of candidates between them. Inevitably, in 1885, there was a reluctance in some Liberal quarters to accept the moral right of the new Liberal associations to monopolise party nominations, and their legitimacy was challenged in some constituencies by Independent Liberals. With the Liberal electors not always prepared to take their cues from local party endorsements, seven Independent Liberals standing in the burghs defeated official representatives of their party. By 1886, however, the rationalisation of the party system and the rise of Unionism rendered such methods unnecessary and electorally suicidal.

Three of the 1885 Independent Liberals were returned in Edinburgh, where there was a struggle between ‘the shrieking brotherhood of Liberals… [making] …a desperate attempt to assert their supremacy by means of what they have chosen to describe as Liberal Associations' (*Scotsman,* 27.11.1885), under Radical domination, and more Whiggish interests, deriving from the old Liberal Aggregate, supported by the *Scotsman*. In Edinburgh East, George Goschen, an English Churchman, sought the candidacy shortly after the passing of the redistribution bill, but he was not acceptable to the Liberal association, whose chairman described him as 'The Goliath of modern Whiggism ...Proud representative of the Holyrood Brewery and the Auld Kirk' (*Scotsman*, 3.10.1885). It was, however, more than a month before Benjamin Costelloe, a candidate acceptable to the voluntaries,[3] was adopted by the Liberal association. Costelloe's critics pointed out that he was a Roman Catholic and a Glaswegian, who had already been rejected as a nominee for Glasgow St Rollox; and in the absence of a Conservative the voters preferred Goschen by seven to three. Edinburgh South Liberal Association, by contrast, had nominated a Radical barrister-at-law, Thomas Raleigh, as their candidate, before Lord Provost Sir George Harrison, a Liberal Churchman, entered the field. The chairman of the local association, Baillie Turnbull, claimed that as the Liberal associations had been established in 1874 for the very purpose of preventing internecine warfare, the lord provost should step down.[4] Sir George's backers, however, held that such rules did not apply in the absence of a Conservative challenge; and in the consequent election the lord provost won 60 per cent of the poll.

In Edinburgh Central there were three Liberals standing in addition to a Conservative. The official nominee, John Renton, had strong Radical connections as the son of a United Presbyterian minister and grandson of William Renton, a father-in-law of Duncan McLaren, former lord provost, MP from 1865 until 1881, and political leader of the Scottish voluntaries. His two Independent Liberal opponents were Adam Black (a Churchman), whose father had been a Whig-supported member for the city, 1856–65, when he had been defeated by McLaren; and a late entrant, John Wilson, former city treasurer and honorary secretary to the Radical Committee which had returned McLaren and Miller in 1865. Wilson won with 42 per cent of the votes, and Renton had to be content with second place. The only official Liberal elected in Edinburgh was a former member for the unitary city, Thomas Buchanan (a disestablisher) in Edinburgh West, against Conservative opposition only. Despite the ideological dimension to the various contests, the choices of the Edinburgh electorate seemed also to indicate a preference for candidates of high social standing: national with respect to Goschen, and local in the case of Harrison and Wilson. It was, however, a measure of the cultural shift caused by the home rule crisis, that in 1886 both Goschen and Wilson were heavily defeated by margins of six to four, following their desertion to Liberal Unionism; and it is likely that had Harrison done so (he died shortly after his election), he, too, would have lost his seat, because his successor, Childers, retained the constituency for Gladstonianism with almost 60 per cent of the votes, as the electors focused on the national issues rather than local personalities.[5] Ironically, Buchanan, the only successful official Liberal in the capital in 1885, was to retain his seat as a Liberal Unionist in 1886, when the former Independent Liberals in Edinburgh were defeated by Gladstonians.

The strains that the new franchise was placing on traditional Liberal organisations and voter allegiances were also evident in Perth and the burghs of Wick, St Andrews, and Kirkcaldy, the other constituencies to fall to Independent

Liberals in 1885.

In Perth the struggle for the Liberal nomination between the Whiggish incumbent, Parker, and a Radical opponent, McDougall, supported by the executive of the Liberal association, was particularly fierce, with the latter carrying the day at an open meeting. Parker, however, received a letter of support from Gladstone, and with the help of the *Perthshire Advertiser* won well as an Independent Liberal, defeating a Conservative and pushing McDougall into third place (Savage: 120-2). As a Gladstonian, Parker received the endorsement of the Perth Liberal Association in 1886, when he defeated a Liberal Unionist. Although Parker was again the official Liberal in 1892, the recently formed Perth Liberal and Radical Association put forward their own candidate as an Independent Liberal in opposition, helping the Conservatives to carry the seat at a trough in Liberal fortunes in eastern Scotland (Craig: *n*. 495). That was the last time an Independent Liberal came forward in Perth, and the only time it was won by a Unionist.

Like Parker, Sir George Campbell, who had represented Kirkcaldy Burghs for the previous decade, lost the Liberal nomination in 1885, but as an Independent Liberal beat his Liberal and Conservative opponents comfortably, and was officially recognised by his local association in 1886, when he withstood a Unionist challenge. By contrast, in St Andrews Burghs, Sir Robert Anstruther, a crusading Churchman, defeated the official incumbent Liberal and disestablisher, Stephen Williamson, in 1885, by two votes. His return signalled a shift towards the right in the constituency, because it was held by three members of the Anstruther family for Liberal Unionism until 1918, save for a short period from a by-election in 1903 to 1906 and from January to December 1910. An Independent Liberal also took the Wick Burghs in 1885, though in this instance from a Radical position, when John Cameron, nominated by the Wick Radical Workingmen's Association and endorsed by the Highland Land Law Reform Association, defeated John Pender, who had represented the constituency since 1872 (Craig: *n*. 521). Cameron retained the seat as an official Liberal in 1886, but was defeated in 1892 by Pender standing as a Liberal Unionist.

Apart from 1885, there was only one occasion in which an Independent Liberal defeated an official Liberal. That was in Glasgow Tradeston in January 1910, when a temperance Liberal, Cameron Corbett, elected as a Liberal in 1885, returned as a Liberal Unionist from 1886 to 1906, having defected from the Unionist camp in 1908 over the attitude of the Conservatives to the licensing question (Pelling: 402), stood as an Independent Liberal, defeating both a Liberal Unionist and a Liberal in a very close three-cornered contest. His peculiar success rested largely on his personal popularity and reputation for 'princely liberality' (Blewett: 373), rendering his position, according to Churchill, 'absolutely unassailable having given parks, fountains and other such things to his beloved native town' (Blewett: *n*. 51, 478). Corbett was the only successful independent candidate in the election throughout Britain in January 1910. The following December he was again returned to Westminster, but this time as an official Liberal.

In addition to the seven burgh cases where Independent Liberals were successful in 1885, there were four constituencies, Aberdeen North, Glasgow Camlachie and Falkirk Burghs (in which there were two Independent Liberals), where they failed to be returned.

James Thom, a local medicinal confectioner in Aberdeen North, and James Martin, a warehouseman standing in Glasgow Camlachie, each secured a derisory 177 votes, largely because their official Liberal opponents were similarly favourable to disestablishment, Gladstonian in orientation, and enjoyed the backing of their local Radical associations. Lacking any institutional support, Thom was defined by the Liberal *Aberdeen Daily Free Press* (16.11.1885) as 'nondescript', refusing to regard him as a Liberal despite his expressed backing for Gladstone. It is, nevertheless, unlikely the Grand Old Man would have endorsed Thom's position, as stated in his election address, that he would 'not vote for a measure to Disestablish the church until an inquiry by Royal Commission or otherwise is made to ascertain upon what title the millions of acres of land in this Country are had by Dukes and Earls, and others who never earned the money to purchase them. Then Disestablish both them and the church *simul et semel*' (*Aberdeen Daily Free Press*, 26.11.1885). He also held there were too many lawyers in parliament – possibly because part of the 'army of long-robed gentlemen' (*Aberdeen Daily Free Press*, 26.11.1885) in the pay of his opponents in the Aberdeen Liberal establishment, were trying to oust him from his business premises, 32a Broad Street, for non-payment of rent.[6]

More important than Thom's eccentricities was the intervention of the Liberal Churchman, Viscount Dalrymple (eldest son of the 10th Earl of Stair), in the Kilmarnock Burghs, for his 20 per cent share of the poll succeeded in narrowly securing the defeat of Dick Peddie, a leading disestablisher, by his Conservative opponent.[7] Dalrymple's Liberal credentials were extremely questionable because it was only his fear that the Church Liberals would refuse to vote for a Conservative that had persuaded him to stand (Hutchison: 159).[8] Opposition to an incumbent was also a feature of the Falkirk Burghs contest, where John Ramsay, a merchant identified with the conservative wing of the party, was unacceptable to certain Advanced Liberal elements. Although he had managed to secure the nomination of the Falkirk Burghs' Liberal Association by eleven votes to six (*Scotsman*, 29.10.1885), partly through sentiment and partly because he reaffirmed his support for disestablishment, Radicals, such as ex-Provost Cassells of Hamilton, were not prepared to back 'an old-fashioned Whig' (*Scotsman*, 15.10.1885). Consequently, most dissident Liberals threw their weight behind a Radical London-based barrister, John Weir, who 'had no sympathy for moderate trimmed Liberals who were always lagging behind' (*Scotsman*, 10.11.1885). A second Independent Liberal, John Roskill from Manchester, also threw his hat into the ring as a Radical. In the event, Ramsay easily retained his seat with just over half the votes cast: nearly four times as many as Weir. Roskill, who at one stage was moved to deny he had retired from the contest, and later did so following arbitration by the SLA, attracted only fourteen electors (Craig: 502). Predictably, Ramsay deserted to the Liberal Unionists, who took the seat with a new candidate in 1886.

The remaining burgh Independent Liberal, ex-Lord Provost Moncur, a local manufacturer, disestablisher and Gladstonian, came forward in Dundee to oppose the officially nominated Charles Lacaita (a disestablisher) and Edmund Robertson (a moderate Churchman), both London-based lawyers standing for the first time. Differences between the three Liberals were minimal and Moncur gained a creditable third place. Undoubtedly the most notable feature of the Dundee contest was the re-emergence of a former Radical member, Edward

Jenkins, as a Conservative Churchman, whose candidacy was endorsed by the established Presbytery. Significantly, his mother was of Belfast Presbyterian stock, and at the time of the election he was living in Ulster. Although coming bottom of the poll in 1885, he returned again ten years later commanding an even smaller share of the votes (Walker: 165, 254-5).

After 1885 there were only three constituencies in which Independent Liberal candidates came forward in the burghs, two having already been mentioned: Perth in 1895 and Glasgow Tradeston in January 1910. The third occasion, in 1892, was in Glasgow Camlachie where the incumbent Liberal, Watt, lost the backing of his constituency association on account of his lukewarm support for Irish home rule, his opposition to disestablishment, and lack of sympathy with the temperance movement (Craig: *n.* 505). Initially he was replaced by Cunninghame Graham, but the latter's left-wing sympathies lost him the nomination also. Standing as an Independent Liberal, Watt secured only 179 votes, but Cunninghame Graham's intervention as a socialist was largely responsible for the Liberal Unionists taking the seat (Craig: 505).

In the counties the tradition of intra-party conflict was almost non-existent, and there were only six cases of Independent Liberals standing: Aberdeen West, Elgin and Nairn, and the Lanarkshire divisions of Mid Lanark and Govan, in 1885, Kincardineshire in 1892, and Caithness in 1900. Apart from the contest in Elgin and Nairn, none of the county Independent Liberals came close to victory.

The 1885 contests in Elgin and Nairn and West Aberdeenshire illustrate the strains the new electorate were imposing on rural Liberalism, for in each case the Independent Liberal was supported by local Radical associations and the Scottish Farmers' Alliance, a body of tenant farmers who were favourable to Chamberlain's views on land reform, and wanted the Irish Land Act introduced to Scotland. The Independent Liberals also had the backing of 'ardent Disestablishers' (*Aberdeen Journal*, 31.10.1885), and, in West Aberdeenshire, the endorsement of Aberdeen Trades Council. So strong was the Radical campaign in Elgin and Nairn that the incumbent Whig laird and Churchman, Sir George Grant, despite receiving a crucial letter of support from Gladstone (Savage: 127), only retained the seat with a majority of 56 over his Conservative opponent and 177 over the Independent Liberal, Charles Anderson, a London QC. The following year Grant deserted to Liberal Unionism, and Anderson, as the official Gladstonian, defeated him by a narrow margin. Quintin Kerr, an Ayrshire farmer and 'valorous tub-thumping spouter' (Farquharson: 41), the Independent Liberal in West Aberdeenshire, was less successful, for although the incumbent, Farquharson of Finzean, was accused of having supported an amendment which had vitiated the intentions of the Agricultural Holdings Act, he was sympathetic to tenant farmers, leant towards disestablishment, and was to back Gladstone over home rule. More centrist than Grant, therefore, Farquharson won more than half the votes in a three-cornered contest, and Kerr received less than a fifth of the poll. The Independent Liberal challenge of Hoey, a Churchman, who received eleven votes in Lanarkshire Govan, was largely accidental, because his decision to stand down following arbitration by the SLA had been too late for his name to be withdrawn from the ballot (Craig: *n.* 546).

Stephen's claim in 1892 to be an Independent Liberal was largely bogus because he was unopposed by the Unionists and his campaign in Kincardineshire, organised through the Church Defence Association, depended on Tory rather than dissident Liberal backing. Significantly, his share of the poll, 36.0 per cent, reflected the performance of Unionist candidates in the region (Dyer). Two Independent Liberals stood in Caithness in 1900. One was Dr Clark, a former MP, who in 1885, 1886 and 1892 had been elected as a Crofter, and in 1895 as a Liberal. His strong Boer sympathies – he had been Consul General of the South African Republic before 1891 – however, lost him his party's nomination in 1900, when they replaced him with Robert Harmsworth, a Liberal Imperialist. Clark also lost the backing of the Land Reform Association of Caithness, who, unwilling to back Harmsworth, put forward a candidate of their own (Craig: *n*. 507). In the event, Harmsworth held the seat with a majority of 28 over a Conservative.

(b) *The Crofters*. A critical development in the 1885 general election was the intervention of Crofting candidates supported by the Highland Land League in Caithness, Sutherland, Ross and Cromarty, Inverness-shire, Argyll and the Inverness Burghs, as a direct result of the extension of the vote to poorer sections of the peasantry.

Hitherto, the Highland electorate had been especially small, and the politics of the region had been dominated by a handful of landed families. The Liberal interest had been locally defined by Whig proprietors – such as the Duke of Sutherland – who had been instigators of the clearances. Consequently, for the new electors, Liberalism was an interest hostile to their own. Just as in Ireland, therefore, much of the peasantry was available for mobilisation by new political forces, and in 1885 the Crofters defeated official Liberal candidates in Caithness, Argyll, and Ross and Cromarty, and both a Liberal and a Conservative in Inverness-shire. Only the Marquis of Stafford in Sutherland, and a Free Churchman, Robert Finlay, in the Inverness Burghs, successfully resisted the challenge. Thereafter, in 1886 and 1892, the Gladstonian Liberals deferred to Crofters. In Inverness-shire, however, in 1886, the incumbent landowning Crofter, Fraser Mackintosh, a former Conservative and Liberal MP for the Inverness Burgh, 1874–1885, stood unopposed as a Crofter opposed to home rule. By 1895, the Crofting candidates were standing as official Liberals.

The survival of Finlay in the Inverness Burghs was illustrative of the peculiarities of Highland politics at this time. Finlay represented the Free Church Constitutional Party, which was opposed to disestablishment, and in 1886 he introduced a bill 'to declare the Constitution of the Church of Scotland in a manner that would facilitate union with the Free Church on the basis of the Claim of Right of 1842. It was backed especially by the Free Church anti-Disestablishers in the Highlands, of whom it was said their main opposition to disestablishment was that it would confiscate the endowments and state support which they hoped to enjoy one day when they returned to a purified Establishment' (Kellas 1964: 38). Free Church establishmentarianism in the Highlands, therefore, complicated the relationship between the crofters and the Scottish Liberals, whose urban Free Churchmen had grown close to the United Presbyterian voluntaries, from which the Liberal Party drew its activist core, and were to join with them in the United Free Church in 1900. The Highland Free Churchmen, however, refused to join the voluntaristic UF Church, thereby sharpening the cultural and political peculiarities of the region.

The incorporation of the Crofters into mainstream Liberalism within a decade, indicates to a certain extent the pressure group nature of the movement and the limited objectives of the Land League's supporters, which had been largely achieved by 1895. It also indicated the realignment that had taken place within rural Liberalism generally following the Third Reform Act. In 1885, the Whig faction within county Liberalism was still influential in many areas, but the home rule issue alienated much of this support because it was closely associated with land reform. Consequently, most Whig landowners deserted to Liberal Unionism in 1886 for largely class reasons, and it is not insignificant that the number of landowning Liberal county MPs fell from nine in 1885 to only three in December 1910. The activities of the Crofters' party, therefore, might be regarded as an extreme case of what was happening more widely within Scottish Liberalism – as was noted in Elgin and Nairn and West Aberdeenshire – and not simply a phenomenon unique to the social structure and history of the Highlands in the nineteenth century.

(c) *The Socialists.*[9] The circumstances that stimulated the various socialist parties to make sporadic attacks on the Liberal Party in urban constituencies and industrialised counties were not unrelated to the stimuli that had created the Crofter phenomenon. Philosophically, many of the early Scottish socialists were Radical Liberals who had been fired by the highland campaign of Henry George; the credibility of their challenge rested on the Third Reform Act, which had greatly extended the franchise to industrial workers; and tactically, they sought to gain recognition from the Liberal Party by posing as a threat to their interests either by winning seats from them, as did the Crofters, or by dividing the radical vote to allow Unionist victories in sufficient divisions to force the Liberals into electoral pacts. In the event, the labour interests failed to achieve even the limited success of the Crofters, and the local Liberal associations kept the Labour leaders at arm's length.

A major problem for the socialists was that the Irish Catholic working class were unwilling to desert the Liberals until the resolution of the home rule question, and Unionism appealed to working class Orangemen. The refusal of the Irish Nationalists to support Keir Hardie in the Mid Lanark by-election of 1888 played a major role in securing his humiliating defeat, despite backing from the Scottish Home Rule Association (Kellas: 1965a). Not that the Labour leader always helped his cause, as when he introduced Alexander MacDonald – one of the first two working men to enter Parliament – to an audience of Lanarkshire miners, comparing him favourably to Martin Luther. Two thirds of those present were Irish Roman Catholics, and the meeting ended in a riot (Stewart: 11).

The 48 socialist interventions, 1885–December 1910, are noteworthy more for the complexity of the party labels spawned by their candidates than the magnitude of their impact. The increased importance given to Clydeside in the redistribution act assisted the socialists in that 18 of their burgh candidatures were in Glasgow, and ten of their 15 attempts to win county seats were in Lanarkshire. The role of Glasgow as the main centre of the left-wing challenge was particularly evident before 1906, in that no fewer than 14 of the 21 socialist candidatures in the general elections, 1885–1900, were in the city. Further-more, the Lanarkshire divisions of Partick and Govan, contested respectively in 1885 and 1895, were within the Glasgow conurbation. Elsewhere, the left intervened five times in Dundee, three times in Aberdeen North, twice in Ayrshire North and Fife West, and once in Aberdeen South, Edinburgh Central, Greenock, Paisley and the burgh districts of Falkirk, Leith and Montrose. Additionally, socialists contested twelve by-elections: three before 1900 and five after 1910. There were only three socialist interventions in county seats before 1906, and only a combined total of twelve in the general elections of 1906 and 1910, despite decisive majorities amongst Scottish Miners for affiliation to the Labour Party in both 1906 and 1908. The unwillingness of the Scottish artisan electorate to follow their industrial leaders in rejecting the Liberal Party makes the observation that the 'problem [with the miners] was to turn general sympathy into support for particular Labour candidates' (Gregory: 94), particularly apposite north of the border.

The first socialists to stand were representatives of the Scottish Land Restoration League, a brand of William Morris' Socialist League, when, in 1885, they contested Lanarkshire Partick, Greenock, and the Glasgow divisions of Bridgeton, Blackfriars and Hutchesontown, and Tradeston. Three of the candidates recorded barely one per cent of the poll, the best performance being in Tradeston, where Greaves won just over fourteen per cent of the votes.

The left-wing standard remained furled in 1886, but in 1892 various parties supported candidates in seven constituencies. Led by Keir Hardie, the Scottish Labour Party – an association of trade unions, political elements, such as the remnants of the SLRL, and individuals including Dr Clark, a Crofter MP, and Cunninghame Graham, the former Lib–Lab member for NW Lanark – endorsed Bennett Burleigh as Labour and Liberal candidate in Glasgow Tradeston, Brodie as Labour and Temperance candidate in Glasgow College, and both Cunninghame Graham and Hugh Watt in the same Glasgow Division, Camlachie, although the latter was essentially an Independent Liberal.[10] The party also gave its support to Woollen in Perth, an Independent Gladstonian, and to Clark, who stood as a Crofter in Caithness, fully outside the orbit of the SLP. Champion, of the Social Democratic Federation, who had broken with the SLP, stood in South Aberdeen as a candidate of the more radical Scottish United Trades Councils Labour Party;[11] and Chisholm Robertson, the Stirlingshire Miners' leader, who had also fallen out with the SLP, came forward under the banner of Liberalism, home rule and Labour. John Wilson stood in Edinburgh Central for the Scottish Socialist Federation against, amongst others, AK Connell, a Labour and Unionist candidate, and in Dundee, J Macdonald represented the SPLP. Excluding Woollen and Clark (neither of whom can be considered as a socialist candidate), none of these aspirants performed with great distinction, the most impressive result being that of Champion who captured almost 16 per cent of the poll in Aberdeen South. The main consequence of these interventions was to enable the Liberal Unionists to capture Glasgow Camlachie and retain Glasgow Tradeston. Nevertheless, the Liberals felt under no pressure to make concessions to Labour representatives, and in 1894 the Glasgow Liberal Council together with the executive of the Scottish Liberal Association closed the door on the socialists by asserting that the difference between them was 'not one of representation but of principle' (Kellas 1968: 328).

The socialists continued to plough a hard and lonely furrow. In 1895 the Independent Labour Party presented seven candidates in Glasgow, Dundee and Lanarkshire Govan, and an Independent Labour (not ILP) offering backed by the local trades council stood in Aberdeen North. With the exception of Macdonald in Dundee, who increased his vote from 354 to 1,313 between 1892 and 1895 amongst an electorate of over 18,000, the results were worse than in 1892. Macdonald's improvement was due to his endorsement by the Dundee Trades Council, which had been denied to him three years earlier because of Irish opposition (Walker: 266-8). Following the poor performance of 1895, AE Fletcher, a member of the Scottish Workers' Representation Committee, a local variant of the Labour Representation Committee (reflecting the autonomous character of many aspects of the Scottish Labour movement), constituted the sole socialist candidate in 1900, when he came forward in Glasgow Camlachie. With the imprimatur of the ILP, Glasgow Trades Council, and the Camlachie Liberal Association, Fletcher won nearly 42 per cent of the votes (Hutchison: 182).

As with the Liberals, 1906 brought a revival in socialist fortunes. The SWRC fought Paisley, Falkirk Burghs, Ayrshire North, and Lanarkshire North East and North West; the Social Democratic Federation maintained a Marxist presence in Aberdeen, where Kennedy contested the North division; and the Labour Party stood in Glasgow Blackfriars and Hutchesontown, Dundee and Lanarkshire Govan. The most notable results were clearly in Blackfriars and Hutchesontown, where the engineer George Barnes defeated both a Conservative and a Liberal with just under 42 per cent of the poll, and in Dundee, where the two-member system enabled a single Labour nominee, Alexander Wilkie, to capture one of the seats. An important element in Barnes' victory was his endorsement by the United Irish League in a constituency where the Irish Catholic vote had secured the election of a Conservative, Bonar Law, in 1900, as a protest against the coolness towards home rule of the incumbent Liberal, Provand, who was seeking to return in 1906 (Pelling: 402). In Dundee, by contrast, the Irish had been told to support the two Liberals, but whereas the continuing Liberal, Robertson, was generally popular, the new Liberal candidate, a London stockbroker replacing a well-liked local newspaper proprietor, was less acceptable, and a third of Robertson's electors also cast a vote for Wilkie.[12]

Elsewhere there were creditable results. Burgess and Hill, the respective candidates in Glasgow Camlachie and Lanarkshire Govan won one in three of the ballots in their constituencies, coming close behind the Liberals and within striking distance of the Unionist victors. Similarly, in Lanarkshire North East and North West, the two socialists received almost 30 per cent of the poll; Kennedy held a quarter of the votes, coming second in Aberdeen North; the miners' leader, Smillie, did almost as well in Paisley; and Brown, another miner, won rather more than a fifth of the ballot in Ayrshire North. Although these advances were sufficient to deny the Liberals victory in Glasgow Camlachie, Lanarkshire Govan, North West Lanarkshire and Ayrshire North, they failed to force the Liberals into an electoral alliance such as Ramsay MacDonald had won for Labour in England (Bealey & Pelling: Ch.4). The most that Labour gained was that in 1910 the Liberals gave Barnes a free run in Glasgow Blackfriars and Hutchesontown, and a local electoral pact was forced on the Liberals in Dundee.

In January 1910, all twelve socialist candidates represented the Labour Party, with the exception of the Social Democrat, Kennedy, in Aberdeen North, and Burgess in the Montrose Burghs, nominated by the local ILP branch against national party advice that there was insufficient funding to mount a campaign

(Craig: *n.* 516). The promise of 1906, however, was largely unfulfilled. Labour's share of the poll fell by 8.2 per cent in Aberdeen North, 7.9 per cent in North Ayrshire, 17.4 per cent and 14.2 per cent respectively in Lanarkshire North East and North West, and by 5.7 per cent in Lanarkshire Govan. The best results, apart from Glasgow Blackfriars and Hutchesontown and Dundee, where there was no Liberal opposition, were Fife West, in which the local Miners' leader, William Adamson, captured nearly 37 per cent of the poll at the first time of asking, and Glasgow Camlachie, in which there was only a small drop in Labour support. Burgess in Montrose Burghs and Smillie in Mid Lanark both emerged with more than a quarter of the vote, but Walker captured a more modest 18.9 per cent in the Leith District. Only in Glasgow Camlachie did Labour intervention punish the Liberals by allowing the return of a Conservative. Quite clearly, the polarised character of the election had persuaded many radical voters of the tactical necessity to vote Liberal. Such sentiments were probably also shared by many Labour activists, and it may not have been financial considerations alone that persuaded them to advance only five candidates in December 1910. Smillie lost only one per cent of his earlier vote in Mid Lanark, but in Glasgow Camlachie Labour's share of the poll fell by almost eleven per cent. In the absence of a right-wing candidate, Adamson carried West Fife against the incumbent Liberal, and Barnes and Wilkie, unopposed by Liberals, retained their seats.

The inability of the left outside the Liberal Party to make a major impact on Scottish representation served to underline the depth of support for Scottish Liberalism amongst working class Scotsmen. It was a measure of that strength that even Lib–Lab candidates (which in this analysis have been classed as Liberals), did not prove especially attractive. As we have seen, in 1885 the electors of Kirkcaldy Burghs preferred to stick with Sir George Campbell than to back Inglis, the Lib–Lab offering endorsed by the Liberal association. Cunninghame Graham, another Lib–Lab candidate, failed to carry Lanarkshire NW, in 1885, despite Liberal victories in adjacent constituencies, although he made amends the following year to record the only Lib–Lab win in Scotland ever. The results of Lib–Lab candidatures in other constituencies: Lanarkshire Govan (1885), Renfrew East (1886), Greenock (1895) and Glasgow Tradeston (1900), offer no evidence to suggest that they enhanced the vote which might have been achieved by a straight Liberal. It was hardly likely, therefore, that if Lib–Lab candidates had a neutral if not negative influence on the size of the Liberal vote, that socialists standing independently would have done better even had they attracted some working class Unionist electors.

As with the Crofters, Liberalism did not ignore the challenge from the left but shifted its ground to incorporate the demands of the new industrial electorate. In 1891 the Scottish Liberal Association came out in favour of the Eight Hour Day, the abolition of the House of Lords, universal adult suffrage and major land reform in the highlands, thereby finessing the positions of moderate socialists like Hardie. More importantly, many Scottish Liberal MPs espoused these policies, which were more advanced than those of the Newcastle programme, and in 1893 some 44 of them supported an Eight Hour Bill (Kellas: 1965a).[13] From 1906 onwards, whatever the misgivings of the Scottish Liberal rank-and-file, the industrial working class responded positively to the reforming government led by Scots-based MPs, amongst whom Campbell-Bannerman,

Asquith, Haldane and Churchill were the most prominent. Furthermore, the replacement of John Morley by Vernon-Harcourt in the Montrose District in 1908 was seen as a move to the left, as were the election of Arthur Ponsonby in Stirling Burghs following the death of Campbell-Bannerman, and the return of John Barran (Hawick District), Percy Molteno (Dumfriesshire), William Pringle (North West Lanark), and Alexander Scott (Glasgow Bridgeton). Between 1910 and 1914, the ranks of social radicals were further reinforced by WGC Gladstone (Kilmarnock District), James White (Glasgow Tradeston), Daniel Holmes (Lanarkshire Govan), and John Pratt (Linlithgow). It was a measure of the threat posed to the left by the new generation of Liberal MPs, that the return of Pratt drew the comment from the socialist organ *Forward* that he was 'a dangerous man. His platform ability, his knowledge of the socialist case, and his strong humanitarian (if not socialist sympathies) could be used to damaging effect against Labour candidates on behalf of the Liberal aspirants for Parliament' (Hutchison: 239-40). These developments were consolidated by the institution of a Royal Commission into the provision of working class housing in Scotland, in association with the trade unions. Consequently, by the end of the pre-war period, the Liberals were in a better position to resist socialism than they had been in 1885, just as they were in a stronger position to incorporate rural radicalism.

In the final analysis, the socialists could never break the umbilical cord with the Liberals. While some working class voters were prepared to take a chance with Labour candidates when the tide flowed strongly to the left, as in 1906, they would rally to the Liberals in times of crisis, as in 1910. Even the socialist leaders, who had been rebuffed by the Liberals, appeared affected by similar sentiments in that they offered no challenge in 1886, presented only a single candidate in 1900, and ran only five aspirants in December 1910. The ambivalence of Labour leaders towards the Liberals at this time is well documented, as for example by Robert Smillie, who in his autobiography *My Life for Labour*, identified WE Gladstone as 'the greatest man I met,' followed by Campbell-Bannerman (Donnachie et.al.: 17).

(d) *Liberals, Liberal Unionists and Conservatives.* The major confrontation of the period, however, was not between the Liberals and combinations of Independent Liberals, Crofters and Socialists, but between Liberals and Conservatives allied to the Liberal Unionists.

The development of the national party system after 1868 had done much to ensure that the Conservatives at least nominally contested most Scottish constituencies. Nevertheless, as late as 1885 the Tories ignored eight burgh constituencies, and failed to challenge in six county seats, including four in the Highlands, where they deferred to the Whigs in their struggles with the Crofters. In 1886, however, the party system was simplified as Independent Liberalism fell away, official Liberalism was identified with Gladstonianism, and Liberal Unionists deserted to form a Unionist alliance with the Conservatives. As a result, the right not only extended its appeal amongst the electorate but became organisationally capable of challenging the Liberals across all constituencies on a routine basis.

Altogether some 22 Scottish Liberal MPs, including Independent Liberals, thirteen of them in the burghs, and one Crofter, opposed Gladstone's home rule

Bill. The most readily identifiable group of Liberal Unionists were a côterie of Liberal landowners including the Marquis of Stafford (Sutherland), Arthur and Hugh Elliot (Roxburgh and Ayrshire North) – the second and third sons of the Earl of Minto – Sir George Grant (Elgin and Nairn), Sir Robert Anstruther (St Andrews Burghs), and Richard Campbell (Ayr Burghs), for whom the proposed reform was the last straw in the anti-landlord drift of the party under Gladstone. To them might be added the lawyer Craig Sellar (Lanarkshire Partick), whose father had been responsible for organising the Sutherland clearances. Not all of the prime minister's opponents, however, were Whigs: John Kinnear in East Fife was a Radical, and Thomas Sutherland (Greenock) had been elected in 1880 as a 'Reformer, Free Trader, and advocate of the Extension of the Franchise, of Religious Equality, of Temperance, and of Education' (Donald: 47). Sutherland's opposition represented mercantile disquiet with the home rule, and two other shipowners, James Barclay (Forfar) and Sir Donald Currie (West Perthshire) also became Liberal Unionists, as did Sir Robert Jardine (Dumfriesshire), a China merchant. The most notable dissentient was the radical landowner and Scottish secretary, George Trevelyan (Hawick Burghs), who emerged as a Liberal Unionist in 1886 because he was opposed to the accompanying land bill. As the author of the Scottish Crofters' Act, 1886, however, Trevelyan cannot be identified with mainstream proprietorial opposition to Gladstone's policy, as was demonstrated by his early return to the Liberal Party.

Of the twelve Liberal Churchmen, seven – Currie, Grant, Anstruther, Jardine, Stafford, Finlay (the pro-establishment Free Churchman from Inverness Burghs), and Goschen (Edinburgh East) – voted against Gladstone; four – Robertson (Dundee), Tennant (Peebles and Selkirk), Marjoribanks (Berwick) and Childers (Edinburgh South) – voted with the prime minister; and McLagan (Linlithgow) abstained (Kellas 1964: 40). Additionally, a Crofter Churchman and landowner, Fraser Mackintosh, (Inverness-shire), also voted against the bill. Buchanan (Edinburgh West), Corbett (Glasgow Tradeston), Sellar, Trevelyan, Henry (Glasgow Blackfriars and Hutchenstown), constituted a small group of disestablishers opposed to home rule. It was significant, however, that while the disaffected Churchmen were lost permanently, the disestablishers, Trevelyan, Buchanan and Corbett later returned to the fold of mainstream Liberalism, along with William Jacks (Leith Burghs), whose distinctly ambivalent attitude towards home rule was probably typical of many Scottish Liberals (Cook). Thus, while Liberal Unionism signalled the end of the Whig association with Gladstonian Liberalism because it was allied to disaffection across a whole range of issues, there were elements within urban Liberal Unionism whose underlying commitment to Liberalism remained, and whose disagreement with the leadership was narrowly restricted to certain aspects of the home rule question.

The consequences for electoral competition was that with so many Liberal MPs declaring themselves Unionists, the poor performance of Conservative candidates in 1885, and the suddenness of the 1886 election, the Liberal Unionists were given the lion's share of the constituencies to fight. In 1886, there were only four Conservatives standing in the burghs (fewer than at any election since 1859), and thirteen in the counties – probably less than at any time since the Union, and certainly since 1832. Of those who had been Liberal MPs, twelve were returned as Liberal Unionists, six were defeated by Liberals, and four retired.

Liberal Unionist candidates continued to dominate burgh constituencies right up to and including the election of 1900, when they and their allies contested all burgh constituencies for the first time (Table 3.1). Thereafter, the Conservatives assumed an ascendancy with 16 candidates in 1906 and 17 in both elections of 1910, whereas the Liberal Unionists slipped to fourteen in 1906 and January 1910, falling away to ten the following December. Conservative candidates were well represented in Glasgow and other western burghs, but in the stronger Liberal areas Liberal Unionists were preferred, and it was not until December 1910 that Conservatives reappeared in Edinburgh. Despite the shifting balance in candidate distribution, Liberal Unionists continued to return more burgh members than the Conservatives – apart from 1900 and January 1910, when the two factions were evenly represented – largely because the Liberal revival after 1900 negated any advantage the Conservatives had in advancing more candidates.

In the counties, the Conservatives rapidly established dominance over the Liberal Unionists. The election of 1892 produced 21 Conservative candidates, rising to 32 in January 1910, whereas Liberal Unionists declined steadily from 22 in 1886 to five in the last election before the war. From 1895, the only region to have a preponderance of Liberal Unionist candidates was Highland in 1900. Throughout the period the Conservatives had more county MPs than the Liberal Unionists, whose only win after 1900 was in Ayrshire North in 1906.

Table 3.1: The Distribution of Liberal Unionist and Conservative Candidates, 1886 – December 1910*

	1886	1892	1895	1900	1906	Jan. 1910	Dec. 1910
Burghs							
Liberal Unionists	23 (8)	20 (6)	16 (9)	17 (8)	14 (4)	15 (2)	10 (3)
Conservatives	4 (1)	11 (2)	13 (5)	14 (8)	16 (2)	16 (2)	17 (2)
Counties **							
Liberal Unionists	22 (8)	17 (5)	14 (5)	12 (9)	10 (1)	7 (0)	5 (0)
Conservatives	13 (9)	21 (7)	25 (12)	27 (11)	29 (3)	32 (5)	27 (4)

* MPs in brackets. ** Unionist/Crofter (1886) excluded.

The urban/county balance in the distribution of Unionist MPs between the two parties was hardly surprising. Conservative dominance in the counties reflected the continuation of a long-established two-party competition, whereas the presence of Liberal Unionists in the burghs arose from 50 years of virtual one-party rule. The exceptions, Glasgow and Highland, proved the rule. The Conservatives had established themselves in Glasgow well before 1886, having returned a member in 1874, whilst the peculiar claims of Liberal Unionists to represent the Highlands arose from their predominantly Whig antecedents. What impact the Conservatives would have made in Scotland had they been the only alternative to Gladstonian Liberalism on the right between 1886 and 1900 is impossible to establish, but it is unlikely they would have matched the performance of the Unionist coalition.

Conclusion

In 1885, Duncan McLaren, who for fifty years had played a major role in the politics of Edinburgh and had been the dominant influence in the development of Radical Liberalism in the city, was made honorary president of the Edinburgh South Liberal Association. As the home rule crisis began to unfold, the Southern Association passed a resolution expressing 'great admiration of Gladstone's talents and sagacity' (Mackie Vol.II: 256), and supported the institution of a parliament in Dublin. Shortly afterwards, McLaren resigned his honorary post, declaring he would vote for any candidate opposed to an Irish parliament 'whether Radical, Whig or Tory' (Mackie Vol.II: 258), regarding Gladstone's attitude as 'a virtual assumption of political autocracy or dictatorship' (Mackie Vol.II: 248). He was to die before the general election of 1886, in which the electorate of his new constituency voted in the home rule candidate by two to one.

The sad resignation of McLaren underlined an important change in urban political culture, distinguishing the politics of 1886–1910 from that prevailing in the five decades after 1832. In mid-Victorian Britain, local notables played a critical role in mediating between national leaders and the electorate, whether as heads of factions and/or as MPs themselves. McLaren, for example, had gone to Westminster as a plenipotentiary from Edinburgh not as Liberal lobby fodder, and earned the sobriquet 'Member for Scotland' (Mackie Vol.II: 116). Even in January 1886, Childers had sought McLaren's imprimatur before fighting a by-election in Edinburgh South. The 'dictator' Gladstone, however, had changed the rules through his charismatic appeal to the activists in the new Liberal associations, who preferred to put their trust in his leadership rather than in that of traditional local leaders such as 'the Nestor of Scottish Liberalism' (Mackie Vol.II: 261). As McLaren himself remarked at the time, 'the present generation of active men who now move in political matters are to an enormous extent men 'who knew not Joseph'[14] (Mackie Vol.II: 251). Gladstone's appeal, of course, critically extended to wide sections of the Scottish electorate (particularly the newly-enfranchised), who increased the status of the Gladstonian Liberal associations by voting for their candidates. The result was to make MPs more subject to parliamentary discipline because their nomination and election rested on activists and voters more committed to the British party leadership than to themselves as individuals. A man such as Corbett was very much an exception.

In rural constituencies, too, the character of Liberalism changed. The transformation was most evident in the Highlands, where the Whig elite, having been rejected by the voters, deserted to Liberal Unionism, leaving the development of Liberal interests and organisation to the Crofters. Similarly, in the other agricultural counties, the Liberal coalition passed from landed proprietors into the hands of tenant farmers, burgh tradesmen, newspapermen, United Presbyterian ministers and lawyers, who were active in the village and small town associations. As a result, Liberal activists no longer looked to local landowners for guidance, but took their cues from the United Kingdom leadership.

One consequence of that was increased influence of the whips over candidate selection, leading to the extensive carpet-bagging which characterised Liberal rural representation after 1886.

By contrast, the right, despite the development of formal party structures, remained dependent on local elites, acting as a counterpoint initially to the Caesarism of Gladstone. Scottish Liberal Unionism failed to produce a Chamberlain, and to the extent he articulated the interests of his party nationally, it was an embarrassment to his supporters in Scotland given his advocacy of protection and their commitment to free trade. Scottish Conservatism also lacked a charismatic figure, and the party associations, especially in rural constituencies, were dominated by small groups of social and economic leaders, who frequently resented attempts to make their party organisation more popular.

In conclusion, the major change in the Scottish party system came with the ending of single party politics in the burghs. Although that change came through the agency of the home rule crisis, the expansion of the electorate had rendered the maintenance of the old Liberal coalition, already under strain, impossible to maintain. The home rule crisis, however, determined how considerations of class, religion, and national identity would shape the parameters of the new party system. Although the developments of 1886 caused 20 years of difficulties for the Liberals, they worked generally to the advantage of mainstream Liberalism, because realignment over home rule enabled Gladstone to minimise the divisive influence of disestablishment sentiment in the new Liberal associations, the desertion of the Whigs facilitated an accommodation with rural radicalism, and religio–ethnic divisions amongst the working class stunted the growth of socialist parties. Most importantly, from a Scottish perspective, these political cleavages, and the parties and leaders who articulated them, were British in character. Thus, in contrast to Ireland, the ending of constituency-focused politics in Scotland resulted in a territorial perspective that leaped over national sub-divisions to the United Kingdom as a whole.

Notes

1. I am much endebted here to Kellas (1964) and Savage.
2. An arrangement not always popular locally, as with Lord Salisbury's diktat to the Ayrshire Conservatives to adopt a Liberal Unionist (Hutchison: 210).
3. 'A Radical candidate, who holds my opinions,' was the verdict of Duncan McLaren, leader of the Scottish Voluntaries (Letter to Adam Black, quoted by Mackie, Vol.II: 38).
4. Ironically, Sir George had himself chaired such a committee in 1880.
5. Childers may also have been helped by the fact he was a Churchman.
6. The 'conspiracy' of lawyers, he claimed, was inspired by the Hunters, Esslemonts and Websters, i.e. the families of local Liberal MPs, or prospective MPs (*Aberdeen Journal*, 14.9.1885).
7. Peddie had introduced a Disestablishment bill in 1884, which produced a strong negative reaction from Liberal Churchmen (Kellas 1965: 33-5).
8. There was also an Independent Conservative standing in Kilmarnock who won 55

votes, having retired from the contest too late to withdraw his nomination.

9. The term 'socialist' simply refers to candidates arising from the working class movement, and involves no ideological test. The information in this section is mostly drawn from Kellas (1964).
10. At least, that is the ascription given by Kellas (1964). Craig, however, classifies Cunninghame Graham as SPLP and Watt as an Independent Liberal.
11. For a full discussion of Aberdeen working class politics at this time see Buckley.
12. The detailed arithmetic of this result is discussed in the next chapter.
13. This was designed not only to finesse the socialists, but also the Liberal Unionists, who continued to espouse the more radical social policies of Joseph Chamberlain to the embarrassment of Gladstonians.
14. A reference to the Pharaoh who enslaved the Israelites (Exodus 1:8). This was a particularly apposite text in that 'Joseph' might well have applied to Joseph Chamberlain, the leader of the voluntaries, most of whom, unlike McLaren, deserted to Gladstone.

References

Aberdeen Daily Free Press.

Bealey, F, & Pelling, H, *Labour and Politics, 1900-1906*, London, 1958.

Blewett, N, *Peers, Parties and the People*, London, 1972.

Buckley, KD, *Trade Unionism in Aberdeen, 1878-1900*, Edinburgh, 1955.

Cook, AB, 'Gladstone's election for the Leith district of burghs, July 1886', *Scottish Historical Review,* Vol. 49, 1970.

Craig, FWS, British Parliamentary Election Results, 1885-1918, London, 1974.

Crapster, BL, 'Scotland and the Conservative Party in 1876,' *Journal of Modern History*, Vol. XXXIX, 355-60.

Crowley, DW, 'The Crofters Party, 1885-92,' *Scottish Historical Review,* Vol. 35, 1956.

Donald, J, *Past Elections in Greenock*, Greenock, 1933.

Donnachie, I, (ed.) et.al., *Forward! Labour Politics in Scotland, 1888-1988*, Edinburgh, 1989.

Dyer, M, *The Politics of Kincardineshire*, (unpublished Ph.D.) Aberdeen, 1974.

Farquharson, R, *The House of Commons from Within*, London, 1912.

Gregory, R, *The Miners in British Politics, 1906-1914*, London, 1968.

Hansard.

Hunter, J, 'The Politics of Highland Reform, 1873-1895,' *Scottish Historical Review*, Vol. 44, 1965.

Hutchison, ICG, *A Political History of Scotland*, Edinburgh, 1986.

Kellas, JG, 'The Liberal Party and the Scottish Church Disestablishment Crisis,' *English Historical Review*, Vol. 79, 1964.

Kellas, JG, 'The Liberal Party in Scotland, 1876-95,' *Scottish Historical Review*, Vol. 45, 1965.

Kellas, JG, 'The Mid-Lanark By-Election (1888), and the Scottish Labour Party (1888-1894),' *Parliamentary Affairs*, Vol. 18, 1965 (1965a).

Kellas, JG, *Modern Scotland: The Nation Since 1880*, London, 1968.

McCaffrey, JF, 'The Origins of Liberal Unionism in the West of Scotland,' *Scottish Historical Review*, Vol. 50, 1971.

Mackie, JB, *The Life and Work of Duncan McLaren*, 2 Vols, London, 1888.

Pelling, H, *Social Geography of British Elections, 1885-1910*, London, 1967.

Savage, DC, 'Scottish Politics, 1885-6', *Scottish Historical Review*, Vol. 40, 1961.

Scotsman.

Stewart, W, *J. Keir Hardie*, London, 1921.
Urwin, DW, 'The Development of the Unionist Party Organisation in Scotland until 1912,' *Scottish Historical Review*, Vol. 44, 1965.

4 *Electoral Behaviour, 1884–1910*

The eight general elections from 1885 to December 1910 fall into three distinct phases. Firstly, the election of 1885, in which the Liberals confirmed their sweeping victory of 1880; secondly, the elections from 1886 to 1900, when the Liberals gradually lost ground to a Unionist coalition which latterly won a majority of both county and burgh constituencies; and thirdly, the elections of 1906 and 1910, that re-established a clear Liberal dominance.

Although electoral trends in Scotland bore similarities to developments in England, the parameters were different (Cornford; Dunbabin). Whereas in 1885 the Conservatives won a majority of English boroughs for the first time since 1832, they carried only one of the 31 Scottish burgh seats; whereas the Unionists, with the exception of 1906, enjoyed English majorities (mostly substantial ones) in every election from 1886 to December 1910, they only won once in Scotland (1900); and whereas the 1906 election proved only a Liberal peak in England, in Scotland it marked a new plateau of achievement (Pelling: esp. 372-413; Blewett: Part I). Scotland remained less Unionist than any of the English regions over the period as a whole, though between 1886 and 1900 the Unionists performed worse north of the border than in Peak–Don, twelve constituencies centred on the South Yorkshire coalfield. Nevertheless, from 1886 Scotland ceded to Wales the accolade of being the most Liberal nation (Pelling: 415; Morgan), which was markedly evident in 1900 when Wales swung to the Liberals. Thus, whilst England became a predominantly Conservative nation in the late nineteenth century, confirming the results of 1874, Scotland, together with Wales and Nationalist Ireland, formed a crucial part of the reduced Liberal coalition.

Despite the decline in Liberal strength being associated with the home rule election of 1886, realignment had been apparent the previous year, especially in those areas where the Unionists were to enjoy their greatest successes. Compared to 1885, there were only marginal changes in the strengths of the major alignments in 1886 in Glasgow and the West, though the Unionists won 15 of the 24 seats. Furthermore, if the votes cast in 1885 for Independent Liberal Churchmen who became Unionists are classified as right-wing ballots, then the 1886 realignment appears even less dramatic.

Ironically, the electoral impact of the home rule crisis and its aftermath was most evident in those parts of Scotland which continued to return mostly Liberal MPs, because it accelerated the emergence of two-party electoral competition in areas which hitherto had been one-party fiefdoms. Consequently, the decline in Liberal support between 1885 and 1886 was most pronounced in the east, where right-wing electors, who had previously supported Whigs against Radicals or Liberal Churchmen against Liberal Dissenters, sided with Unionists against the Gladstonians. The underlying strength of Gladstonian Liberalism in eastern Scotland, however, meant that increased voter support for the right was not greatly reflected in the transfer of seats.

The recession in Liberal fortunes, following a shallow revival in 1892, deepened in 1895, as the endemic problem of Irish home rule was compounded by the party's less necessary advocacy of disestablishment and temperance, which were significantly less popular with the electors than activists. It was, however, the South African War and the desertion of the Irish which finally broke seven decades of Liberal dominance in Scottish general elections.

The Scottish Liberal Association was cripplingly split over the Boer War, but nowhere was the confusion and division more evident than in the attitudes of Liberal MPs. Although 27 Scottish Liberals (in common with the majority of their party) abstained on a pro-Boer amendment to the Queen's speech moved by the Irish in 1899, four of them – Dr Clark, Caithness; Wedderburn, Banffshire; MacLeod, Sutherland; and Souttar, Dumfries – voted for the amendment; whilst ten Liberal Imperialists – Asher, Elgin Burghs; Ferguson (the Scottish Whip), Leith Burghs; Dunn, Paisley; Gibson-Carmichael, Midlothian; Asquith, Fife East; Haldane, Haddington; Crombie, Kincardine; Douglas, NW Lanark; Ure, Linlithgow; and Kinloch, East Perth – voted with the Conservatives to secure its defeat (*Hansard*, 77: 157-60). The following year, eight Scottish Liberals, including five who had supported the government on the Irish motion – Asher, Dunn, Gibson-Carmichael, Crombie and Douglas – failed to vote for a Liberal front-bench motion critical of the conduct of the war (*Hansard*, 79: 824-8). Disharmony was further exacerbated by the factional bias of Ferguson, who drew strong criticism from within the SLA – including Campbell-Bannerman, a moderate – for his attempts to force Liberal Imperialists on reluctant constituency associations. Consequently, three weeks before the 1900 election he felt forced to resign his position as Scottish whip (Hutchison: 178). The impending debacle was completed by the refusal of the Irish Nationalist leaders to urge support for Liberal candidates because of their opposition to the founding of a Roman Catholic university in Ireland. The election of 1900, therefore, symbolised a decade and a half in which the Scottish Liberals had become disoriented and seemingly incapable of rediscovering the pulse of the electorate.

Continuing Liberal dissension throughout the 1890s enabled the Unionist parties to sustain the initiative they had gained in 1886. There were even signs that the infusion of Radical Liberal Unionists had enabled the new coalition to devise social policies more appealing to the crofters and working men than those of their Gladstonian opponents (Hutchison: 200-1). Chamberlain's call for protection in the summer of 1903, however, dealt a severe blow to the credibility of Scottish Unionism, because its challenge to free trade questioned the approach to political economy which had informed the British Union of 1707, and had become an article of faith for the Scottish middle classes of the nineteenth century. Thus, the Liberals, by emerging as the guardians of a threatened national consensus, were able to transcend the conflicts which had divided them after 1885 to win a substantial victory in 1906.

The new government led by Campbell-Bannerman and Asquith, both MPs for Scottish constituencies, proved popular in Scotland, whose electors stoutly supported its struggle with the upper chamber over Lloyd George's 1909 budget, designed to pay for the introduction of old age pensions with a land tax. Not only were working class electors positively disposed towards state pensions, but middle class electors and small farmers, who might have been less sympathetic, had become ill-disposed towards the House of Lords. A 1904 decision of the Law Lords to award the continuing Free Church ('Wee Frees') all the property of the Free Church, following the decision of the Free Church as a whole to join with the United Presbyterians in 1900, had angered urban Presbyterian sensibilities; and Upper House 'outright rejection of the reintroduced Scottish Smallholders' Bill,' and wrecking amendments to the Scottish Land Values Bill (forcing its withdrawal), in 1908, renewed the spirit of rural revolt against the parliamentary allies of the big landlords (Blewett: 48). Balfour himself admitted that 'The feeling...[was]...so strong against the House of Lords that it seems quite hopeless [for the Unionists] to think of contesting a Highland seat...until the question of the House of Lords is settled' (Blewett: 403).

Thus, the Scottish voters, unlike the English, were disinclined to rally to the defence of hereditary rule. The problems of Scottish Unionists were further compounded by their continued adherence to tariff reform. Consequently, the broad coalition of forces which had produced the 1906 result were mobilised to confirm their previous decision in 1910.

Participation

The extension of the franchise to the rural peasantry and the routinisation of two party competition in the burghs sharpened ideological conflict, so that despite a vastly increased electorate, the combination of a deepened socio-political polarisation and an intensified partisanship helped to maintain the high levels of participation that had been established between 1868 and 1880.

There were, however, significant fluctuations in the level of turnout closely related to the popularity of the Liberals. In 1885, the last election for twenty years in which Scottish Liberalism could claim to represent unequivocally the national will, an average of 83 per cent of the electorate voted in each contested seat (see Table 4.1). The following year, however, participation dropped to 72 per cent (the lowest of the period), as the home rule crisis found Liberal candidates and associations sounding a variety of uncertain notes. Turnout continued to remain stubbornly below 80 per cent in the three subsequent contests, which were also associated with an unpopular and divided Liberal Party. Significantly, the Unionist triumph of 1900 was accompanied by the second lowest turnout of the period. In 1906, however, Scottish Liberalism rediscovered its equilibrium as the disparate elements in its coalition flocked to defend free trade; and in 1910, the party's social reform programme and opposition to the Upper House appeared hardly less popular. Consequently, the turnout of 1885 was almost equalled in 1906, as Scotland reaffirmed its faith in the historic Liberal creed, and surpassed it in 1910. Thus, the inverse relationship between Unionist success and turnout observed generally in British elections of the period was more or less confirmed by the Scottish experience (Cornford: 53-58; Dunbabin: 96).

Regional modifications to the overall pattern of participation depended on the relative strengths of the parties from one area to another. Where Unionists were strong not only were there fewer Liberals to abstain, but more right-wing electors positively motivated by the same issues which depressed Liberal support. Consequently, there was a contrast between regions of higher turnout with lower fluctuation from one election to another, where electoral competition between the parties was keen, and regions of lower turnout and higher fluctuations, where the Liberal Party was clearly dominant.

Table 4.1: Average Percentage Turnout in General Elections, 1885–December 1910, by region

	1885	1886	1892	1895	1900	1906	Jan 1910	Dec 1910	All: 1886–Dec. 1910
Burghs									
Aberdeen	74		66	62	68	72	80	69	70
Dundee	84	68	77	75	70	82	86	84	78
Edinburgh/Leith	82	73	79	74	74	81	87	81	79
Glasgow	81	77	78	63	73	83	87	85	78
Highland	90	81	83	84	80	90	91	91	86
East	84	62	75	77	74	82	87	84	78
Central	84	65	75	73	76	76	82	85	76
West	86	77	84	85	80	87	88	84	84
Borders	92	88	88	87	85	91	93	91	89
All Burghs	**83**	**75**	**79**	**74**	**76**	**83**	**87**	**83**	**80**
Counties									
Highland	77	59	68	66	68	70	76	74	70
East	79	63	73	77	72	80	82	81	76
Central	83	70	77	80	76	77	82	78	78
West	84	78	82	83	78	83	85	84	82
Borders	87	78	85	88	84	88	90	90	86
All Counties	**82**	**71**	**78**	**79**	**76**	**80**	**83**	**80**	**79**
All	**83**	**72**	**78**	**77**	**76**	**81**	**85**	**81**	**79**

Voting was at its highest in the counties and burghs of the Borders, where a combination of small constituencies and a strong tradition of inter-party rivalry assisted voter mobilisation, so that in no fewer than sixteen of the 60 constituency battles of the period turnout was over 90 per cent. Not only did the underlying strength of Unionism in this region minimise the decline in turnout, 1886–1900, but in the county constituencies participation was fractionally greater in 1895 than ten years before. Similarly, in the West the traditional Conservatism of the counties, plus the immediacy of the home rule issue in an area heavily populated by Irishmen of both religious communities, ensured that the drop in turnout, 1886–1900, was relatively small compared to 1885. Consequently overall participation averaged above 80 per cent in the counties and burghs of greater Clydeside, and would have done so in Glasgow had not the election of 1895 coincided with a public holiday (Pelling: 403).

Outside the Highlands (which are a special case), the lowest turnouts and greatest fluctuations in turnout were in the East, where between 1885 and 1886 the proportion of those voting dropped by sixteen per cent in the counties and in Dundee, and by 22 per cent in Perth and the burgh districts. Although there was some recovery in 1892 and 1895, turnout remained generally depressed until

1906. In Aberdeen, where overall participation was as poor as in the Highlands, the only high turnout was 80 per cent in January 1910. These regions were the most Liberal part of Scotland because they were the most homogeneously Presbyterian and isolated (apart from Dundee), from the social impact of Irish immigration. Thus, while many Liberal electors in the East appeared to have had reservations regarding Gladstone's Irish policy, many of them were more likely to abstain in 1886 than to switch their allegiances to the Unionists. Disestablishment, however, was more immediately controversial in the county constituencies, where the established church and Episcopalianism were influential, and may well have been responsible for boosting turnout against the Liberals in 1892 and 1895.

Participation in Central Scotland, 1885–December 1910, averaged 76 per cent in the smaller burghs, 79 per cent in Edinburgh/Leith, and 78 per cent in the counties. In this strongly Liberal area, between 1885 and 1886, turnout declined nine per cent in the metropolis, thirteen per cent in the counties, and a massive 19 per cent in the burghs. In this respect, the parallels with the East were strong.

Attendance at the polls was at its lowest in the Highlands and Islands, where turnout averaged only 70 per cent over the period. In many respects this indicated a society whose structure and concerns were somewhat tangential to the wider polity. Significantly, the highest turnout, 77 per cent, was recorded in 1885, with the first thrust of Crofter enthusiasm.

The problem for the Highland electorate was that the post-1885 political cleavages cut across the unity which the crofters had found in their own party, and they found it more difficult than their national leaders and MPs to identify with Gladstonian Liberalism. Many of the crofters were members of the pro-establishment Free Presbyterian Church, and supported that section which chose to remain 'Wee Free' following unification with the United Presbyterians. Their unreconstructed Calvinism rendered them at least ambivalent towards Irish home rule and openly hostile to disestablishment. Furthermore, as a fertile source of recruitment for the armed services and the colonies, many Highlanders were critical of the pro-Boer stance taken by Liberal MPs in Sutherland and Caithness. Thus, while Gladstonian Liberalism was attractive for its instincts on land reform, it had distinctly less appeal on other locally significant dimensions. It was, perhaps, only their greater hostility towards the Conservatives and Liberal Unionists as the party of rapacious landowners that recommended Liberalism to many crofters. Consequently, only when conflicts between landowners and tenants were to the fore was the Liberal Party unequivocally attractive in this region, and that was seemingly reflected in turnout variations.

Voter Alignment

The Burghs

From 1832–1880 the Scottish burgh constituencies had been almost exclusively Liberal, and there was little reason to suspect the situation would change in 1885 as more lower class electors came onto the register. Liberal hegemony, however, had tended to suppress the real extent of Conservative sentiment, so that support for the right not only gained from the desertion of Liberal Unionists, but the emergence of a modern two-party system liberated a hidden Tory vote. From 1886–1900 it appeared that the change had revolutionised Scottish burgh representation, although the Liberal revival from 1906 indicated that the change had been less fundamental in the smaller burghs than the large cities.

The election of 1885 seemed to confirm a continuance of the traditional pattern, as the Conservative vote declined as a proportion of the registered electorate in Aberdeen, Dundee, Edinburgh/Leith and the Eastern burghs, and no Tory stood in either of the Highland burgh districts. Unofficial Liberals polled three times more votes than the Conservatives in the East and almost twice as many in Edinburgh, while the official Liberal share of the enrolled increased in Aberdeen and Glasgow (see Table 4.2). On the other hand, the division of Glasgow appeared to stimulate Tory morale as their proportion of the registered electorate rose from 19.6 per cent in 1880 to 35.2 per cent in 1885, bringing the party within striking distance of its main opponent. The Conservatives achieved similarly critical improvements in the West burghs, where they reduced the gap between themselves and the official Liberals from nearly 27 per cent in 1880 to under six per cent in 1885. There were also signs of an emerging Tory vote in Central and Borders, although not in any way threatening to the Liberals.

The somewhat confused nature of the 1885 election, containing both traditional as well as novel features in electoral behaviour, was clarified in 1886, the most critical election in Scottish burgh constituencies since 1832. Under the catalyst of a divisive and polarised election, the latent tensions caused by the expansion of the electorate, and the division of three major cities, the Liberal coalition fractured, completing the transition from a locally-focused electoral culture of uncontested returns and conflicts between rival Liberal candidates, to elections routinely fought between Liberals and Unionists on national issues

The consequences of the home rule election were most apparent in ethnically-polarised Glasgow and the West. In Glasgow the Liberals led the Unionists by less than half a per cent overall and lost three seats – Tradeston, St Rollox and Central – while in the West burghs, the Unionists outpolled the Liberals, capturing Greenock and the districts of Falkirk and Ayr, where the Liberal share of the vote collapsed from 53.7 per cent in 1885 to 35.9 per cent in 1886. The fielding of candidates returned as Liberals in 1885 assisted the Unionist cause in St Rollox, Greenock and Ayr Burghs. In the Falkirk District, too, the Liberal elected in 1885 had become a Unionist, although he did not stand in 1886.

These developments, however, were not unprecedented. Both Glasgow and the Ayr Burghs had returned Conservatives in 1874; and while the Falkirk Burghs, dominated by the Lanarkshire towns of Hamilton and Airdrie, had been solidly Liberal, 1868–1880, they had elected three Conservatives between 1841 and 1857, and the Conservatives had established a respectable vote in Greenock prior to 1885 without winning the seat.

The Liberals, however, performed sufficiently well in the Kilmarnock Burghs to recapture the constituency from the incumbent Conservative, Sturrock, whose vote only increased by 135, as the previously divided Liberals reunited; and the Unionists made almost no impression on Paisley, where there were few Catholic immigrants (Pelling: 403).

In the burghs outside greater Clydeside the 1886 developments were more fundamental. For example, in Edinburgh/Leith, the Unionist proportion of the electorate rose from the 15.3 per cent cast for the Conservatives in 1885 to 30.3

per cent in 1886, the combined Liberal and Independent Liberal share collapsed from 65.8 per cent of those enrolled in 1885 to 42.3 per cent, and the Unionists captured the West division as Buchanan transferred his allegiance. Nevertheless, given the successes of the Independent Liberal Churchmen in 1885, the Gladstonians performed well in carrying the three remaining Edinburgh seats, while Gladstone, himself, was unopposed in the Leith Burghs (Cook).

Significant changes were also evident in the Wick and Inverness Districts, neither of which had been contested by the Conservatives in 1885. Pender, defeated as the official Liberal in Wick Burghs the previous year, re-emerged as a Unionist, and captured 43 per cent of the poll; whilst Finlay, who commanded the antidisestablishmentarian Free Presbyterian vote in the Inverness Burghs, retained the seat as a Unionist. Similarly, the Unionists took St Andrews Burghs, a constituency in which no Conservative had stood since the passing of the First Reform Act, when the incumbent Independent Liberal Churchman, Sir Robert Anstruther, having declared for Unionism, had passed the torch to his son. Across the four East burghs, Unionists more than doubled the support attracted by the Conservatives in 1885, reducing the Liberal lead from 24.1 per cent to 8.1 per cent of the electorate.

The major exceptions to the trend were Aberdeen, where the Unionists failed to contest either constituency in 1886, and Dundee, the most radical of the major cities, in which the Liberals performed almost as well as in 1885, and the Unionists made little progress. The pace of change in Dundee was probably delayed because it remained an undivided constituency. The Liberals also benefited in Dundee from the presence of an Irish Nationalist population without the countervailing influence of Ulster Orangemen. Consequently, the hostility towards Roman Catholics, so evident in the west, was less a feature of the Dundonian social culture. Furthermore, the number of Irish-born in the city had declined after 1866 (Walker: 114-5, 120-1).

With nine Unionist victories in the burghs in 1886, the urban seats began to lose their common Liberal identity. Nevertheless, it would be wrong to discount the strength of burgh Liberalism. Even in the crisis of 1886, Aberdeen and Dundee, as we have seen, remained strong Liberal bastions, and Liberals commanded almost 60 per cent of the votes cast in Edinburgh/Leith, together with a group of Central and Border burghs, comprising Kirkcaldy, Stirling, Dumfries and Hawick, where Trevelyan, the member since 1868, was narrowly beaten as a Unionist.

In 1892, as the immediacy of the home rule crisis abated, the Liberals made a firm recovery in the burghs of industrial Scotland outside the major cities. In the West, the Liberal share of the electorate grew by more than a fifth on 1886, surpassing the share official candidates won in 1880, and the Unionist vote eased by a little over one per cent. Ayr Burghs, which had become permanently marginal following the death of Campbell in 1888, reverted to the Liberals, and the Unionists lost their narrow majority in the Falkirk District. In Central and Borders burghs, Liberal support grew from 44.1 per cent of the electorate to 50.0 per cent, as the Unionist share stagnated at less than a third.

Table 4.2

Electoral Support for the Main Parties in Burgh Constituencies, 1880–1910, expressed as a percentage of the enrolled electorate

(Unionist includes Conservatives and Liberal Unionists)*

	1880	1885	1886	1892	1895	1900	1906	Jan 1910	Dec. 1910	Change 1880–D.1910	Change 1886–D. 1910
Aberdeen											
Liberals	52.9	58.1		45.0	42.7	39.6	49.5	46.4	42.3	–10.6	– 2.7
Unionists	22.1	14.6		14.9	16.4	28.4	13.9	28.3	27.3	+ 5.2	+12.4
The Left				5.6	3.2		8.2	5.6			
Liberal Lead	*+30.8*	*+43.5*		*+30.1*	*+25.7*	*+11.2*	*+35.6*	*+18.1*	*+15.0*	*–15.8***	*–15.1*** *(from 1892)*
Dundee											
Liberals	54.6	44.3	48.1	45.5	42.4	41.6	39.6	30.3	25.5	–29.1	–22.6
Unionists	17.1	16.5	20.2	29.8	27.7	28.0	18.3	23.2	28.1	+11.0	+ 7.9
The Left					4.9		24.1	27.8	24.5		
Liberal Lead	*+37.5*	*+27.8*	*+27.9*	*+15.7*	*+14.7*	*+13.6*	*+21.3*	*+7.1*	*–2.6*	*–40.1***	*–30.5***
Edinburgh/Leith											
Liberals	61.4	37.8	42.3	43.7	39.4	37.7	50.3	48.2	45.3	–16.1	+ 3.0
Unionists	19.8	15.4	30.3	34.1	35.0	36.0	29.7	34.8	34.9	+15.1	+ 4.6
The Left				0.9				4.1			
Ind.Liberal		28.0									
Liberal Lead	*+41.6*	*+22.4*	*+12.0*	*+ 9.6*	*+ 4.4*	*+ 1.7*	*+20.6*	*+13.4*	*+10.4*	*–31.2***	*– 1.6***
Glasgow											
Liberals	40.9	42.8	38.8	39.8	27.5	27.7	40.7	38.6	39.6	– 1.3	+ 0.8
Unionists	19.6	35.2	38.4	35.6	32.2	42.0	35.2	36.6	38.5	+18.9	+ 0.1
The Left		2.9		2.4	3.0		6.3	8.0	6.6		
Ind.Liberal								3.4			
Liberal Lead	*+21.3*	*+ 7.6*	*+ 0.4*	*+ 4.2*	*– 4.7*	*–14.3*	*+ 5.5*	*+ 2.0*	*+ 1.1*	*–20.2***	*+ 0.7***

* Where possible adjustments have been made for unopposed returns.

** Net Liberal gain over the Unionists.

Table 4.2 (cont)

	1880	1885	1886	1892	1895	1900	1906	Jan 1910	Dec. 1910	Change 1880–D.1910	Change 1886–D. 1910
West Burghs											
Liberals	55.5	42.0	38.2	45.8	42.1	39.9	46.7	52.3	48.9	– 6.6	+10.7
Unionists	27.4	36.3	39.4	38.1	43.1	40.7	33.0	35.1	33.7	+ 6.3	– 5.7
The Left		0.2					3.1				
Ind. Liberal		7.2									
Liberal Lead	*+28.1*	*+5.7*	*–1.2*	*+7.7*	*–1.0*	*–0.8*	*+ 13.7*	*+17.2*	*+15.2*	*–12.9***	*+15.4***
Borders/Central Burghs											
Liberals	61.5	36.2	44.1	50.0	49.4	46.0	53.7	56.0		–5.5	+11.9
Unionists	14.3	25.0	31.5	31.4	30.0	34.0	24.3	30.0		+15.7	– 1.5
Ind. Liberal		25.9									
Liberal Lead	*+47.2*	*+11.2*	*+12.6*	*+18.6*	*+19.4*	*+12.0*	*+29.4*	*+26.0*		*–21.2*** (to Jan 1910)	*+13.4*** (to Jan 1910)
East Burghs											
Liberals	54.6	35.6	34.9	39.8	42.7	42.2	52.6	49.1	50.6	– 4.0	+14.7
Unionists	23.5	11.5	26.8	29.2	32.8	30.8	27.7	28.5	31.1	+ 7.6.	+ 4.3
The Left								8.4			
Ind.Liberal		35.2		4.7							
Liberal Lead	*+31.1*	*+24.1*	*+8.1*	*+10.6*	*+9.9*	*+11.4*	*+24.9*	*+20.6*	*+19.5*	*–11.6***	*+11.4***
Highland Burghs											
Liberals		46.3	40.5	41.1	40.2	36.7	48.0	52.6	50.1		+ 9.6
Unionists			41.4	42.4	44.7	43.7	41.8	38.5	40.2		– 1.2
Ind.Liberal		44.1									
Liberal Lead			*–0.9*	*–1.3*	*–4.5*	*–7.0*	*+6.2*	*+14.1*	*+9.9*		*+10.8***

* Where possible adjustments have been made for unopposed returns.

** Net Liberal gain over the Unionists.

By contrast, in Edinburgh/Leith, a small Liberal advance was more than offset by a continuing improvement in Unionist support, and Buchanan, having been converted to Gladstonianism, was beaten in Edinburgh West by a Unionist, thereby emphasising the essentially right-wing character of this constituency.[1] In Dundee the Unionists increased their strength by a half to 29.8 per cent of the electorate (a pre-1914 apotheosis), as the Liberals lost a little ground; while in Aberdeen, where the Unionists did hardly better than the Conservatives in 1885, the Liberal share of the electorate collapsed from 58.1 per cent in 1885 to 45 per cent, in the city's first post-home rule contest, establishing a reduced parameter of Gladstonian strength.

Elsewhere change was more marginal. Glasgow remained the least Liberal of the major cities, and despite a small increase in Liberal voting the rise was substantially less than in the other Western burghs. Although a drop in the Unionist vote enabled the Liberals to recapture St Rollox, a socialist intervention in Camlachie produced a balancing Unionist gain. The Unionists improved their relative strength in the Highland burghs, but both parties commanded more of the electorate than in 1886, and both seats changed hands, with Inverness Burghs falling to the Liberals as Pender regained the Wick District for Unionism. Similarly, in the East, each party mobilised more electors than in 1886, but although the Liberals improved their popular lead, the Unionists captured Perth on a split Liberal vote.

The steady attrition in Liberal burgh strength resumed more generally in 1895, stimulated by a severe trade depression. In the West burghs the Unionists achieved their best performance of the period, leading the Liberals by one per cent of the electorate in retaining Greenock, capturing the districts of Ayr, Falkirk and Kilmarnock, and leaving the Liberals a solitary seat in Paisley. The coincidence of the election with a public holiday in Glasgow assisted in reducing the Liberal share of the enrolled from 39.8 per cent per cent to 27.5 per cent, as the Unionists won the most votes, and – by retaking St Rollox and winning College – most seats, for the first time. In Edinburgh/Leith, the distance between the parties was reduced to less than five per cent of the enrolled, and the Unionists captured the South division, where the middle class Unionism of Newington and Morningside vied with the Liberal working class electorate of Dalry and Fountainbridge for political dominance (Pelling: 388).

Antidisestablishmentarian sentiment found both the Highland burgh constituencies falling to the Unionists, who recorded their best performance before 1914; and in Aberdeen the Unionists increased their share of the poll in the city as a whole despite standing down in the North division. The Unionist advance, however, was halted in Dundee, where both the major parties lost support following an Independent Labour Party intervention; and in the East burghs, where each party increased its popularity and the Gladstonians recaptured Perth, the distance between the alignments hardly changed. The best Liberal performances, nevertheless, came in the burgh districts of Borders and Central, where their increased share of the poll in Stirling, Dumfries and Hawick, continued an improvement relative to the Unionists that had been evident in 1892.

The Khaki election of 1900 underlined the changed nature of burgh politics, when the Unionists won more votes than the Liberals and carried 16 of the 31 seats. Unionists were returned in each of Glasgow's seven divisions, and continued to hold all the seats in the West, except Paisley. In Edinburgh/Leith, where 20 years before the Liberals had enjoyed a 44 per cent advantage over the Conservatives, the Unionists were within less than two per cent of becoming the more popular faction – less than half a per cent in Edinburgh itself – and in Aberdeen a Liberal lead of 43.5 per cent in 1885 was reduced to 11.2 per cent.

Although there were undoubtedly exceptional political circumstances prevailing at the time, it is important to emphasise that outside Glasgow, where the peculiar features of the 1895 election clouded the picture, the swings to the Unionists were mostly undramatic, indicating a continuing trend rather than any peculiar deviation. Indeed, there were signs that the Unionist post-1885 surge was running out of steam. In the West, East and Highland burghs the Unionists mobilised a smaller proportion of the electorate than in 1895; in Dundee and Edinburgh/Leith the Unionist share of the enrolled increased by only 0.3 per cent and 1.0 per cent respectively, and by only four per cent in Borders and Central following poor performances in both 1892 and 1895. The relative improvement in the Unionist position was assisted as much by a decline in Liberal support, ranging from 3.5 per cent in the Highland burghs to 0.5 per cent in the East, as to their own popularity. The Liberals even improved their position relative to the Unionists in Dundee, Edinburgh East, Greenock, and the districts of Falkirk, Kilmarnock, Montrose and St Andrews. A further measure of the ambivalent nature of the outcome were the swings recorded against Munro Ferguson (Leith Burghs), Asher (Elgin Burghs), and Sir William Dunn (Paisley), who had all been more supportive of the government than their own party leaders over the prosecution of the South African War.

The impact and long-term implications of the 1900 election were at their most significant in Glasgow, where by almost any standard Unionism had replaced Liberalism as the dominant electoral alignment. Although less popular as a proportion of the electorate than in the other Western burghs, the Glaswegian Unionists in 1900 mobilised a higher percentage of the enfranchised than any party in the city after 1885, so the general observation that 'the chief factor in Conservative success was lack of enthusiasm amongst Liberals' (Cornford: 35) did not hold in this case. A second major feature of the 1900 result in Glasgow was the disastrous 27.7 per cent Liberal share of the enrolled – substantially worse than in any other Scottish region – which not only enabled the Unionists to enjoy a 14.3 per cent lead and to capture the two remaining Liberal seats, Blackfriars and Hutchesontown and Bridgeton (their only burgh gains in 1900), but demonstrated how soft the Liberal vote had become in the second city of the empire. Although the Liberals were to perform much better in Glasgow in the three subsequent contests, the seeds of their post-Great War vulnerability had been sown. The Unionists also made a significant advance in Aberdeen, where their share of the enrolled increased from 14.9 per cent in 1892 – the last time they had contested both divisions – to 28.4 per cent, and the Liberal share fell marginally below 40.0 per cent for the first time, despite the absence of socialist candidates, thereby completing the redefinition of underlying voting patterns in the major cities.

The election of 1906 was truly dramatic in that it negated most of the progress made by the right after 1885, as the tariff issue divided Unionist voters, and revived a Liberal electorate which had been perplexed by the issues that had dominated the four previous contests. The pro-Liberal swings (expressed in terms of proportions of the registered electorate) were especially strong in the central lowlands: 9.9 per cent in Glasgow, 9.5 per cent in Edinburgh/Leith, 8.7 per cent in Central and Borders, and 7.3 per cent in the West burghs.

In Aberdeen the movement to the Liberals was 12.2 per cent, as the Unionist vote fell by more than half on 1900, and in the North division the Conservative came third to Kennedy of the Social Democratic Federation. The success of Kennedy in winning a quarter of the votes despite an extra 600 voting Liberal indicated the emergence of a left-wing constituency independent of Liberalism, and was in conformity with the high number of Labour plumpers in Dundee. The success of Labour in splitting the Liberal vote in Dundee reduced the Unionist–Liberal swing to 3.9 per cent as the city shifted firmly to the left, returning its first Labour MP.

The 6.6 per cent movement to the Liberals in the two Highland burgh districts was due almost entirely to a 13.3 per cent increase in the Liberal share of the electorate in the Inverness Burghs, where John Bryce defeated Sir Robert Finlay, who had represented the constituency, apart from a short interlude, since 1885. By contrast, in the Wick Burghs the Unionist majority of 113 in 1900 was only reduced to 96. An important factor stemming the Liberal challenge appears to have been the philanthropy of the incumbent MP, Sir Arthur Bignold, who had bestowed a hospital on Wick, established public parks in Wick and Kirkwall, supported local charities with an open purse, and was generous towards the poor (Pelling: 383). A 6.8 per cent pro-Liberal swing was recorded in the Eastern burghs, where the party's share of the electorate grew by more than 10.0 per cent on 1900, but the Unionists regained St Andrews Burghs, which they had lost at a by-election in 1903.

Following the 1906 debacle, the Unionists only retained six of their sixteen burgh seats: Edinburgh West, Glasgow Camlachie and Tradeston, Ayr Burghs, Wick Burghs and St Andrews Burghs. Glasgow Camlachie was only held because of Labour intervention, and only the peculiar popularity of incumbents enabled the Unionists to resist the tide in Tradeston, where Corbett held sway, and the Wick District. The Liberals recaptured Edinburgh South, Falkirk District (despite an SWRC intervention), Glasgow Bridgeton, Central, College and St Rollox, Greenock, and the Inverness and Kilmarnock Districts, to hold 23 burgh constituencies; and Labour took Blackfriars and Hutchesontown from the Conservatives in Glasgow, and one of the Liberal seats in Dundee.

The significance of the 1906 result is best measured against the contest of December 1910, for not only was it the last election of the period, but indicates the extent to which the result of 1906 was the product of short-term or more long-term factors.

The most notable feature of the 1910 elections was the consolidation of burgh Liberalism outside the major cities. In January 1910, Liberal candidates improved their support in most of the single member burghs, and despite a small decline in December these constituencies emerged more Liberal than in 1906. In the West burghs Liberals attracted two per cent more of the enrolled in December 1910 than four years previously; and a small swing against the Unionists, 1906–December 1910, afforded the Liberals a 15.2 per cent advantage, where a decade earlier they had been in second place. The swing of 8.0 per cent between 1900 and December 1910 in the West burghs was similar to an 7.7 per cent movement in Glasgow, but substantially ahead of the 3.7 per cent in their associated counties.

The Liberal recovery was so strong in the two Highland districts that in January 1910 their 14.1 per cent lead over the Unionists was more than twice that of 1906, as Wick was carried for the first time in general elections since 1886. The defeat of Sir Arthur Bignold, despite his strong personal vote and his minimalist view that tariffs should only be applied to counteract dumping (Blewett: 321-322), underlined how popular the Liberals had become in the north, as developments in the Highland burghs reflected a similar movement of opinion in their associated county constituencies.

In the four districts of Central and Borders the Unionists were so overwhelmed in January 1910 that they failed to contest the burghs of Kirkcaldy, Stirling and Hawick the following December. Consequently, these predominantly working class burghs constituted the most Liberal region in Scotland. In the East, the Liberals continued to command the support of half the electorate in both elections of 1910 and captured St Andrews in the January contest. At the same time, however, the Unionists also improved their position, and with 31.1 per cent of the electorate supporting them in December 1910 they were more popular than in 1900 and retook St Andrews.

In the big cities the large swings of 1906 had been less a springboard for a higher level of underlying Liberal support than recovery from an abysmal result in 1900. Consequently, the new parameters of support in these constituencies were little different from those immediately following the home rule crisis. In Glasgow, for example, the popularity of both the Liberals and Unionists 1906–December 1910 was broadly similar to that of 1885 to 1892, and in Aberdeen Liberal strength in 1910 reflected the outcome in 1892 and 1895. Only in Edinburgh did the Liberals appear somewhat stronger in 1910 than in the post-1885 decade. In Aberdeen the Unionists were as strong in 1910 as they had been in 1900, and in Edinburgh they sustained a position established in 1892, having restored their losses of 1906. Thus, between 1886 and December 1910 the relative strengths of the two major parties hardly changed in Glasgow and Edinburgh, whilst in Aberdeen the Liberal advantage closed from 30.1 per cent of the electorate in 1892 to 15.0 per cent in December 1910.

A critical factor inhibiting a strong Liberal resurgence in the big cities was the emergence of a left-wing vote that would only support socialist candidates. In Glasgow, for example, George Barnes captured Blackfriars and Hutchesontown for Labour in 1906 against both Liberal and Unionist candidates, and only faced Unionist opposition in 1910. It was indicative of the reluctance of some working class voters to support Liberals, that in Aberdeen North, where Labour stood down in December 1910, having polled 1,344 votes the previous January, the Liberal vote remained static. Indeed, the Liberals commanded a higher share of the enrolled electorate in middle class Aberdeen South than in the working class North Division. It is noteworthy that Edinburgh, where the socialists were weak, emerged as the most Liberal of the four major cities.

It was, however, in Dundee that the Liberals came under greatest pressure from the left. In 1906, Wilkie had taken a seat from the Liberals, when no fewer than 2,553 electors had plumped for his candidacy. Labour also contested a by-election in 1908, though Wilkie and his major backer, the Jute and Flaxworkers Union, seeking an electoral pact with the Liberals, were opposed to the intervention (Walker: 286). Despite dissension on the left, the Labour candidate won 24.9 per cent of the votes cast, and a second leftwing candidate,

Scrymgeour, a Prohibitionist, captured a more modest 4.1 per cent of the poll. The combined vote for the left, therefore, was greater than the 27.1 per cent won by the Unionist. The result, which restricted the victor, Churchill, to 43.1 per cent of the votes, left the Liberals both fearful of Labour and sufficiently grateful to Wilkie to come to an understanding that neither of their parties would subsequently advance more than one candidate (Walker: 290). At the elections of 1910, the Unionists polled more strongly than in 1900, and with the Liberals only presenting a single candidate, they were arguably the strongest single party in the December contest. Indeed, the Liberals only led Labour by the narrowest of margins in what had become a three-party conflict. Dundee, therefore, had become the least Liberal city, the least Unionist city (with the possible exception of Aberdeen), and the most Labour of all the burghs. Thus, to a large extent, parliamentary politics in Dundee was already anticipating the post-1918 dispensation.

Table 4.3: Summary of Support for the Liberals and Unionists (Conservatives and Liberal Unionists), 1880–December 1910, in Burgh Constituencies
(expressed as a percentage of the enrolled electorate*)

	1880	1885**	1886–1900	1906–1910
Liberals				
Major Cities	49.2	43.1 (10.9)	37.8	42.4
Other Burghs	57.6	40.1 (19.4)	42.4	50.8
All Burghs	51.9	42.2 (13.5)	39.4	45.5
Unionists				
Major Cities	19.6	25.2	33.5	32.6
Other Burghs	21.8	25.9	36.3	32.1
All Burghs	20.4	25.4	34.5	32.4

* Where possible adjustments have been made for uncontested seats.
** The brackets indicate support for Independent Liberals.

The major development in voting behaviour in the Scottish Burghs, 1885–1910, was growth in underlying support for the right from a fifth of the electorate in 1880, to a quarter in 1885, and to around a third thereafter (Table 4.3), with a peak in 1900 (37.2 per cent), followed by a trough (29.7 per cent) in 1906. Overall levels of Unionist support across the four cities were essentially the same as in the other burgh constituencies as a whole. Variations in absolute Unionist burgh strength, therefore, were less a function of size and type than of ethnic geography.

The performance of the Liberals, however, did relate in some measure to size and type. Even in 1880 the absolute level of Liberal strength had been greater in the smaller burghs than in the large cities, and although the differential was eroded in 1885 – if the performances of independent Liberals are excluded – the differences between the two remained significant. (Indeed the differential between the cities and smaller burghs of 8.4 per cent, 1906–1910, was similar to the 7.4 per cent differential in 1880.) Broadly, the political changes, 1885–86, reduced the Liberals' share of the burgh electorate from around a half to two fifths. The Gladstonians lost further ground down to the election of 1900, when they attracted only 36.3 per cent of the electorate, but recovered to 46.6 per cent in the revival of 1906, and was sustained in January (45.9 per cent) and December (44.2 per cent) 1910. Thus, following the set-backs of the post home rule decade, the burgh Liberals polled two per cent better in December 1910 than the official Liberals in 1885 (Table 4.5). The improvement, 1906–1910, however, was more marked in the smaller burghs than the big cities, so that while half the electorate in the former voted Liberal (+10.7 per cent on 1885), barely two fifths did so in the latter (-0.7 per cent on 1885). The main reason for this difference was less the Unionism of the cities, than the unwillingness of many of their working class electors to vote for other than socialist candidates.[2]

The election of 1885, when the Conservatives only carried the Kilmarnock Burghs,[3] marked the last hurrah for the virtual Liberal monopoly over burgh representation stretching back to 1832. In 1886 the Unionist allies won nine burgh constituencies, fourteen in 1895, and sixteen in 1900, when the textile town of Paisley was the only burgh out of twelve to return a Liberal in the west. Even in December 1910 the Unionists won five burgh seats and Labour retained two. In eight general elections, official Liberals carried Edinburgh West and St Andrews Burghs only once; Glasgow Camlachie, Central and Tradeston, and Ayr Burghs only twice; and Wick Burghs only three times. Thus, there were seven burgh constituencies, just over a fifth of the total, which were not predominantly Liberal.

Although urban Liberalism undoubtedly weakened after 1880, the Liberal Party, nevertheless, still remained the dominant force in burgh constituencies. Including the Independent Liberals of 1885, there were no fewer than thirteen seats which returned Liberals at every election of the period. All of them – Aberdeen North and South, Dundee (1), Edinburgh Central and East, and the districts of Leith, Stirling, Hawick, Elgin, Montrose and Kirkcaldy – were in the eastern half of the country, apart from Dumfries Burghs and the notable exception of Paisley. Perth only went Conservative on a split Liberal vote in 1892, and Glasgow Bridgeton only fell to the Unionists in 1900. Edinburgh South was Liberal on six occasions, while Glasgow St Rollox and the burgh districts of Falkirk, Inverness and Kilmarnock, together with the second Dundee seat, returned a Liberal in five elections.

It was a measure of Liberal strength that in December 1910 they were unopposed in the districts of Hawick, Kirkcaldy and Stirling; and polled more than 70 per cent of the votes in the Elgin Burghs, more than 60 per cent in the Kilmarnock and Montrose Districts, Paisley, Perth, Aberdeen North, Edinburgh East and Central, and Glasgow Tradeston, and more than 55 per cent in Aberdeen South, Greenock, the Glasgow divisions of Bridgeton and St Rollox, and the districts of Falkirk, Inverness and Dumfries. By contrast, the most secure of the five Unionist burgh constituencies were Glasgow Central and Edinburgh West, where in each case the Unionist share of the poll was only 53.8 per cent. Consequently, while recognising the qualitative changes in the nature of burgh representation after 1885, the quantities suggested the Liberals survived the traumas of realignment, 1886–1900, to reassert their traditional dominance.

The Counties

Although 1880 had been an *annus mirabilis* for county Liberalism, the equalisation of the franchise, bringing poorer tenant farmers and working class artisans onto the register, was expected to further entrench its position. In the event, despite a radical transformation in the character of the county electorate, the relative positions of the parties in December 1910 were substantially as they had been in 1880 (Table 4.4).

Initially it appeared that the Liberals had benefited greatly from the new dispensation, when in 1885 they consolidated a strong lead in the rural East, and substantially improved their position in the Borders and Central region (Table 4.4). In Central, dominated by the Fife and Lothian coalfields, the Liberal share of the registered electorate grew to 56.9 per cent, as they established a 30.3 per cent lead over the Conservatives, whose strength was never to match their support in 1880. Thus, having been hotly contested between the parties, 1868–1880, Central became the most Liberal region for more than twenty years, as the Conservatives lost control of Haddington. Predictably, as in 1880, the Liberals took all nine seats in the East, extending from the Moray Firth to Fife East (Table 4.6), although their share of the electorate had marginally fallen. The recession in Liberal support was due in part to the intervention of Radical Independent Liberals in Elgin and Nairn and West Aberdeenshire, whose share of the poll, 31.2 and 19.6 per cent respectively, reflected the proximity of these constituencies to the Highlands, in which Crofting candidates were upsetting the old political order. The Liberals also performed remarkably well in the Borders, due to good results in Dumfries, Peebles and Selkirk, and Roxburgh. In Galloway, however, there were swings to the right, so that Wigtown remained Conservative, and a new Liberal candidate lost Kirkcudbright to Mark Stewart, a much respected local Conservative landowner (Pelling: 409).

Whereas the new working class electorate had considerably strengthened the Liberals in the Central region, their enfranchisement in the West hardly changed the relative strengths of the major parties because sectarian divisions over Ireland cut across the politics of class interest. Trailing the Liberals by only 2.4 per cent of the electorate in 1885, the Conservatives carried five of the twelve constituencies, including Bute, the most Conservative constituency in Scotland since 1832, Dunbartonshire, Tory since 1841, the new suburban constituency of Renfrew West, Lanarkshire Govan, which returned William Pearce, the owner of Fairfields shipyard (Pelling: 408), and Lanarkshire North West, whose electors favoured an Inverness landowner, John Baird, over 'Don Roberto' Cunninghame Grahame, a Lib–Lab landowner, 'elegant literary stylist and horseman' (Donnachie et.al.: 9). The capacity of the Conservatives to command substantial working class support in this expanding region was the most significant feature of the 1885 election, because it enabled them to break away from their reliance on a politically declining landed interest, and establish a base that was to bear even greater fruit in the twentieth century. The most dramatic feature of the 1885 election, however, was the emergence of the Crofters who, with more than a third of the electorate behind them, trounced the Whigs and Tories in the Highlands, a turbulent area which was effectively adjusting to a popular electoral system for the first time.

Table 4.4

Electoral Support for the Main Parties in County Constituencies, 1880–1910, expressed as a percentage of the enrolled electorate

(Unionist includes Conservatives and Liberal Unionists)*

	1880	1885	1886	1892	1895	1900	1906	Jan 1910	Dec 1910	Change 1880–D.1910	Change 1886–D. 1910
Highland											
Liberals	47.2	26.4	6.7	6.4	37.7	33.6	46.1	50.4	46.7	–0.5	
Unionists	36.3	8.9	21.0	28.3	29.8	30.9	20.6	23.9	23.3	–13.0	
Crofters		33.8	30.7	32.8							
Liberal Lead	*+10.9*				*+7.9*	*+2.7*	*+25.5*	*+26.6*	*+23.4*	***+12.5*	
East											
Liberals	51.8	48.9	36.0	41.0	41.4	39.1	50.9	50.7	47.6	–4.2	+11.6
Unionists	32.9	25.9	26.5	33.1	35.9	33.2	29.4	31.8	31.9	–1.0	+5.4
Liberal Lead	*+18.9*	*+23.0.*	*+ 9.5*	*+7.9*	*+5.5*	*+5.9*	*+21.5*	*+18.9*	*+15.7*	**–*3.2*	***+6.2*
Central (+Berwick)											
Liberals	50.5	56.9	43.5	44.7	43.4	41.0	49.8	48.1	44.0	–6.5	+0.5
Unionists	34.0	26.6	27.9	32.2	37.3	35.2	27.2	28.4	26.2	–7.8	–1.7
The Left				1.1				5.4	6.8		
Liberal Lead	*+16.5*	*+30.3*	*+15.6*	*+12.5*	*+ 6.1*	*+ 5.8*	*+22.6*	*+19.7*	*+17.8*	***+1.3*	***+2.2*
Clydeside											
Liberals	45.0	42.5	37.7	41.0	39.3	38.1	39.5	42.1	43.0	–2.0	+5.3
Unionists	42.4	40.1	40.2	41.8	42.6	40.9	34.8	37.1	38.3	–4.1	–1.9
The Left		0.1			0.3		8.1	6.4	1.8		
Liberal Lead	*+2.6*	*+2.4*	*–2.5*	*–0.8*	*–3.3*	*–2.8*	*+4.7*	*+5.0*	*+4.7*	***+2.1*	***+7.2*
Borders (–Berwick)											
Liberals	45.0	49.4	35.4	40.1	39.9	36.6	47.1	45.8	46.0	+1.0	+10.6
Unionists	44.1	38.5	43.9	45.5	46.8	46.9	41.7	44.4	44.3	+0.2	+ 0.4
Liberal Lead	*+ 0.9*	*+10.9*	*–8.5*	*–5.4*	*–6.9*	*–10.3*	*+5.4*	*+1.4*	*+ 1.7*	*+0.8***	*+10.2***

* Where possible adjustments have been made for unopposed returns.

** Net Liberal gain over the Unionists.

Crofters took Inverness from the Conservatives, and Argyll, Caithness, and Ross and Cromarty from the Liberals. Only Sutherland, retaining the Marquis of Stafford in its first contested election since before 1832, declined to elect a Crofter, and no Crofter stood in Orkney and Shetland.

The encouragement flowing to the Liberals in 1885 was rudely shaken by the 1886 home rule election, when a severe haemorrhaging of support in the East, West, Central and Borders, left them with a smaller proportion of the county electorate (34.5 per cent), than in any general election from 1885 to December 1910 (Table 4.5). Only the failure of the Unionists to attract more than a small proportion of Liberal dissenters restricted the exchange of seats.[4] Even so, the 18 county constituencies carried by the Liberals was one fewer than in the debacle of 1900, and only one more than the Unionist tally.

The Borders, a traditionally Conservative region, moved most strongly to the right, when, following an exceptional result in 1885, a 14 per cent drop in the Liberal share of the electorate and a 5.4 per cent recovery by their opponents ensured that all five seats were carried by the Unionist coalition (Table 4.4). The swing against the Liberals in Roxburgh – where the incumbent, Arthur Elliot, second son of the Earl of Minto had deserted to Liberal Unionism – was more than 18 per cent of the poll, and 13.5 per cent in Dumfries, where Sir Robert Jardine had also changed sides. Desertion, however, could not explain similarly high shifts of allegiance in Peebles and Selkirk, where a faithful moderate Gladstonian, Sir Charles Tennant, was defeated. Only in Kirkcudbright, which had switched to the Conservatives in 1885, was the swing infinitesimal. The election of 1886 re-established the Border counties as the most Unionist region, with a steady level of support around 44 per cent of the electorate.

In the West, where the new political parameters were already evident, the popularity of the Unionists remained virtually static. A relatively small decline in Liberal strength (-4.8 per cent), however, was sufficient to produce a Unionist lead of 2.5 per cent in the popular vote, similar to that in the region's burghs outside Glasgow. As a result, the Unionists captured six formerly Liberal constituencies. Both seats in strongly Protestant Ayrshire transferred their allegiance, following the desertion in the North division of Hugh Elliot, the third son of the Earl of Minto, to Liberal Unionism, and the defeat of Eugene Wason, a Gladstonian and 'temperance advocate' (Hutchison: 178), in the mining Southern constituency. Renfrew East, a suburban seat on the edge of Glasgow, was captured by Michael Shaw-Stewart, scion of a locally well-known Tory family, who defeated a new Lib–Lab candidate; and the incumbent Liberal, Craig Sellar, delivered Lanarkshire Partick, with its 'almost solid Tory vote' in Kelvinside and Hillhead, to Liberal Unionism (Pelling: 408). Agricultural Southern Lanarkshire also moved to the right, and only Lanarkshire North West, a mining and suburban seat, bucked the trend, replacing the incumbent Conservative, Baird, with Cunninghame Graham. In total, the Unionists captured nine of the twelve constituencies in the West, their best performance in the region before 1931.

The strong negative reaction against the Liberals in Central (-13.4 per cent), and in the East (-12.9 per cent), where the party attracted a smaller proportion of the electorate than in the West, was almost as great as in the Borders. Relatively small increases in Unionist popularity from low bases, however, ensured the maintenance of comfortable Liberal leads. All the seats in Central returned

Gladstonians, but in the East the voters of Forfar temporarily followed their MP, John Barclay, into Liberal Unionism; while West Perthshire – in which Liberal organisation was weak and the influence of the Duke of Atholl and the Earls of Breadalbane and Ancaster was strong (Pelling: 394) – transferred its allegiance, as did the MP, Sir Donald Currie, on a more permanent basis.

In the Highlands and Islands, the Liberals only contested Orkney and Shetland, where they emerged as strong as in 1885. Elsewhere, the anti-Unionist standard was carried by the Crofters, although not unambiguously so, as was demonstrated in Inverness, where the incumbent Crofter, Fraser Mackintosh, having declared his opposition to home rule, was returned unopposed. In Sutherland, the Marquis of Stafford having stood down for a commoner, fell to a Crofter, and incumbent Crofters polled very strongly in Caithness and Ross and Cromarty. The Unionists, however, took Argyll from the Crofters, having failed to contest the constituency in 1885. Argyll was the most right-wing of the Highland seats, partly because it shared the antipathy of western counties towards home rule, and also because of a significant middle class electorate in Dunoon and on the Cowal coast (Pelling: 408). The general improvement of the Unionist vote from 8.9 per cent in 1885 to 21.0 per cent in 1886 in the region as a whole, however, was less a function of the home rule question than a major restructuring of electoral competition.[5]

The Unionists continued to record steady progress in 1892 and 1895 in all regions, and remained the dominant alignment in the West and Borders. The improvement in the Unionist position, however, did not necessarily imply absolute Liberal losses.

In 1892, the Liberal share of the enrolled improved more than that of their opponents in the West and Borders, and in the East a Unionist increase of 6.6 per cent was strongly countered by a five per cent surge in Liberal voting. Consequently, the Liberals recovered half the seats they had lost in 1886, as they took Dunbartonshire – which was moving to the left with the development of Clydebank, for the first time in more than 50 years – and reclaimed Forfar, Roxburgh, South Ayrshire, and Lanarkshire Govan. Local factors played their part in contributing to Unionist reverses. In Govan and Dunbartonshire friction between the Conservatives and Liberal Unionists over the selection of candidates found the coalition divided on the eve of the election (Hutchison: 210). Roxburgh returned to the Liberals because a significant number of Liberal Unionists with disestablishment sympathies switched to the Gladstonian candidate (Hutchison: 201), and Forfar was a 'natural' Liberal seat which had probably voted Unionist in 1886 out of deference to the radical incumbent, but refused to do so a second time. In the Highlands, the Unionists lost Argyll and Inverness to Crofters, who now held five of the six seats in the region. The only compensation for the Unionists was their recapture of Lanarkshire North West, which had gone against the trend in 1886.

In 1895, the Unionists polled a higher proportion of the registered county electorate (39.0 per cent) than in any election, 1885–1910, so that although the Liberals lost little overall support, the right recovered its position of 1886. The Unionist improvement was most clearly marked in the Central region (+5.1 per cent on 1892), where its attempts to meet working class concerns – including, for some candidates, endorsement of a miner's eight hour day, housing reform to provide working men the right to purchase rented property, the revival of

Chamberlain's old age pensions scheme, and a compensation scheme for miners – had a strong appeal. Significantly, McKillop, a coalmaster who took the marginal seat of Stirlingshire for the Unionists, was a supporter of the eight hour day,[6] as was Sir William Arrol, who recaptured South Ayrshire from the Liberals. Similarly, Alexander Wylie, a popular local dyer sympathetic to working class concerns, who retook Dunbartonshire following the restoration of peace within the local Unionist coalition, benefited from the assistance of his employees (Pelling: 407). The only Unionist set-back in industrial Scotland was in North West Lanark, which once again bucked the regional trend, although it was in conformity with a slight weakening of the Unionist position in its neighbour, Lanark North East.

Not only did the Unionists exploit working class discontent with the Liberals, but in the Highlands (where the Crofters had metamorphosed into the Liberal Party), they embarrassed the government too, by promising to introduce property rights that had been extended to the Irish peasantry. Consequently, highly marginal Argyll reverted to Unionism, following the conversion of the Duke of Argyll to a land purchase scheme for smallholders (Hutchison: 204-5); and in Inverness, where the Crofter, Dr MacGregor, had already resigned his seat on Rosebery's refusal to help the landless cottars, the electors reinforced the outcome of the consequent by-election, which had returned JEB Baillie, a Tory laird favourable to land reform (Hutchison: 205). Significantly, a third Unionist gain, Elgin and Nairn, which shared some social characteristics with the crofting counties, was contiguous with Inverness and Argyll. The relative positions of the parties in the Borders remained static, with the Liberals offsetting the loss of Roxburgh with the capture of Dumfries.

The election of 1900 was a great Unionist triumph in terms of seats, when, as in the burghs, the party carried just over half the county constituencies. The defeat, however, was less than an unmitigated disaster for the Liberals, because the outcome was characterised more by its negative features than a positive assertion of Unionism. Across the counties as a whole, the Unionists polled 1.5 per cent less of the electorate than in 1895, and whilst the Liberals were down 2.2 per cent they still received more votes than their opponents. Although the Liberals lost ground in every region, the Unionists, compared to 1895, were also less popular in the East, Central and the West, remained virtually static in the Borders, and advanced by a mere 1.1 per cent in Highland. Thus, although the right won a majority of county seats in 1900, there were signs that Unionism had already past its peak. Its relative advance derived principally from Liberal divisions over the South African War, which perplexed an electorate that was apparently neither jingoistic nor unpatriotic. Unionist gains in Orkney and Shetland, Sutherland and Aberdeenshire East, set against the loss of Inverness, signalled a false dawn.

The balance between jingoism and patriotism was nowhere better illustrated than in the Highlands, where the Unionists made most regional progress. Much of that improvement had come in Caithness, in which the Unionist share of the electorate increased by 11.1 per cent, and in Sutherland, where it grew by a massive 25.2 per cent. Significantly, both constituencies had been represented by pro-Boer Liberals, Clark and MacLeod, who had voted for the Irish motion of 1899 (see Chapter 3). In Caithness, the Liberals replaced Clark with an Imperialist, Robert Harmsworth, but with the former MP running as an

Independent, Liberal disunity was highlighted, and their majority over the Unionists fell from 55.2 per cent to a mere 0.8 per cent of the poll. MacLeod retained the Liberal nomination in Sutherland, but fell to a relative of the noble duke on a swing of 32.4 per cent of the votes cast. By contrast, the Unionists lost ground both relatively and absolutely in Ross and Cromarty and Inverness. The Liberal capture of Inverness on a small swing of 3.4 per cent was probably assisted by their adoption of an Imperialist, JE Dewar, a whisky distiller, and the retiral of Baillie, the popular Conservative member. Dewar's performance, however, was not so impressive as that of the former Crofter, James Weir (neither Imperialist nor pro-Boer), who increased his share of the poll from 53.7 per cent in 1895 to 68.7 per cent in 1900 in Ross and Cromarty. Personal considerations, however, were less evident in Orkney and Shetland, where Lyell, a mainstream incumbent Liberal since 1885, lost a quarter of his voters, and an increased 4.8 per cent Unionist share of the electorate gave his opponent, Wason, a majority of 40. It seems likely that the strong military and naval connections with Orkney proved the decisive factor (Pelling: 382).

Significantly, the two Unionist gains outside the Highlands also underlined the apparent desire of the electorate to punish overt pro-Boers. Souttar, who had voted for the Irish motion, lost Dumfries, although his majority of thirteen in 1895 was only transformed into a Unionist majority of 449. None of the Scottish Liberals who voted with the Irish in 1899 was returned in 1900, because the fourth, Wedderburn, retired on the eve of the election. His marginal seat, Banffshire, however, was retained by his party. A substantial movement of patriotic opinion also ousted Thomas Buchanan, who had represented Aberdeenshire East following his 1892 defeat in Edinburgh West. Although Buchanan had not supported the Irish amendment, he had been one of six Scottish Liberals who in July 1900 backed a motion of censure against the colonial secretary moved by Sir William Lawson, an ardent pro-Boer, during a discussion on the service estimates.[7]

In 1906, the Liberals set aside the vicissitudes of the previous two decades, capturing a marginally higher proportion of the county electorate than in 1885. In the predominantly rural regions they ran more than 10.0 per cent ahead of their performances in 1900, as they consolidated their vote in Highland, captured more than half the electorate in the East, and established a clear lead over the Border Unionists for the first time in five general elections (Table 4.4). Similarly, in Central a Liberal lead that had been reduced to 5.8 per cent in 1900 shot up to 22.6 per cent. Only in the West, where Labour candidates attracted 8.1 per cent of the electorate (mostly in Lanarkshire), did Liberal support fail to register a sharp increase as it became the least Liberal region for the first time.

For the Unionists 1906 was a disaster, as their share of the electors dropped 10.3 per cent in Highland, 8.0 per cent in Central, 6.1 per cent in the West, 5.2 per cent in Borders and 3.8 per cent in the East, and their party ceased to be the dominant alignment in the Borders and the West for the first time since 1885. Swings from the Unionists to the Liberals rose from 3.8 per cent in the West, to 7.8 per cent in East, 7.9 per cent in the Borders, 8.4 per cent in Central, and 11.4 per cent in Highland. The Unionists lost all their county seats except Wigtown and North Ayrshire, but gained Lanarkshire Govan and North West Lanarkshire (again defying the trend), as a result of Labour interventions.

The combination of rural radicalism and collectivist social reform, which characterised the policies of the government, 1906–1910, consolidated the Liberal position in Scotland, so that the elections of 1910 broadly confirmed the results of 1906. Indeed, overall Liberal strength in the counties was greater in January 1910 than in 1906, and hardly less the following December. In January 1910 more than half the electorate in the East and Highland turned out to support the Liberals, and in the Borders the Liberals performed rather better in December 1910 than in the previous January. In the West the Liberals improved their vote in both elections of 1910, though this was partly because in December the Labour Party stood down in all seats except Mid Lanark.

By contrast, the Unionists recovered less than two fifths of the ground lost in the debacle of 1906, which was insufficient to rebuild their parliamentary strength. It was symptomatic of Unionist difficulties that while in January 1910 they recaptured Perth West, Kirkcudbright, Renfrew East and Bute, Wigtown remained the only 1906 constituency they retained, because Ayrshire North, which they had held since 1886, Lanarkshire North West (continuing its eccentric career), and Govan fell to the Liberals, despite continuing Labour interventions in all three divisions. December 1910 was even less productive for the Unionists, with Kirkcudbright returning to the Liberals, leaving them with only four county seats.

The most novel feature of the December 1910 county elections was the victory of William Adamson in West Fife, which was significant in two respects. Firstly, it was the first success of a Labour candidate in a Scottish county, and secondly, it highlighted the general inability of his party in Scotland to match the inroads Labour had made in English mining constituencies. Of all county seats West Fife was the most likely to fall to Labour, for with more than half the electorate employed as colliers, the division was easily the most mining constituency in Scotland. Although hitherto a safe Liberal seat, the reluctance of many electors to cast a ballot, particularly in 1906, hinted at the existence of a working class vote independent of the Liberal coalition (Pelling: 395). That seemed confirmed in January 1910, when Adamson, standing for the first time, won 4,736 votes, with the Liberal only 353 below his party's record poll in the constituency four years before and the Conservative enjoying a 213 rise in his tally. Despite the Conservative standing down in December, 'Liberal dominance of the division was ended once and for all' (Pelling: 395). West Fife had begun its long career as the most left-wing Scottish constituency.

It was remarkable, given the fundamental changes to the county franchise in 1885, that the proportion of county seats won by the Liberals, 1885–1910, (71 per cent), was exactly the same as between 1868 and 1880, and that the Liberal vote lead over the Unionists in December 1910 (10.9 per cent) was hardly different from their advantage in 1880 (9.7 per cent). Most of the improvement had come in the Highlands (+12.5 per cent), but even in the troublesome West the Liberals were 2.1 per cent stronger.

By the close of 1910 the Liberals had overwhelmingly dominated representation in the East and Central regions over eight general elections since 1885, and Highland, following 20 years of realignment, had fallen firmly into the Liberal camp. The Unionists, by contrast, had failed to establish themselves as the major force in any region, although they had a challenging position in the marginal West and Borders. Twelve county constituencies – Aberdeen West, Banff, Kincardine, Fife East, Perth East, Clackmannan and Kinross, Berwick,

Haddington, Edinburgh, Linlithgow, North East and Mid Lanark – were constantly Liberal. Wigtown was the only seat consistently to return Unionists, and only six other seats – Bute, Ayr North, Renfrew East and West, Kirkcudbright, and Perth West – were predominantly Unionist. Apart from Dunbarton, Lanark South and Partick, and Peebles and Selkirk, which split their allegiance, the remainder favoured the Liberals. Thus, with Labour confined to West Fife, the Liberals had established a position in the counties equal to that of 1880.

Conclusion

The strength of the Liberal Party in the 50 years after 1832 had rested on its social comprehensiveness, incorporating a broad coalition of landowners, farmers, shopkeepers, industrialists and artisans. By contrast Conservatism failed to establish a credible position in the burghs and relied heavily on the declining political influence of Tory landowners. Consequently, in 1880 the Liberals polled almost twice as many votes as the Conservatives, and won all but seven county constituencies (Table 4.5). In December 1910 the Unionists found themselves with even fewer seats, but they were 8.4 per cent more popular than the Conservatives in 1880, whilst the proportion of the electorate voting Liberal had fallen by 6.2 per cent (Table 4.5).

Although the franchise extension in 1884 was far greater in the counties, it was in the burghs that change was most evident, because the introduction of a modern two-party system had revolutionised their political culture. The home rule crisis of 1886 effected an alignment of Conservatives, Liberal Unionists and Orangemen to create a Unionist coalition commanding the allegiance of around 34 per cent of the electorate – compared to 20.4 per cent for the Conservatives in 1880 – and reduced support for Gladstonian Liberalism to around two fifths of the enrolled (Table 4.5). In 1900 the Unionist lead over the Liberals in the burghs was sufficient to make them the most popular party in Scotland as a whole by around 150 votes. In the counties, by contrast, both major parties were less popular with the registered electorate in 1910 than in 1880, and their relative positions hardly changed. As a consequence of these various developments, overall differences in the level of party strength in burgh and county constituencies were eliminated, reflecting the equalisation of the franchise.

The success of the Unionists between 1886 and 1900 was in large measure a function of low turnout, and the subsequent change in party fortunes was less a consequence of Unionist decline than a surge in Liberal support. The Unionist triumph of 1900, for example, was with only 37.4 per cent of the electoral enrolment, and the average Unionist share of the electorate in the depths of 1906–1910 was only 2.9 per cent below their share between 1886 and 1900, their years of prosperity. Even in December 1910, the Unionists ran 13.7 per cent ahead of their performance in 1880 in the burghs: a level of popularity only marginally below their breakthrough in 1886 (Table 4.5). The transformation of Liberal fortunes, 1906–1910, therefore, was mostly a function of a 7.0 per cent increase in support compared to 1886–1900.

Table 4.5
Summary of Electoral Support for the Liberals and Unionists, 1880–1910, expressed as a percentage of the enrolled electorate (Unionist includes Conservatives and Liberal Unionists)*

	1880	1885	1886	1892	1895	1900	1906	Jan 1910	Dec 1910	Change 1880–D.1910	Change 1886–D. 1910
Burghs											
Liberals	51.9	42.2	40.3	43.2	37.6	36.3	46.4	45.9	44.2	–7.7	+3.9
Unionists	20.4	25.4	34.2	33.2	33.3	37.2	29.7	33.4	34.1	+13.7	–0.1
Liberal Lead	*+31.5*	*+16.8*	*+6.1*	*+10.1*	*+4.3*	*–0.9*	*+16.7*	*+12.5*	*+10.1*	***–21.4*	***+4.0*
Counties											
Liberals	47.9	44.8	34.5	37.4	40.4	38.2	44.9	45.9	44.6	–3.3	+10.1
Unionists	38.2	29.9	32.9	36.7	39.0	37.5	31.3	33.6	33.7	–4.5	+0.8
Liberal Lead	*+9.7*	*+14.9*	*+1.6*	*+0.7*	*+1.4*	*+0.7*	*+13.6*	*+12.3*	*+10.9*	***+1.2*	***+9.3*
ALL											
Liberals	50.7	43.7	36.8	39.9	39.2	37.4	45.6	45.9	44.5	–6.2	+7.7
Unionists	25.5	28.1	33.4	35.2	36.5	37.4	30.6	33.5	33.9	+8.4	+0.5
Liberal Lead	*+25.2*	*+15.6*	*+3.4*	*+4.7*	*+2.7*	*0.0*	*+15.0*	*+12.4*	*+10.6*	***–14.6*	*+7.2*

* Where possible adjustments have been made for unopposed returns.

** Net Liberal gain over the Unionists.

While it was true that, as in England, Scottish politics became more class-based after 1885, the Liberals emerged as the dominant party in Scotland from 1906 because they had reconstructed a broad social consensus based on general support for free trade, widespread sympathy for the claims of tenant farmers, and a measure of social reform, to remain a centre party, marginalising the socialist left and holding off the Unionist right. Although the gap between the Liberals and Unionists in 1910 was substantially less than that between the Liberals and Conservatives in 1880, the spatial distribution of the votes seemed to have secured a continued Liberal hegemony. In regional terms, the Liberals had a heartland which included the county and burgh constituencies of Highland, the East and Central, but the Unionists lacked any secure base. Wigtownshire remained the only consistently Unionist constituency between 1885 and 1918: a slender strand, indeed, from which to assault the Liberal Dardanelles.

Notes

1. In 1888, on returning to the Liberal Party, Buchanan had chosen to fight a by-election, which he won with a majority of 46 against Raleigh, a Radical Liberal Unionist. In 1892 he lost by 512 votes to Viscount Wolmer. Edinburgh West, with its large business vote, returned a Liberal Unionist in all general elections, 1886–December 1910.
2. It is noticeable that Edinburgh, where the Labour movement was weak, was the most Liberal city.
3. Even there the Conservative win was due to the division of the Liberal vote between two candidates.
4. Between 1885 and 1886 while the Liberal share of the electorate fell by 10.3 per cent, support for the Unionists only rose 3 per cent (Table 4.5).
5 In 1885, Conservatives only stood in Orkney and Shetland and Inverness. The main conflict in Argyll, Caithness, Sutherland, and Ross and Cromarty had been between Crofters and Liberals. In 1886, apart from Inverness, there were straight fights between Crofters and Unionists on the mainland, and between a Liberal and Unionist in Orkney and Shetland.
6. 'McKillop won a good section of the mining vote and also polled well on the western side of the county, where a residential population dependent on Glasgow was building up' (Pelling: 395).
7. Scottish supporters of Lawson included Bryce (South Aberdeen), Clark (Caithness), MacLeod (Sutherland), Morley (Montrose Burghs), Shaw (Hawick Burghs) Wedderburn (Banff), and Buchanan (East Aberdeen) (*Hansard*, 84: 1259). During the election campaign Buchanan protested against his presentation in the press as a straightforward pro-Boer. His actual position, however, was somewhat complicated and obscure; but it would seem the electors regarded him as having too many pro-Boer sympathies.

References

Blewett, N, *Peers, Parties and the People*, London, 1972.

Cook, AB, 'Gladstone's election for the Leith district of burghs, July 1886, *Scottish Historical Review,* Vol. 49, 1970.

Cornford, J, 'The Transformation of Conservatism in the Late Nineteenth Century, *Victorian Studies*, Vol.7, 1963.
Craig, FWS, *British Parliamentary Election Results, 1885-1918,* London, 1974.
Dunbabin, JPD, 'Parliamentary Elections in Great Britain, 1869-1900: A Psephological Note,' *English Historical Review*, Vol. 86, 1966.
Gregory, R, *The Miners in British Politics, 1906-1914*, London, 1968.
Hansard (4th Series).
Hutchison, ICG, *A Political History of Scotland*, Edinburgh, 1986
Morgan, KC, *Wales in British Politics*, Cardiff, 1963.
Pelling, H, *Social Geography of British Elections, 1885-1910*, London, 1967.
Walker, W, *Juteopolis*, Edinburgh, 1979.

5 *The Members 1885 and December, 1910*

The composition of Scotland's parliamentary contingent changed substantially at the general election of 1885, when only 33 of the 58 members at the dissolution were returned in a new complement of 70 MPs. In the burghs two thirds of those elected had not previously sat, while in the counties just over half the members were new, if one includes Craig Sellar and Fraser Macintosh, who had formerly represented burgh constituencies.

The change of personnel in the burghs was largely a function of redistribution, which not only eliminated two burgh districts and increased the number of MPs in the four big cities from eight to fifteen, but introduced burgh divisions for the first time in Aberdeen, Edinburgh, and Glasgow. It was not entirely surprising, therefore, that John Webster, only first chosen to represent Aberdeen in 1880, along with an Edinburgh colleague and two of the three Glasgow MPs, chose 1880 as the moment to retire. A parallel decision of the two Dundee MPs and the member for the Leith Burghs also to leave parliament after relatively short periods at Westminster, meant that of the sixteen members returned in 1885 from the four major cities and Leith, only two had sat in the previous parliament. Other retirees included an elderly William Baxter of the Montrose Burghs, and Stewart Clark, a local merchant, who had momentarily held Paisley following a by-election in 1884; while Fraser Macintosh, the maverick member of the Inverness Burghs, was translated to the county of Inverness as a Crofter. Redistribution also brought an end to the political career of Rear-Admiral Sir John Hay, a former Conservative lord of the admiralty, with the suppression of the Wigtown District, and occasioned the removal of Sellar from the Haddington Burghs.

Only three burgh MPs seeking re-election were defeated in 1885. John Pender, the official Liberal was displaced in the Wick Burghs by John Cameron, an Independent Liberal; in the St Andrews Burghs, the Cheshire shipowner and official Liberal, Williamson, fell to a local landowner, Sir Robert Anstruther, standing as an Independent Liberal; and in the Kilmarnock District, Dick Peddie surrendered his constituency to a Conservative, Peter Sturrock.

The most significant development in 1885 was the impact of the new franchise in the Highland region, because it undermined the suzerainty of both Whig and Tory landlords. Recognising the new order, three sitting Liberal MPs – Samuel Laing (Orkney and Shetland), Sir John Sinclair of Ulbster (Caithness), and Lord Colin Campbell (Argyll) – and one Conservative, Cameron of Lochiel (Inverness), decided that discretion was the better part of valour and stood down, opening the way for more advanced Liberals and Crofters. In Ross and Cromarty, the sitting Liberal, Munro Ferguson, stood his ground, but was defeated by a Crofter, and although the Marquis of Stafford defied the Sutherland peasantry successfully in 1885, he failed to stand in 1886, following his conversion to Liberal Unionism, and he, too, was replaced by a Crofter.

Change in the rural areas outside the Highlands was relatively minor, confirming the Liberal gains of 1880. In the East there were two new members due to the division of Perth and Fife, and only one of the seven regional members elected in 1880 was missing from the parliament of 1885, Alexander Gordon – the second son of the Earl of Aberdeen – having made way for Peter Esslemont in East Aberdeenshire. Similarly, in the Borders, five of the six MPs returned in 1880 were successful in 1885, the only change being in Wigtown, where the seat was regained by the Conservatives following the retiral of the former Liberal MP.

Redistribution inevitably had a major impact in the West with the creation of four extra seats in Lanarkshire and the bifurcation of Renfrew. Consequently (with Sir Thomas Colebrooke stepping down following the suppression of his old division, Lanarkshire North; the retiral of Alexander Crum, the former MP of a united Renfrew; the defeat of Conservative incumbents in the two Ayrshire divisions; and a change of Tory MP in Bute) only three of the twelve regional members elected in 1885 – Orr-Ewing (Dunbartonshire), James Hamilton (South Lanark), and Craig Sellar (Lanarkshire Partick) – had sat in the old parliament. The only change in Central, however, was the defeat of the incumbent Conservative in Haddington.

The election of 1885 not only witnessed a substantial turnover of Scottish MPs, but a significant deepening of the trend evident in 1880 away from traditional sources of recruitment, especially in the counties. Prior to the Third Reform Act, representation, both Liberal and Conservative, had been dominated in the rural areas by landowners, lawyers and service officers, whose roots and interests lay in large family estates centred on the counties for which they were returned. In 1880, such individuals accounted for 28 (almost half) of Scotland's 58 members, but in 1885, only 21 out of a contingent of 70. Their replacements and recruits to the new division came from an increased number of merchants and manufacturers, together with a significant rise in the proportion of those with a professional background.

The Members, 1885[1]

The Liberals and Crofters

The Burghs

The rise of the new professional middle class MP with a cosmopolitan background was a distinctive feature of the development of Liberal representation within the burghs. In Aberdeen, Webster, a locally-based advocate from a long-established local family, was replaced by two academic lawyers, William Hunter (Aberdeen North) and James Bryce (Aberdeen South). Hunter, the son of an Aberdonian granite merchant, had attended the city's grammar school and university in his youth, but had subsequently taken the road south to practice law at the Middle Temple, and was later appointed Professor of Jurisprudence, Roman Law and International Law at University College, London. Politically a Radical, his support for a unicameral parliament, the disestablishment and disendowment of the church, and the introduction of old age pensions strongly recommended him to his predominantly working class constituents, his nomination being largely due to backing from the Aberdeen Radical Association, which had close connections with the Trades Council (Buckley:

100). James Bryce, born in Belfast the son of a Glaswegian, and educated at both Glasgow and Oxford Universities, was particularly cosmopolitan. Following his call to the bar at Lincoln's Inn he became Regius Professor of Civil Law at Oxford before unsuccessfully seeking to represent the Wick District in 1874. In 1880, he was returned for the London borough of Tower Hamlets, several hundred miles further south; but having served his constituents for only one parliament he repaired to Aberdeen South, whence he embarked on a distinguished political career as chancellor of the duchy of Lancaster, president of the board of trade, and chief secretary for Ireland, before his appointment as ambassador to Washington.

Table 5.1: Backgrounds of Scottish Members of Parliament returned in 1885

	Liberals			Cons	Crofters	All
	Burghs	**Counties**	**All**			
Landowners	2	7	9	2	-	11
Landowners/Soldiers	2	2	4	2	-	6
Landowners/Lawyers	1	1	2	2	1	5
Landowners/Academics	1	-	1	-	-	1
(All Landowners)	**(6)**	**(10)**	**(16)**	**(6)**	**(1)**	**(23)**
Soldiers	-	1	1	-	-	1
(All Soldiers)	**(2)**	**(3)**	**(5)**	**(2)**	**(-)**	**(7)**
English Bar Lawyers	3	4	7	-	-	7
Scottish Bar Lawyers	1	2	3	-	-	3
Lawyer/Academic	3	1	4	-	-	4
(All Lawyers)	**(8)**	**(8)**	**(16)**	**(2)**	**(1)**	**(18)**
Businessmen	10	9	19	-	1	20
Businessman/Naval Architect	-	-	-	1	-	1
Businessman/Civil Engineer	-	-	-	1	-	1
(All Businessmen)	**(10)**	**(9)**	**(19)**	**(2)**	**(1)**	**(22)**
Farmer	1	-	1	-	-	1
Surgeon/Newspaper Proprietor	1	-	1	-	-	1
Journalist	1	-	1	-	2	3
Doctor/Surgeon	1	-	1	-	1	3
(All Physicians)	**(2)**	**(-)**	**(2)**	**(-)**	**(2)**	**(4)**
Chemist	1	-	1	-	-	1
Academics	2	1	3	-	-	3
(All Academics)	**(6)**	**(2)**	**(8)**	**(-)**	**(-)**	**(5)**
ALL	30	28	58	8	4	70

A third lawyer/academic, Edmund Robertson, was elected in Dundee. Reflecting the social mobility of his time, his father having been a schoolmaster, Robertson went to Lincoln College, Oxford, after graduating from his local university, St Andrews. Thence he followed the familiar route of a call to the bar at a London Inn of Court, and later became a fellow of Corpus Christi and a public examiner in law.

English influences in the Eastern burghs, where the Oxford academic Charles Parker continued to hold Perth, were reinforced following the adoption of London-based barristers by the Liberals in the Inverness and Montrose Burghs and Dundee. In the case of Charles Lacaita (Dundee), whose home was in Leatherhead, Surrey, only his birth in Edinburgh provided a Scottish connection to offset a classic upper middle class English background centred on Eton, Balliol and Lincoln's Inn. More typical, however, were Robert Finlay (Inverness Burghs) and John Will (Montrose Burghs), who combined a strong Scottish upbringing with a career in England. Finlay had been educated both at school and university in Edinburgh, his native city, prior to his call to the bar at the Middle Temple; while Will, who also practised from the Middle Temple, had previously attended Brechin Grammar School and Edinburgh University before completing his education at King's College, London. The Anglo– Scottish ambience of Eastern MPs was somewhat modified by Alexander Asher, the son of a Banffshire minister, who following his education at the universities of Aberdeen and Edinburgh had practised at the Scottish bar before his return for the Elgin Burghs at a by-election in 1881, when he was appointed solicitor general.

In Glasgow, the seven-fold division of the city helped to break the near monopoly which local merchants had hitherto exercised over its representation, and its six new Liberal members, who joined Charles Cameron (College), the proprietor of the *North British Daily Mail*, reflected a variety of backgrounds. Only Gilbert Beith (Central) represented the commercial life of the city. The son of a Free Church minister and former pupil of Stirling Academy, he rose from being an apprentice to head the firm of Beith, Stevenson and Company, established an export company in Glasgow and Manchester, and later became chairman of the Glasgow Chamber of Commerce. The only other merchant, Hugh Watt (Camlachie), a native of Kilmarnock, and graduate of the University of Geneva, had business interests centred on London. Two of the new members, Mitchel Henry (Blackfriars and Hutchesontown) and Edward Russell (Bridgeton) were Englishmen with no apparent Scottish connections. Henry's father, the owner of a Huddersfield and Manchester mercantile company, had been MP for South Lancashire, his mother and wife were Irish, and he had sat for Galway from 1871 to 1885. A fellow of the Royal College of Surgeons, having received his training at University College, London, Henry subsequently pursued his profession at the Middlesex Hospital. His retreat to Glasgow was a welcome bolt-hole from the revolutionary changes in Irish politics following the Third Reform Act. Russell's adoption reflected the sharpening ideological edge to politics in the west of Scotland. Born in London and educated privately, he had followed a career in journalism, rising to the position of leader writer on the *Morning Star* (later the *Daily News*), and latterly edited the *Liverpool Daily Post*. Active in politics, he became chairman of the Liverpool Reform Club and president of the local Literary and Philosophical Society. As an advanced Liberal he supported home rule and was opposed to the heredity principle in the House of Lords. Although John McCulloch (St Rollox) held views common to most progressive Liberals of his time, as an agriculturist he might have been more appropriately adopted in a county division. His father had been a Wigtownshire farmer, and he had been educated in local schools before working on the land and becoming a farmer himself. McCulloch was also a writer: a propagandist for the cause of tenant farmers, and had published a report on agricultural leasing – a matter of constant friction between landlord and tenant at that time. He supported reform of the land system, and advocated the establishment of a land court. Amongst his other causes were reform of the House of Lords, and the need for an independent government for Ireland. The sixth new member for Glasgow was Archibald (better known as Cameron) Corbett, who represented Tradeston until his elevation as Baron Rowallan in 1911. He belonged to a family with landed interests in both Warwickshire and Ayrshire, and had unsuccessfully stood for North Warwick in 1884. In 1886 he deserted to the Liberal Unionists, but his free trade and temperance sympathies led him to resign the Liberal Unionist whip in 1909, and by December 1910 was once again the official Liberal nominee.

The splitting of Edinburgh into four divisions introduced three new members (all Independent Liberals) to the burgh. Two of them, John Wilson (Central) and George Harrison (South), were by no means new to the capital's commercial life and politics. Wilson, a local merchant, was a native of Edinburgh, a product of its High School, and in the course of his public career had served as chairman of the Edinburgh Liberal Association, as deputy-chairman of the chamber of commerce, as a magistrate, and as city treasurer. Similarly, Sir George Harrison, a director of the North British Railway Company, had been chairman of the chamber of commerce, and both treasurer and lord provost of the municipality. George Goschen, by contrast, was an archetypal carpet-bagger, whose sojourn in Edinburgh was appropriately brief. An ex-pupil of Rugby, graduate of Oriel College, Oxford, and resident of Kent, Goschen was very much a south-east Englishman, quite untypical of his constituents. Before coming to Edinburgh he had represented both the City of London and Ripon, Yorkshire, and following his defeat as a Liberal Unionist in 1886 and failure in Liverpool Exchange (1887) he finally gained acceptance with the electors of St Georges, Hanover Square, London. Goschen was later to hold several high offices of state, and as chancellor of the exchequer devised the method of calculating the proportion of public expenditure awarded to the various parts of the United Kingdom (the Goschen Formula). The one continuing Edinburgh MP was Thomas Buchanan (West), the third son of a Glasgow merchant, who following schooling at Glasgow High and Sherbourne graduated from Balliol. Prior to his unsuccessful attempt to capture Haddingtonshire in 1880 and his return at the Edinburgh by-election of 1881, he had become a fellow of All Souls. The neighbouring seat, Leith Burghs, witnessed the election of William Jacks in 1885, whose background as the son of a Berwickshire shepherd was the most working class of any member hitherto returned in Scotland, at least since 1832. Educated at a village school in the borders, Jacks began work as an apprentice to a firm of shipbuilders in West Hartlepool. He later rose to become manager of the Sutherland and Seaham Engine Works and Foundry Company, and latterly established an iron and steel business of his own in Glasgow. A lad o' pairts, he also wrote and gave lectures on social, economic and literary subjects. Although a home ruler, he voted against the home rule Bill of 1886 because it failed to promise the Scots what was being offered to the Irish, and was forced out of Leith in somewhat dubious circumstances to provide a seat for Gladstone. In 1892, however, he came back in Stirlingshire as a supporter of the Grand Old Man (Cook).

In the remaining burghs, Richard Campbell (soldier/landowner, Ayr Burghs), Ernest Noel (landowner, Dumfries Burghs), Sir George Campbell (lawyer/landowner, Kirkcaldy Burghs), George Trevelyan (academic/ landowner, Hawick Burghs), Campbell-Bannerman (merchant, Stirling Burghs) and James Ramsay (merchant, Falkirk Burghs), retained the seats they had held in 1880, and Thomas Sutherland, a local shipowner, held Greenock, which he had won at a by-election in 1884. They were joined in 1885 by three new members – William Barbour (Paisley), John Cameron (Independent Liberal, Wick Burghs), and Sir Robert Anstruther (Independent Liberal, St Andrews Burghs) – who each in their different ways represented varying strands of nineteenth century Liberalism. William Barbour came from the local capitalist tradition, for although he lived in Devon and London, he was the son of a Paisley businessman and burgh councillor. The weakening of his ties with Paisley had been occasioned by the family interests being transferred to Liverpool and Manchester in order to improve their trading connections with South America. John Cameron, an Independent Liberal enjoying the support of the Land League, had a professional background not unlike that of the Crofter candidates. Born in Ballantrae, Ayrshire, educated at local schools and Sharp's Institution, Perth, he later graduated from the Royal School of Mines in London as a chemist. Professionally, he worked for the inland revenue and in the chemical laboratory of the Royal School of Mines. By contrast, Sir Robert Anstruther sustained the landed interest which had remained strong in the burgh districts even after 1832. An old Harrovian, Anstruther was a landowner/soldier who reached the rank of lieutenant-colonel in the Grenadier Guards. At the time of his election he was deputy-lieutenant of Caithness and lord lieutenant of Fife, the county he had represented in parliament from 1864 to 1880. As a landowner and Churchman, he somewhat predictably became a Liberal Unionist, and although he retired in 1886, the seat passed without difficulty to his son.

The Counties

Amongst county constituencies it was in the Highlands that the MPs of 1885 provided the sharpest contrast with their predecessors, due to the breakthrough of the Crofters following the liberalisation of the franchise. Although crofter demands and attitudes dictated Highland politics for at least a decade after 1884, no crofter sought to become a member of parliament. Lacking both the financial security and skills to become MPs themselves, the crofters looked to the middle class leadership of the Highland Land League to represent their case in the House of Commons. Consequently, the distinction between the new Highland MPs and their predecessors was less social – indeed, some were not without landowning connections – than ideological.

The closest the crofters came to direct representation was in Sutherland, where Angus Sutherland, born in Helmsdale the son of a crofter, replaced the Duke of Sutherland when he retired from the House in 1886. At the time of his election, however, Sutherland no longer lived locally, for after a short period as a pupil teacher at the Free Church School in the Strath of Kilconan he entered Glasgow University, and was subsequently appointed a mathematics teacher at Glasgow Academy. By contrast, Dr Gavin Clark, the son of a Kilmarnock insurance agent, who replaced Sinclair of Ulbster in Caithness in 1885, had no close Highland connections, and following his graduation from Glasgow and Edinburgh Universities had pursued his career as a surgeon at King's College, London. Nevertheless, his strong radical views, his support for the Land League, his home rule principles, and residence in London, made him an ideal candidate for the majority of his constituents. Defeated in 1900, having lost the Liberal nomination for his pro-Boer sympathies, Clark subsequently joined the Labour Party, and was its Glasgow Cathcart candidate in 1918. Similarly, Dr Roderick MacDonald – who defeated the incumbent Liberal landowner/soldier, Munro Ferguson, in Ross and Cromarty – although born in Skye, had only a marginal connection with the region, because shortly after his birth, his father had moved to Glasgow, in common with many other West Highlanders. Following attendance at schools in Glasgow, and Glasgow and Edinburgh Universities, he became a Fellow of the Royal College of Surgeons, and like Clark worked in England, first as coroner for North East Middlesex and later as medical officer of health for Durham. While in London he became treasurer to the London Crofters' Aid and Defence Fund, and espoused the causes of home rule and reform of the House of Lords.

Whereas Sutherland, Clark and MacDonald were new to the House of Commons and reflected the emergence of a new type of member, two of the Crofter MPs, Donald Macfarlane and Charles Fraser Macintsoh, had both been members before the Third Reform Act, and came from traditional sources of MP recruitment. Macfarlane, who represented Argyll, 1885–6, was the son of a Caithness magistrate, and had previously been returned for Carlow in Ireland. Educated privately before becoming an East India Merchant, he had homes in London and Norwich, but despite his conventional background was a supporter of Irish home rule and land reform for small tenants. A former Conservative, Fraser Macintosh, who carried Inverness-shire in 1885, had been born in Inverness, where he later practised as a solicitor and represented the burgh district in parliament from 1874 to 1885 as a Liberal. He was also a landowner and magistrate in his new constituency. Unlike the other Crofter members, however, he was opposed to home rule, and in 1886 was returned unopposed as a Unionist Crofter. It wasn't until 1892 that he was defeated by a member of Lord Napier's Crofters' Commission, Dr Donald MacGregor, who had secured the backing of the Land League. MacGregor was yet another medical graduate of Edinburgh University who subsequently continued his career in England, where he became identified with the Crofters' cause. He, however, only strayed as far as Penrith in Cumberland, and on his adoption as candidate in Inverness was medical superintendent at Barnhill Hospital and Asylum, Glasgow.

In contrast to the mainland, Leonard Lyell, who replaced Samuel Laing in Orkney and Shetland, was a Liberal, the Land League not presenting a candidate. He had been born in London, and at the time of his election was the professor of Natural Sciences at University College, Wales. Lyell's Scottish connections were through his famous uncle, the geologist, Charles Lyell, on whose death he inherited the family estate in Forfarshire, where he became a magistrate. Politically a Gladstonian, he remained loyal to the Grand Old Man in

1886.

The second region of major change was the West, where only seven of the twelve county members were Liberal in 1885, and six of them were new representatives: Craig Sellar (Lanarkshire Partick) and Donald Crawford (Lanarkshire North East) were both members of the legal profession; James Finlayson (Renfrew East) and Stephen Mason (Mid Lanark) were businessmen; and Hugh Elliot (Ayrshire North) and Eugene Wason (Ayrshire South) were landowners. The one surviving Liberal was John Hamilton, a landowner/ soldier, in Lanarkshire South.

Although the insertion of Sellar in the Haddington Burghs at a by-election in 1882, following an unsuccessful foray in Plymouth Devonport in 1880, was in conformity with traditional Whig influence in the seat, his translation to suburban Glasgow seemed a less appropriate move. His father, Patrick, had been the notorious factor of the Duke of Sutherland, who between 1807 and 1816 had masterminded the clearances. On leaving the duke's service in 1818 Patrick became a sheep farmer on the Sutherland estates until his death in 1851 (Stephen & Lee). Craig Sellar had been born in Sutherland, but received his education at Rugby and Balliol. Unlike many of his upper middle class contemporaries, however, he returned to Scotland, where he was called to the bar in 1862, and became legal secretary to the lord advocate, 1870–74, and a magistrate and deputy lieutenant in Argyll. Predictably, given his background, he deserted to Liberal Unionism in 1886, holding Partick until his death in 1890. Two years younger than Sellar, Donald Crawford, a home ruler, was also called to the Scottish bar in 1862, following an education at Glasgow University, Balliol, and Heidelberg. He was also a fellow of Lincoln's Inn. Crawford is perhaps most distinguished for having cited Sir Charles Dilke as co-respondent when divorcing his wife, Virginia.

James Finlayson, the senior partner of a Johnstone flaxspinning and thread manufacturing business, and a director of an insurance firm and the Glasgow and Southwest Railway Company, as a disestablisher, home ruler, and advocate of House of Lords reform, reflected the Radical temper of Liberalism in the west, as did the Fifeshire-born merchant, Mason, a home ruler and land reform pamphleteer, who became director and president of the Glasgow Chamber of Commerce. The Whig tradition was sustained by Hugh Elliot, who defeated an incumbent Conservative in North Ayrshire. The third son of Lord Minto, he had received his education at Eton and Cambridge, and although in favour of disestablishment he was not a home ruler, and successfully deserted to the Unionists in 1886. Eugene Wason, the son of an Ayrshire landowner, educated at the Rugby and Oxford before being called to the bar at the Middle Temple, also came from a traditional background. Nevertheless, he was a Radical, and his support for both universal adult suffrage and reform of the House of Lords probably appealed to the miners in his constituency. Less popular in this Covenanting county, however, was his support for home rule, which occasioned his defeat at the hands of a Unionist in 1886.

Changes in county constituencies outside the Highlands and the West were more incremental. In the Borders, all the Liberals who had been elected in 1880 were returned with the exception of John Maxwell, who retired from Kirkcudbright (he was replaced by a Conservative); and in the East, the only newcomers were Peter Esslemont (East Aberdeenshire), Robert Menzies (East

Perthshire) and John Kinnear (East Fife), occasioned by the division of Perthshire and Fifeshire. Similarly, Haldane (Haddington) was the only new arrival in the six counties of the Central region.

The return of Esslemont, who replaced the heir to the dukedom of Gordon in East Aberdeenshire, was a reflection of the rising tide of rural radicalism. The son of a tenant farmer, Esslemont had only received an elementary education at Belhelvie Parish School, but had subsequently become senior partner in a firm of Aberdeen drapers, Esslemont and Macintosh, president of the Chamber of Commerce, magistrate, and lord provost of Aberdeen, 1880–3, before his return to Westminster in 1885. The ideological trend was further sustained by John Kinnear, a graduate of St Andrews and Edinburgh Universities, who had been called to the bar at Lincoln's Inn in 1856 following six years practising in Scotland. His nomination in East Fife displeased the Whig leadership in the new division, but a greater dislike of the Tories kept the Liberals united (Hutchison: 155). It was ironic, therefore, that in 1886 Kinnear joined the small band of Radical Unionists and lost his seat to Asquith. Coming from a landed family, the third newcomer, Menzies, had a more conventional background. In common with other members of his class he had been to school and university in England (Harrow and Christ Church), before practising law at Lincoln's Inn. Nevertheless, despite landed interests in Forfar, Perth and Midlothian, he remained loyal to Gladstone until his death in 1889. The most significant new arrival at the election of 1885 was Richard Haldane – a lawyer/academic – in the mining seat of Haddington, who translated Shopenhauer into English. His selection marked not only the rise of a class of intellectual MPs within the parliamentary Liberal Party, but provided a strong link with the politics of the twentieth century, for following a distinguished career as secretary of state for war, 1905–12, when he became lord chancellor, this former Liberal Imperialist later became leader of the Labour Party in the House of Lords.

Those remaining from 1880 included seven landowners – Hon E Marjoribanks (Berwick), Hon ARD Elliot (Roxburgh), Hon RD Bruce (Fife West), Dr R Farquharson (Aberdeenshire West), Sir George MacPherson Grant (Elgin and Nairn), RW Duff (Banff), and P McLagan (Linlithgow); half a dozen with a predominantly mercantile background but in the process of acquiring landed property – WE Gladstone (Midlothian), Sir Robert Jardine (Dumfries), Sir Charles Tenant (Peebles and Selkirk), Sir Donald Currie (West Perth), JW Barclay (Forfar), and JC Bolton (Stirling); a professional soldier, Sir George Balfour (Kincardineshire); and JB Balfour (Clackmannan & Kinross), a Scots lawyer.[2]

The Conservatives

Whereas Liberal representation had begun to detach itself from reliance on landed families as a source of MP recruitment, the Conservative members remained almost exclusively a party of landlords. Even Peter Sturrock, the only one of their number to represent a burgh constituency, the Kilmarnock District, was the son of a large farmer, though he himself had qualified as a civil engineer following an education at Kilmarnock Academy and Glasgow University. Later he became a colliery owner, and served variously as treasurer, dean of guild, and provost of Kilmarnock. In 1886, his fortunate success of 1885 was overturned by a Gladstonian Liberal.

Of the seven Conservatives elected in Scottish county constituencies in 1885, only two of them, Archibald Orr-Ewing (Dunbartonshire), and Sir Herbert Maxwell (Wigtownshire), both landowners, had sat in the previous parliament. All the new men, with one exception, were landed proprietors, though unusually (and in contrast to the Liberals), they did not include representatives of titled families. Sir Mark MacTaggart Stewart, for example, first returned for Kirkcudbright in 1885, had been educated at Winchester and Christ Church before practising law at the Inner Temple. He was also a deputy-lieutenant of Kirkcudbright and Wigtown, and an honorary colonel of the Ayrshire and Galloway Artillery Volunteers. In 1874 he had seemingly stood with success in the Wigtown Burghs, but the result was subsequently declared void. Equally typical was Sir Archibald Campbell (Renfrew West), vice-lieutenant and county convenor of Renfrewshire, a Crimean War veteran who had risen to the rank of lieutenant-colonel in the Argyll and Sutherland Highlanders. In conformity with his social status, the new member for the recently created division of North West Lanarkshire, a deputy lieutenant and landowner from Inverness-shire, John Baird, was yet another product of Harrow and Oxford. Somewhat eccentrically, he supported a measure of Irish home rule and a relaxation of laws inhibiting the transfer of land. Neither consideration, however, prevented his defeat by the Liberals in 1886. A fourth landowner, James Robertson, sat for the island of Bute. He was distinguished in having had a Scottish education at Edinburgh University, and in practising at the Scottish bar. The landowner/soldier/lawyer mould was only broken by Sir William Pearce in the shipbuilding division of Lanarkshire Govan. Appropriately, he was a naval architect by training who became chairman of the Govan Shipping Line and a director of the Scottish Oriental Company.

The Members, December 1910

The Liberals

After a quarter of a century of internal divisions, splits and an increasingly partisan electoral conflict, the Liberals by 1910 had reasserted themselves as the clearly dominant force in Scottish politics. With 58 seats in December 1910, they held one more than in 1885, although they carried five fewer constituencies in the burghs. The major change in the profile of Liberal MPs was a reduction in the number of landowners from fourteen to five, and their replacement by lawyers in county constituencies, where members of the legal profession increased from eight to seventeen. Developments in the burghs were relatively minor.

The Burghs

In contrast to the counties, members with a legal training in the burghs fell from eight in 1885 to three in December 1910, and those with landowning connections were reduced from five to two. Consequently, the relatively static number of businessmen and other professionals assumed a greater proportionate importance.

Table 5.2: Backgrounds of Scottish Members of Parliament returned in December 1910

	Liberal			Conserv.	Labour	All
	Burghs	Counties	All			
Landowner/Soldiers	2	3	5	5	-	10
Soldiers	-	1	1	-	-	1
Soldiers/Busnessmen	1	-	1	-	-	1
(All Soldiers)	**(3)**	**(4)**	**(7)**	**(5)**	**(-)**	**(12)**
English Bar Lawyers	1	6	9	-	-	9
Scottish Bar Lawyers	1	6	6	2	-	8
Lawyer/Academics	-	4	4	1	-	5
Lawyer/Businessmen	1	-	1	-	-	1
(All Lawyers)	**(3)**	**(17)**	**(20)**	**(3)**	**(-)**	**(3)**
(All Academics)	**(1)**	**(4)**	**(5)**	**(1)**	**(-)**	**(6)**
Businessmen	10	10	20	1	-	21
(All Businessmen)	**(12)**	**(10)**	**(22)**	**(1)**	**(-)**	**(23)**
Other Professionals	7	3	10	-	-	10
Trade Union Officials	-	-	-	-	3	3
ALL	**26**	**34**	**58**	**9**	**3**	**70**

Six of the eight Liberals returned in the burghs of East and Highland in December 1910 had been educated within Scotland, and four of them had subsequently pursued their various occupational interests north of the border. Robert Munro (Wick Burghs), John Bryce (Inverness Burghs), and Alexander Whyte (Perth), had each attended provincial academies before entering Edinburgh University, while John Sutherland (Elgin Burghs) graduated from Aberdeen University after attending a state school in the fishing village of Lossiemouth. Duncan Pirie (Aberdeen North) had also been educated within Scotland, although at the more socially exclusive Glenalmond, before entering the army. On graduating, Munro had proceeded to practise law at the Scottish bar; Whyte, having lectured at the Sorbonne became principal of New College, Edinburgh; and Sutherland ran a business in Portsoy. On his retirement as a captain in the 3rd Hussars, Pirie became a director of the family paper-making company on Donside; and similarly, George Esslemont (Aberdeen South), son of the former member for East Aberdeenshire, studied at Aberdeen Grammar School before joining the family drapery business. Far less parochial was Bryce, who moved from Edinburgh University to Balliol, and while at Oxford became treasurer and later president of the Oxford Union. Consequently, while for other Scots in these burghs a local education was followed by a career within Scotland, for Bryce it was a prelude to the acquisition of banking and insurance interests based on London, railway directorships in India and Burmah, chairmanship of the Rangoon Chamber of Commerce, and membership of the legislative council of Burmah, reminiscent of the strong earlier association between Scottish representation and the East India Company. Supporting the Scots were Vernon-Harcourt (Montrose Burghs), a Hampshire-born diplomat and lieutenant in the RNVR, who although educated at Eton and Trinity College, Cambridge, was identified with the left-wing of his party; and Winston Churchill, Old Harrovian, soldier, spy, journalist and minister of the crown, who held one of the seats in Dundee. It was a measure of Vernon-Harcourt's commitment to Scotland that he had unsuccessfully sought to represent Hastings only weeks before Montrose in 1908; but his illustrious father had contested the Kirkcaldy Burghs in 1859.

Table 5.3: Characteristics of Scottish Members of Parliament, December 1910

	Liberals n=58			Unionists n=9	Labour n=3	All n=70
	Burgh	**County**	**All**			
Scotsmen	24	19	43	8	3	54
Englishmen	8	5	13	1	-	14
Other	2	-	2	-	-	2
Attended Scottish schools	15	17	32	5	3	40
Attended English schools	15	7	22	4	-	26
Attended Scottish university	11	11	22	3	-	25
Attended English university	7	7	14	3	-	17
Scottish Local Govt. Cllrs.	4	4	8	1	1	10
English Local Govt. Cllrs	4	2	6	-	1	7
Main Location of Econ.Interest.						
Scotland	14	11	25	8	1	34
England	19	13	32	1	2	35
Other	1	-	1	-	-	1
Represented English constituency	3	5	8	-	-	8
Attempted to repr. an English. constituency.	2	2	5	1	1	7

The claims of Esslemont and Sutherland were enhanced by a strong involvement in local politics. George Esslemont, whose family members were closely connected with a variety of social and public bodies in Aberdeen, was a member of the town council, the school board and harbour board; while Sutherland was chairman of his local Fordyce School Board and a member of Banffshire County Council. Sutherland also had national credentials as chairman of the Scottish Temperance and Social Reform Association, which would have commended him to not only to Liberal activists in his constituency, but also to the petite bourgeoisie and puritanical religious sects that thrived in the fishing burgh of Peterhead, the major component of his burgh district.

The tradition of local men representing Glasgow and the Western burghs was in sharp decline by December 1910, and was only clearly sustained by John McCallum, a soap manufacturer, educated at the Neilson Institute in his native town, Paisley, which he represented from 1906 until his death in 1920. Godfrey Collins, the managing director of W Collins and Sons, the Glasgow and London publishers, could also claim a strong family connection with the region, although he himself had been to school at Temple Grove, East Sheen, in England, and resided in London. Nevertheless, after a short career as an officer in the Royal Navy, following his graduation from HMS *Britannia*, and his return for the second time in December 1910 as 'an ardent supporter of Free Trade and Land and Temperance reform, including the Taxation of land' (Donald: 54), he established a close connection with his constituency, Greenock, which lasted until his death in 1936.

Although Alexander Scott (Glasgow Bridgeton), Henry Watt (Glasgow College), and John Macdonald (Falkirk Burghs), graduated from Glasgow University after attending Scottish academies, all of them subsequently pursued their careers in London. Scott repaired to the Middle Temple, Watt to Gray's Inn (although retaining a business connection with Glasgow), while Macdonald served on the London School Board and wrote articles for the journal *Nineteenth Century.* Prior to his adoption in Bridgeton, Scott had been a member of Lewisham Town Council, and Macdonald had represented Bow and Bromley in parliament before defeat led him to the Falkirk District. Similarly, Adam Rainy (Kilmarnock Burghs), although educated at Edinburgh Academy and Edinburgh University, practised as an eye surgeon in London following the completion of his training at the universities of Vienna and Berlin. The son of Robert Rainy, principal of New College, Edinburgh, who had dominated the Free Church in the decades after the disruption, he was a vehement exponent of the disestablishment and disendowment of the Kirk,

The two other West of Scotland burgh Liberals – Thomas Wood (Glasgow St Rollox), and Archibald Corbett (Glasgow Tradeston), a survivor of the 1885 general election, who held the seat under a variety of labels during the intervening twenty five years (Craig: 509) – were Anglo–Scots chasing Scottish seats. Wood, born in London of Scottish antecedents, attended Mill Hill School before proceeding to University College, London. From 1892 to 1909 he was a member of London County Council, on which he was leader of the Progressive Party, and chairman, 1898–9. In 1885 he was returned to Westminster for Islington East, but lost the seat ten years later. Before winning St Rollox in 1906 he had unsuccessfully contested the division in 1900, and stood at a by-election in Orkney and Shetland with a similarly disappointing result in 1902. Later he was to fight Hackney Central (1922) following a heavy defeat in St Rollox at the 1918 general election. Despite his less than total commitment to Scotland, he nevertheless served as Scottish secretary, 1912–16.

The eight burgh Liberals elected in Central Scotland and the Borders were evenly divided between locals and Anglo–Scots or Englishmen.

Of the locals, two, Sir James Gibson (Edinburgh East), and John Gulland (Dumfries Burghs) were both merchants, graduates of Edinburgh Royal High School and Edinburgh University, and Edinburgh councillors, Gibson having been lord provost, 1906–9. First elected in 1906, Gulland had risen to prominence through the activities of the Young Scots, who had done much to revitalise the Scottish Liberals both organisationally and intellectually in the industrial counties following the rout of 1900 (Hutchison: 233, 240). As author of *Christ's Kingdom in Scotland or the Social Mission of the United Free Church of Scotland*, published in 1906, he had tended to see the problem of poverty largely as a function of drinking and gambling, but by 1911 had begun to identify with the state interventionist programmes of Lloyd George (Hutchison: 240). Charles Price, who represented Edinburgh Central from 1906 to 1918, was a retired partner in the Edinburgh and London-based biscuit company, McVitie and Price. The fourth Scotsman and sometime private secretary to Lord Rosebery and Scottish whip, Ronald Munro Ferguson (Leith Burghs), a former lieutenant in the Grenadier Guards with property in Ross and Fife, where he was vice-lieutenant of the county, came from the almost extinct Liberal recruiting ground of landowner/soldiers. He had been defeated by a Crofter in Ross and Cromarty in 1885, and by a Conservative in Dunbarton-shire the following year. His inappropriate adoption as MP for Leith in 1886 was entirely due to his influence with Gladstone, the previous member (Cook: 186), and he held the seat until 1914, despite attempts to exchange it for Kirkcaldy Burghs, which bordered onto his estates. Nevertheless, reflecting the times rather than his Whiggish instincts, he had become convinced by 1912 in the need for a minimum wage and the nationalisation of the mines (Hutchison: 240).

In strictest terms, James Dalziel (Kirkcaldy Burghs), having been born in Kirkcudbright, was Scots, but after a period at Borgue Academy he was removed to Shrewsbury High School and completed his education at King's College, London, where he later became proprietor of *Reynold's News*, a popular working class newspaper. Appropriately, as the representative of a Fife mining constituency, he 'held advanced views on all political and social questions' (Stenton & Lees Vol.III: 88). Charles Lyell (Edinburgh South), the only son of Lord Lyell, a Fifeshire landed proprietor, also had Scottish antecedents. Nevertheless, as a product of Eton and New College, and as MP for East Dorset from 1904, his culture and ambitions were shaped south of the border. It was only electoral defeat in January 1910 that sent him scurrying back to the land of his ancestors.

The two remaining burgh Liberal members, Arthur Ponsonby (Stirling Burghs) and John Barran (Hawick Burghs), were both Englishmen strongly identified with advanced Liberalism. Ponsonby, the son of Queen Victoria's secretary, had been page of honour to the Queen from 1882–87. He had attended Eton and Balliol prior to a period in the diplomatic service and a stint as Campbell-Bannerman's secretary. In 1906 he had attempted unsuccessfully to win Taunton for the Liberals, but was returned by Stirling Burghs in 1908 following the death of Campbell-Bannerman, and held the seat until its demise in 1918. After coming forward in Dunfermline in 1918 as an Independent Democrat he joined the Labour Party, in whose interest he represented Sheffield Brightside from 1922, serving in the two Labour governments of Ramsay MacDonald. Barran, a native of Ripon, Yorkshire, pupil of Winchester and graduate of Trinity College, Cambridge, was a Leeds textile manufacturer. He held Hawick Burghs from March 1909 until it disappeared at the end of the First World War.

The Counties

The decline of the Crofters left its mark on the Highlands, whose representation by December 1910, although still markedly different than before the passing of the Third Reform Act, seemed less vibrant than in the decade after 1885, and suggested more the influence of the whips than the expression of strong preferences by local Liberal associations. Not only were the region's MPs less locally based than before 1885, but they were significantly less involved than had been the Crofter members in local issues and organisations, and had mostly weak Scottish connections.

The most clearly Scottish of the Highland members was the whisky distiller, John Dewar, born and educated in his native city, Perth, where he became lord provost, 1893–99, prior to his election to parliament in Inverness-shire in 1900. His selection owed much to the influence of the Imperialist wing of the party organised by Munro Ferguson, then Scottish whip (Hutchison: 178). James Weir (Ross and Cromarty) was also a native of Perthshire, and had attended Dollar Academy. He had spent most of his life, however, in London, where his father had developed business interests, and in the same year that he won his Highland seat from Fraser Macintosh – 1892 – having failed to carry Falkirk Burghs in 1885, he was also elected to serve on London County Council. A home ruler and supporter of the Crofting Acts, he held his constituency until his death in 1911. The member for Orkney and Shetland, John Wason, had similarly tenuous Scottish connections. Born in Ayrshire, the son of the MP for Ipswich, he was educated, like his brother Eugene, member for Clackmannan and Kinross, at Rugby, after which he farmed in New Zealand, where he sat in the national legislature. On his selection to contest Orkney and Shetland as a Liberal Unionist in 1900 he was practising law at the Middle Temple. He later changed his political allegiance, precipitated a by-election in 1902, which he won as an Independent Liberal, and held the seat as a Liberal from 1906.

The three other Highland members were all Englishmen. The most famous of the trio was Robert Harmsworth, son of Alfred Harmsworth, the newspaper proprietor, who took Caithness as a Liberal Imperialist in 1900. His life centred completely around London, where he went to school, practised as a barrister at the Middle Temple, and became company chairman of the family business. The neighbouring county, Sutherland, provided a haven for another Londoner, Alphaeus Morton, a resident of Clapham and member of the City of London Corporation, who had sat for Peterborough from 1889 to 1895. John Ainsworth (Argyll), also had strong metropolitan connections, in that he was educated at University College School and graduated from University College, London. His home, however, was in Cumberland, where his family had interests in iron mining, and he was chairman of the Cleator and Workington Junction Railway. In 1886 he had failed to be elected for his local seat of Barrow-in-Furness, but prior to the 1900 general election he gained the nomination for Argyll, and eventually won the constituency at a by-election in 1903.

Coupled with its attraction as a region of Liberal strength, Eastern Scotland also became a focus of penetration by non-local influences following the defection of Whig landowners to Unionism. Only two members, Walter Waring (Banff) and Alexander Murray (Kincardine), approached the traditional model of the rural Liberal MP, and neither of them was local to the constituency he represented. Waring, an Old Etonian, had been a captain in the Life Guards and had served in South Africa before resigning his commission in 1906. A resident of Devon (his father being MP for Poole), he had no Scottish connections before marrying a daughter of the 10th Marquis of Tweeddale, who doubtless used his influence to secure his son-in-law a parliamentary seat. Murray, the fourth son of the first Viscount Elibank, whose family home was in the Borders, was also a soldier and had fought in China. His brother, the Liberal chief whip, was principally responsible for securing his nomination to the Kincardineshire seat in 1908. By contrast, a changing social order was reflected by James Falconer (Forfar) and William Young (Perth East), both sons of farmers who had made good. Born in Forfarshire and educated at a local secondary school, Arbroath Academy, Falconer graduated in law from Edinburgh University, and became a writer to the signet. He retained a strong interest in rural affairs, however, and founded the Scottish Rural Workers' Society, which strengthened his claim to represent his native county. William Young had received only an elementary education at Ballater Public School, Aberdeenshire, but proved his capacities by founding a firm of merchants and bankers with offices in London and Mexico.

Three further Eastern members – Archibald Williamson (Elgin and Nairn), William Cowan and James Henderson (Aberdeenshire East and West, respectively) – were English-based businessmen with weak Scottish connections. All, however, had been born and educated north of the border. Williamson and Cowan were graduates of Edinburgh University, and Henderson had attended the University of Aberdeen. Williamson, a native of Forfarshire, lived in Liverpool, where he served on the city council, 1890–94, and operated a number of companies in South America, including the Central Argentine Railway and Lobitos Oil Fields Limited. Cowan lived in Sussex, where he was a JP, and prior to his move north had been MP for Guildford. Similarly, Henderson, an inhabitant of Felixtowe and JP in Surrey and Suffolk, had sought, though without success, to be returned for East Essex before turning to West Aberdeenshire, where his natal claim was reinforced by a directorship of the Great North of Scotland Railway. The eighth Liberal to sit for a county seat in Eastern Scotland in December 1910 was Herbert Asquith, Yorkshireman, graduate of the City of London School and Balliol, QC at Lincoln's Inn, fellow of Balliol, and prime minister. Like others of his fellow MPs, he gave little personal attention to his constituency, which, when added to a less than glorious conduct of the war, was to occasion his humiliating defeat in 1918 (Ball).

In the Borders, the pattern of loose connection between Liberal MPs and their constituents was perhaps even more marked than in the Highlands and East. None of the five, for example, had been educated in Scotland. Sir John Jardine (Roxburgh) and Percy Molteno (Dumfriesshire) appeared especially marginal. Jardine had been born of English parents in Dunstable, and at the time of his election was living in Godalming, Surrey. He attended Eton before graduating in law from Christ Church, whereupon he entered the Bombay civil service, and rose to become a judge of the Bombay High Court and vice-chancellor of Bombay University. As a lawyer/academic, he published works on Buddhism and Chinese law. It was only on retirement at the age of sixty two that he entered parliament. Molteno, son of the first prime minister of the Cape Colony, South Africa, had attended the Cape University before moving to Trinity, Cambridge. Thereafter, he pursued a career at the Inner Temple from his home in Guildford, though he was to acquire landed property in Perthshire.

Although Gilbert McMicking (Kirkcudbright), and Donald Maclean (Peebles and Selkirk), both had Scottish ancestry, they, too, had been raised in the social culture of southern England. McMicking had attended school at Cheltenham and Wimbledon before moving to the Royal Military Academy, Woolwich; while Maclean, whose father came from Tiree, was a solicitor in Middlesex, and had only sought a Scottish constituency following his defeat as the member for Bath in January 1910. The most Scottish Border member was Harold Tennant (Berwickshire), the son of a manufacturer and former MP for Peebles and Selkirk, whose family owned property in Strathdon, Aberdeenshire.

Nevertheless, reflecting the social aspirations of his times, he had been educated at Eton and Trinity, and lived in Kent, where he was a justice of the peace.

The strong influence of the English bar was evident in the Liberal representation in the industrial counties of West and Central Scotland. Arthur Allen (Dunbartonshire), William Beale (Ayrshire South), James Greig (Renfrew West), Eugene Wason (Clackmannan and Kinross), and Haldane (Linlithgow), were all associated with the London Inns of Court. Apart from Haldane, they had all been raised in England and had little claim to represent constituencies north of the border. Allen and Beale were no more than carpet-baggers looking for safe havens following defeat in their former English constituencies. Arthur Allen, a native of Prestwich, Lancashire, was the son of a publisher and son-in-law of the founder of *The Manchester Guardian*. Following his education at Rugby and University College, Oxford, he had pursued his political ambitions as a member of the LCC from 1899 to 1913, and as MP for Christchurch, Hampshire, until defeat in January 1910. Only then did he show an interest in representing a Scottish seat. Similarly, William Beale, whose father had been a Welsh solicitor and mother a native of Birmingham, had sat for North Warwick, Central Birmingham and Aston Manor before his 1906 return in South Ayrshire. Greig and Wason were hardly more locally rooted, for although they had Scottish connections by family and birth, they were culturally English. Eugene Wason's background has already been considered; while Greig, the son of a writer to the signet, had gone first to school at University College, London, before completing his studies at University College itself, and the Sorbonne. Only Haldane in this group could claim a firm Scottish background.

In contrast to the rural constituencies, however, the industrial counties not only returned London barristers, but also an equal number of lawyers practising within Scotland. William Hunter (Lanarkshire Govan), Thomas Wilson (Lanarkshire North East), Andrew Anderson (Ayrshire North), and Alexander Ure (Linlithgow) had all attended Scottish grammar schools – Hunter: Ayr Academy; Wilson: Glasgow High School; Anderson: Dundee High School; and Ure: Larchfield Academy, Helensurgh – before Glasgow (Ure and Wilson) or Edinburgh (Hunter and Anderson) Universities. Wilson's claims to a Clydeside seat were further enhanced by a period of fifteen years on Lanarkshire County Council, where he held the important post of convenor of the public health committee. Ure, a lawyer/academic, who had at one time lectured in constitutional law and history at his alma mater, had strong local political connections through his father, a former Glasgow lord provost.

Only five of the fifteen Liberals elected in the county divisions of the West and Central in December 1910 were unconnected with the law, and they came from a variety of backgrounds. The traditional elite were represented by Alexander Murray (Midlothian), the eldest son of Viscount Elibank, a graduate of Cheltenham College and a lieutenant in the Lothian Yeomanry. Between 1905 and 1909 he served as the Scottish Liberal whip before his appointment as under secretary for India. In 1910 he became the Liberal chief whip and parliamentary secretary to the treasury in charge of patronage, where he gained a laudable reputation for advancing the careers of 'many unknown men without a big bank balance' (*Westminster Gazette* as quoted by Blewett: 280-1). Lanarkshire South was also represented by a Scotsman, Sir Walter Menzies, a graduate of Glasgow High School, who as head of the Phoenix Tube Works,

Glasgow, was one of a small band of manufacturers to sit in parliament. Although Robert Balfour (Lanarkshire Partick) was also Scots by origin and had attended St Andrews University, the merchant company in which he was a partner was based in Liverpool and London, and he was living in Essex at the time of his adoption.

The MP for Stirlingshire, Dr William Chapple, who for a few months in 1908 had sat in the House of Representatives in New Zealand, and in 1910 was living in London, had seemingly little to associate him with his constituency. Perhaps his authorship of *The Fertility of the Unfit* and *The Evils of Alcohol* appealed to the teetotal sympathies of his selectorate, but less so, one suspects, to his electors. The member for Mid Lanark in December 1910, John Whitehouse, was a more practical social philanthropist. Although an Englishman, he had established Scottish connections, when, following his education at the Midland Institute, Birmingham, he became the first secretary of the Dunfermline Carnegie Trust in 1902, and wrote *Problems of a Scottish Provincial Town*. From 1904 to 1907 he was the secretary of Toynbee Hall, and in 1909 and 1910 was the warden of Manchester University Settlement. Between 1908 and 1911 he edited *St George*. He was a founder of the Ruskin Society and the Secondary Schoolboys Company, and honorary secretary of the National League of Workers with Boys. Following his defeat in 1918 he founded Bambridge School, where he was headmaster until 1954. Between 1922 and 1935 he unsuccessfully contested five different constituencies for the Liberals, but none of them was in Scotland.

The Conservatives and Liberal Unionists

With only nine MPs returned in December 1910, and eight of them connected with the law, army and the land, the contingent of Conservative and Liberal Unionist members appeared hardly more broadly-based than the Tories elected in 1885. On the other hand, with the lawyers coming from urban middle class families rather than a traditional landowner/lawyer background, and five elected in urban constituencies, the reduced Unionist ranks continued in some measure to reflect the realignment of 1886.

In social terms the leading Conservatives were the Marquis of Tullibardine (West Perthshire) and Viscount Dalrymple (Wigtownshire). Although both were educated outside Scotland (Tullibardine at Eton; Dalrymple at Harrow and Sandhurst), they and their families were firmly rooted in Scottish society and politics as landed aristocrats, and were closely connected with the constituencies they represented: Tullibardine as the eldest son of the Duke of Atholl, and Dalrymple as heir to the earldom of Stair. Both were soldiers before entering politics. Tullibardine, whose father owned a private army, served in the Royal Horse Guards, and rose to the rank of brigadier-general in the Scottish Horse Brigade Imperial Yeomanry, while Dalrymple served as a captain in the Scots Guards. On leaving the army, Tullibardine not only returned to his native Perthshire, but became a member of its county council, and assumed national responsibilities as Grand Master Mason of Scotland.

The strength of local connection and military service were also evident in the backgrounds of William Anstruther-Gray (St Andrews Burghs), Sir John

Gilmour, Bt. (Renfrew East), and Harry Hope (Bute), representatives of the traditional gentry. Anstruther-Gray came from a family of landowner/soldiers with property in Caithness and Fife, and both his father and brother had sat for St Andrews since the enactment of the Third Reform Act. He himself had risen to the rank of lieutenant-colonel of the 13th Hussars, whom he had joined on leaving Eton, and in 1902 had been appointed inspector general of concentration camps in the Transvaal. In 1903 he had failed to win a by-election in St Andrews, but was successful in 1906 and again in December 1910, following his defeat the previous January. Sir John Gilmour, too, had served in South Africa, and later became a brigadier in the socially prestigious Royal Company of Archers. Although not intimately associated with Clydeside, he had strong Scottish connections, for despite attending Trinity Hall, Cambridge, he had been to school at Glenalmond before a spell at Edinburgh University, was a director of the Caledonian Railway, and as a landowner had served on Fife County Council from 1901 to 1910. Similarly, Harry Hope, sometime captain in the Haddingtonshire and Berwickshire Artillery, and a product of the Collegiate School, Edinburgh and Edinburgh University, was an active member of Forfar County Council and a leading member of the Scottish Chamber of Agriculture. It was, perhaps, his Scottish education which helped draw him from Conservatism into Liberal Unionism in 1887 because he had noted in the constituencies 'a very strong feeling for continued, well-considered Liberalism which I admire' (Hutchison: 200).

The rest of the Unionist contingent was composed of two lawyers, Charles Dickson (Glasgow Central) and James Clyde (Edinburgh West), a lawyer/academic, Halford Mackinder (Glasgow Camlachie), and a brewer, George Younger (Ayr Burghs). Apart from Mackinder, they were all raised and worked within Scotland. Dickson, the son of a Glasgow doctor, and a graduate of Glasgow High School and University, had been called to the Scottish bar in 1877, and served as lord advocate, 1903 to 1905. In like manner, Clyde, after attending Edinburgh Academy entered the local university, where his father taught classics, and practised at the Scottish bar from 1887. Between October and December 1905, he was solicitor general. Mackinder is noteworthy as the only Unionist not to be closely associated with Scotland. The son of a doctor, he went to school in Gainsborough and Epsom before graduating from Christ Church, Oxford. Thereafter he was called to the bar at the Inner Temple, became a reader in geography at Oxford University, and director of the London School of Economics and Political Science from 1903 to 1908. His first attempt to enter parliament had been in Warwick and Leamington in 1900 as a Liberal Imperialist, and after rejection as a Unionist in the Hawick Burghs, 1909, was accepted by the voters of Camlachie in January 1910.

Undoubtedly the most politically involved Conservative MP was George Younger who, following his schooling at Edinburgh Academy joined the family brewing business in Alloa, later becoming its chairman. He was also a director of the National Bank of Scotland, Lloyd's Bank, and the North British and Mercantile Insurance Company. From 1895 to 1906 he was convenor of Clackmannan County Council, and president of the Scottish County Councils' Association from 1902 to 1904. In 1904 he served as president of the National Union of Conservative Associations in Scotland. After three attempts to wrest Clackmannan and Kinross from the Liberals and defeat in the Ayr Burghs at a by-election in 1904, he was elected for the Ayr District in 1906, and represented the seat until he retired in 1922. Fully appreciating the need for Scottish Conservatism to broaden its appeal, he was to play a major role in bringing various tranches of Liberals into a grand Unionist anti-Labour coalition that came to full fruition in 1931.

Labour

Three members of the Labour Party – Alexander Wilkie (Dundee), William Adamson (West Fife), and George Barnes (Blackfriars and Hutchesontown) – secured election in December 1910. Appropriately, Adamson and Wilkie were born in Fife, whose miners, virtually enslaved before the Union (Arnot), could be counted amongst the longest-surviving industrial working class communities in Britain. Barnes, born in Lochee, Dundee, also came from the east of Scotland. The three were completely different from the Liberal and Conservative members in that they were working class. None of them had attended secondary school – Adamson had been to a dame school – let alone a university. Their political credentials lay in their experience as trade union organisers and leaders.

Wilkie, who began work as a seaman, later became a ship constructor on the Clyde, where he joined Glasgow Trades Council and was elected secretary and treasurer of the local Shipwrights Society. On moving to Newcastle, he was elected general secretary of the Shipconstructors and Shipwrights Association, and was elected to serve as a member of the school board and town council. In 1900 his first attempt to enter parliament in Sunderland failed, but he succeeded in removing a Liberal from Dundee in 1906, and survived as a Labour member until he retired under pressure in 1922 (Walker 1970; 1979). Also elected for the first time in 1906 was George Barnes, a former Dundee engineer, who was appointed assistant general secretary of the Amalgamated Society of Engineers in 1892 and general secretary from 1896 to 1908. After his election to parliament Barnes became more committed to the political side of the working class movement. In 1908 he was elected as vice-chairman of the Parliamentary Labour Party, and was elevated to the chairmanship, 1910–11, following his appointment as head of the Independent Labour Party organisation department the previous year. During the war, Lloyd George took him into the cabinet as minister of pensions. He broke with Labour over its decision to withdraw from the coalition government, as both he and Wilkie found themselves outflanked by the leftward drift of the labour movement during the war.

Adamson, whose father and mother had both been miners, left school aged eleven, and worked down the pit for27 years. Active within his local union he became assistant secretary of the Fife, Kinross and Clackmannan Miners Association from 1902 and general secretary from 1908, which provided the springboard for his election in 1910. In common with many of his fellow Baptists and numerous Labour leaders, he was an active teetotaller and founded the Dunfermline Temperance Council (Knox: 58-61). Although his talents were limited, he became chairman of the Parliamentary Labour Party in 1917, and its leader from 1918 to 1921. In 1924 and 1929–31 he served as Scottish secretary.

Conclusion

The Scottish MPs returned in December 1910 can be broadly classified into three types: traditionals, locals, and metropolitans. Traditionals consisted of around a dozen soldiers and landowners with roots in the social and economic life of Scotland as members of long-established county families, but having had an education in common with their English counterparts formed part of an integrated United Kingdom-based upper class. Around a third were locals: middle class businessmen and professionals raised in a predominantly Presbyterian environment, educated at Scottish academies and universities, and whose economic interests were based in Scotland. The dominant group, around half, were metropolitans: Anglo–Scots and Englishmen representative of those Scottish commercial interests which during the course of the nineteenth century had formed strong links with the City of London, and members of the professional classes, especially lawyers, who were attracted to the imperial capital. Many of the metropolitans had enjoyed an English education, and their connections with Scotland were remote. The Labour MPs formed yet another category, for while they were neither traditionals nor metropolitans, as members of trades unions recruiting on both sides of the border, they represented a movement that was forging links between the Scottish working class and industrial workers in northern England and South Wales. Perhaps at no time before or since have Scottish MPs been less locally-based.

A critical element reshaping the profile of Scottish MPs, 1885–1910, was the extension of the rural franchise, because it accelerated the decline of proprietorial support for Liberalism amongst the Whigs, thus diminishing landowners as a source of parliamentary candidates. As there was no local counter-elite of sufficient standing, the rural Liberals were inevitably forced to select candidates with little obvious prior connection with their constituents. The ubiquity of London-based members in such constituencies, therefore, was less a function of sinister manipulation by the whips than the absence of convenient alternatives. Both the geographical location of parliament and the organisation of its business to fit in with the law courts and the City, rendered the metropolitan elite a natural reservoir of candidate recruitment which could be drawn upon when local resources were found wanting.

The loose connection between county Liberal MPs and their seats, however, was not simply confined to rural areas, for although in the industrial seats of the central belt some members had been born and even educated in Glasgow and Edinburgh, as a whole they do not appear to have been closely linked to the political and economic life of their divisions. By 1910 ten of the fifteen members in these seats were lawyers, of whom half practised in London. Only one, a tube-maker, was connected with the major manufacturing or extractive activities of the region, and only two were politically active locally prior to their adoption: one as standing counsel to the Scottish Liberal Association, and the other as a member of Lanarkshire County Council. Thus, the introduction of elected county government in 1889 had done nothing to add to the pool of potential Liberal parliamentary candidates, which reflected the reluctance of Liberals to party-politicise local government.

There were also changes in the burgh constituencies. Prior to 1885, mercantile interests, united by their chambers of commerce and control of their respective burgh councils (though divided by religion), had dominated the politics and representation of the major cities. After 1885, however, their influence over parliamentary elections was much diminished, not only because their members became more politically divided following the home rule crisis, but also due to the division of Aberdeen, Edinburgh and Glasgow, which decentralised political power and enhanced the importance of the new constituency associations. As in the counties however, there was no emergence of a new class of locally-based parliamentary candidates to replace the traditional local source. It is perhaps significant that, in 1910, no Glasgow MP and only one Edinburgh MP had served on his city council, and only four Liberal MPs in all Scotland's burgh constituencies had been elected to a Scottish local authority. None of the four Glasgow Liberal MPs had business interests based in Scotland, and one of the two Edinburgh Liberals with commercial connections in the city had extended his company activities to London. In Aberdeen locality was strong because both members were local businessmen and one had served on the city council, but in Dundee the return of Churchill indicated a preference for the English elite. In the remaining burghs, apart from Greenock, Paisley and the Elgin District, local or regional links between the MP and his constituency were equally weak.

By 1910 Scotland was a region in which the Liberal party had best recovered from the crises which followed the Third Reform Act, and that was mirrored by a significant Anglicisation of its representation. Thirteen of its Liberal MPs were English, 22 had been educated at English schools, fourteen had been to English universities, 32 were economically based south of the border, eight had previously sat for English constituencies, and a further five had fought English seats before coming to Scotland.

Although there were undoubtedly mechanical reasons for Anglo–Scottish penetration – e.g. the loss of the landed Whigs and the difficulties for Scots-based merchants, manufacturers, lawyers and other professionals in sitting in parliament without neglecting their business interests – it was perhaps also the reflection of a local culture which discounted aspirations to national political leadership. The most publicly-oriented Scots had been the Whigs and the Tories, whose civic values, transmitted through the English public schools and universities, which had assisted in the consolidation of the English and Anglo–Scottish upper and upper middle class into a ruling class, fostered aspirations to political leadership. Consequently, the defection of the Whigs and Churchmen left Scottish Liberals organisationally and culturally more dependent on Scottish-educated Presbyterian elements that had grown out of dissent and disruption, and whose preoccupations had been more focused on religion than politics. The obsession of the post-1885 Liberal activists with disestablishment, disendowment, and local option, marked the parameters of their political vision. In a social context where ministers were more important than politicians, resistance to the ambitions of Anglo–Scottish metropolitans was likely to be weak.

The social backgrounds of right-wing MPs obviously fluctuated in the 30 years after 1885. The infusion of Liberal Unionists, for example, increased the proportion of businessmen up to the election of 1900, but as the Unionists retreated the changes seemed to have been transient. Pinned back to nine constituencies, the Unionist MPs in December 1910 appeared little different from their Conservative predecessors of 1885 and earlier. Five of them were landowner/soldiers, three lawyers, and one a businessman. As traditionalists they were proportionately more rooted in Scottish society than the Liberals, and only one of them (a Liberal Unionist) could be classified as a metropolitan. There were, nevertheless, signs of evolution. The lawyers of 1910, unlike their predecessors, were drawn from middle class rather than proprietorial backgrounds, two of them having been to school and university in Scotland; and the businessman, Younger, also Scots-educated, was politically active in local government. Similarly, Sir Harry Hope, a landowner/soldier, had enjoyed an unequivocally Scots upbringing, and that was manifested by his sensitivity to majoritarian Scottish values. Consequently, there was some evidence to suggest that the movement of the professional classes towards the right after 1885 continued to be reflected in the social background of Unionist MPs even in the depths of 1910.

Though only a third the size of the enfeebled Unionists, the Labour contingent was unique in being composed of members of the Scottish working class, and like the Crofters represented a new form of linkage between members and their seats. In the case of the Crofters, the Highland Land League had formed an umbilical cord between mostly London-based Anglo–Scots and a peripheral peasantry, while two of the Labour members were secured to the localities they represented through national unions. The third Labour member, Adamson, represented the replacement of a traditional elite by an organised territorially-based counter elite, that is, a miners' county union: a working class redefinition of the landed interest. For the time being, however, most Scottish working class electors preferred to be represented by the lawyers, businessmen and professional class politicians who dominated the Edwardian Liberal Party in parliament.

Notes

1, 2. Most of the details are drawn from Forster and Stenton & Lees

References

Arnot, RP, *A History of the Scottish miners, from the earliest times,*London, 1955.
Ball, SR, 'Asquith's Decline and the General Election of 1918,' *Scottish Historical Review*, LXI, 1982.
Blewett, N, *The Peers, The Parties, and The People*, London, 1972.
Buckley, KD, *Trade Unionism in Aberdeen, 1878-1900*, Aberdeen, 1955.
Cook, AB, 'Gladstone's Election for the Leith district of Burghs, July 1886,' *Scottish Historical Review*, LXIX, 1970.
Craig, FWS, *British General Elections, 1885-1918*,
Donald, J, *Past Elections in Greenock,* Greenock, 1933.
Forster, J, *Members of Parliament: Scotland*, London, 1892.
Hutchison, IGC, *A Political History of Scotland*, Edinburgh, 1986.
Knox, W (ed.), *Scottish Labour Leaders, 1918-1939*, Edinburgh, 1984.
Stenton, M and Lees, S, *Who's Who of British Members of Parliament, Vol. II, 1886-1918*, Sussex, 1978
Stenton, M and Lees, S, *Who's Who of British Members of Parliament, Vol. III, 1919-1945*, Sussex, 1979
Stephen, Sir L, & Lee, Sir S, *The Dictionary of National Biography*, Vol. XVII, London, 1917.
Walker, W, 'Dundee's Disenchantment with Churchill', *Scottish Historical Review*, Vol. 49, 1970.
Walker, W, *Juteopolis*, Edinburgh, 1979.

6 *The Reforms of 1918–1928*

The reforms of 1884/5 marked a high point for those wanting a widely-based franchise without conceding the principle of democracy, but further reform could not be postponed indefinitely. Following the Liberal victory of 1906, bills were passed in the Commons against plural voting, the question of female suffrage was highlighted by extra-parliamentary agitation, and a Royal Commission on Electoral Systems was established in 1909, to consider, *inter alia*, Proportional Representation (PR), which it opposed, and the Alternative Vote (AV), which it favoured unanimously (Butler: 7-8). It took the exceptional circumstances of the Great War, however, for the government to concede the momentous principle that the ballot was less a reward extended to 'capable citizens' than a universal adult right that could be claimed even by the 'improvident' drinkers of Paisley. That metamorphosis distinguished the Fourth Reform Act from its predecessors, making it less the fulfilment of 1832 than the precursor of a basically different electoral system. Leading politicians, themselves, were consciously aware that the restrictive notions they had espoused in the late Victorian–Edwardian era were no longer defensible, Asquith admitting that his endorsement of female suffrage in 1918 was something of a 'palinode' (*Hansard*, 93: 469).

The 1918 Act was not only a new departure in principle, but also in the method of its construction. Previous reforms had been a series of openly-bargained deals in which the Whigs had played a pivotal role, restraining the Radicals and reassuring the Tories, whose Lords majority could be mobilised to frustrate the wishes of a Liberal-dominated Commons. The outcome had been franchise extensions vitiated by redistribution schemes giving undue recognition to rural regions. The Third Reform Act, however, hastened the end of the Whigs, and with the Unionists loosing ground to rural radicalism but performing strongly in suburban constituencies, the right had lost its traditional fear of redistribution. Thus, given that the democratic principle would have to be conceded, discussion on the franchise could focus on the details of implementation rather than on caveats to restrict its application, and the way was open for redistribution to become a more technocratic exercise than hitherto. Instead, the focus of attention shifted towards the most appropriate method by which votes could be translated into seats (Pugh: ix).

The timing of the reform process, initiated during the crisis of 1916, when Asquith's beleaguered government was seeking to maximise a social consensus behind the war effort, reduced narrow partisan influences. Following a somewhat tortuous gestation, it was agreed that a conference of MPs not directly involved in the administration of the conflict, meeting under the neutral chairmanship of the Speaker, should attempt to devise a broadly agreed scheme of electoral reform (Pugh: chaps. 5 & 6). In addition to the Speaker, the committee was composed of five Peers and 27 Commoners. All the parties were represented, the Scottish MPs including William Pringle (Liberal, North West

Lanark), MacCallum Scott (Liberal, Glasgow Bridgeton), and Sir Robert Finlay (Unionist, Edinburgh and St Andrews Universities). Lord James Bryce, the former Liberal MP for Aberdeen North, an authority on the United States constitution, was also appointed, but withdrew because of ill health before the committee met. On the question of women's suffrage, Scott was 'a radical opponent' and Finlay, leader of the Unionist faction on the committee, 'absolutely irreconcilable', but Pringle was counted amongst 'recent converts' by the National Union of Women's Suffrage Societies (Pugh: 73-74).

The Speaker's Report (*PP* 1917-18, Vol. XXV, cmnd. 8463), published in January 1917, formed the basis of the 1918 legislation. Universal adult male suffrage, it would appear, was accepted unanimously, and the members were particularly insistent on the need for special arrangements to register servicemen. Female enfranchisement, however, proved a more divisive issue (in fact it was the only matter on which consensus could not be found),[1] but a majority favoured a restricted female franchise in order to concede the principle without permitting women to form a majority. The conference further recommended a reduction in the residential qualification from one year to six months, and the production of two registers per annum under the supervision of county and burgh clerks. Plural voting continued to enjoy support, but no elector was to have more than two ballots. Non-Irish constituencies with estimated 1914 populations of less than 50,000 inhabitants were to be liberated (well above the 15,000 standard of 1885), and new seats created on the basis of 70,000 persons per constituency. As previously, Scottish burgh districts were to be considered as groups for redistribution purposes, and regrouping was encouraged. The two Scottish University constituencies were to be amalgamated, and return three members, using the Single Transferable Vote (STV). For the first time elections were recommended to take place on the same day. More controversially, AV was unanimously suggested for single member constituencies, and STV for multi-member constituencies in the larger parliamentary burghs.[2] To discourage frivolous (and working class?) candidates, a deposit of £150 was to be lodged with nomination papers, which would only be returned if the candidate received a minimum of 12.5 per cent of the poll.

In March 1917, Asquith, the former prime minister, thanked the Speaker for his services, and moved a motion recommending legislation based on the conference's resolutions. Although Lloyd George pledged the government's support for the proposals, he indicated he did not consider PR as essential to reform as other matters. A wrecking amendment moved by dissident Unionists was defeated by 62 votes to 341, and the main motion was carried without a division. Scottish MPs, who voted 41:1 against the amendment (the dissentient, Anstruther-Gray, Unionist, whose St Andrews Burghs was threatened with dismemberment), demonstrated a more enlightened attitude than their 1831 predecessors. Scottish Unionists not only wanted reform, but Halford Mackinder (Glasgow Camlachie) gained the backing of five party colleagues for an amendment (not called), which sought to extend reform to the House of Lords and the settlement of Irish home rule before the end of the war.

Maintaining the spirit of consensus, the coalition government committee charged with preparing the legislation was 'composed of men representing many shades of political opinion' (*Hansard*, 93: 1492), and when presented to the House in May 1917 closely followed the Speaker's recommendations, including the introduction of AV in single and two-member constituencies, STV in boroughs with three or more members, and the enfranchisement of most women 30 years and over. For the first time, all aspects of reform, the franchise, registration and redistribution covering all four nations was included in a single bill, symbolising that although the measure was a compromise, a democratic electoral system was an integrated whole.

The progress of the bill continued to reflect the consensual nature of its origins, although not necessarily reflecting the conclusions of the Speaker's committee. The female franchise, for example, was easily carried by nearly 400 in favour to fewer than 60 against, and leaders of all parties were conspicuous in its support; but STV and AV, which had been unanimously supported in the Speaker's committee, generated much heat. During debates on instructions to the Boundary Commissioners, an amendment that they work on the assumption that STV would *not* be introduced was carried by 149:141, with the Unionists 7:3 against STV, Labour evenly divided, the Liberals only 6:4 in favour, and only the 14 participating Irish Nationalists fully supportive (Butler: 7-12). That decision was later confirmed at the committee stage by a majority of 32 against STV, and by a single vote majority AV was extended to all constituencies. Significantly, AV produced a much more partisan division than STV, when only two Unionists voted in favour out of 115, but was supported by 98 to 13 Liberals and all Labour and Irish Nationalists who voted. The reason, of course, was that whereas the probable consequences of STV would have been a close correspondence between the share of votes and seats, AV was especially attractive to the Liberals because they were likely to get the second preferences of both Labour and Unionists voters. It was hardly surprising, therefore, that the Unionist majority in the Lords rejected AV, and reintroduced STV for the larger boroughs, leaving first past the post (FPTP) elsewhere. Predictably, the Commons rejected the Lords' amendments, reasserting their uncertain commitment to AV in all constituencies. The impasse was apparently resolved by a conference between the two Houses, which agreed to abandon AV and instruct the Boundary Commissioners to produce a scheme for STV covering 100 seats only. These proposals, however, proved unacceptable to the Commons, and following a series of resolutions and procedural manoeuvres the status quo was retained (Pugh: 165-167).

Apart from Mackinder, a member of the Proportional Representation Society favouring STV (Pugh: 71), Scottish members contributed little to the above debates. In the lobbies, Scottish MPs (usually around 35 in all), voted similarly to their party colleagues elsewhere in the United Kingdom. It is nevertheless instructive to note that while Scottish Liberals generally favoured STV, those from Glasgow and Edinburgh, where it would have been introduced, were against. Ironically, events were to show that some form of proportional representation was the only means by which the Liberals could have survived in Glasgow (and later Edinburgh), whilst Mackinder's party gained most from the retention of the status quo. Uncertainty as to the consequences of the democratisation of the franchise was clearly a complicating factor in the politics of reform, 1917–18.

The issue which most concerned Scottish members was redistribution, for while the Speaker's conference had indicated that the number of seats in Great Britain should remain broadly the same, it had not specified (apart from Ireland, where the status quo was expressly preserved), how many should be allotted to each country. Although the instructions to the boundary commissioners studiously avoided the imposition of a precise population quota for each constituency, on a strict pro rata basis Scotland stood to lose half a dozen seats to England. Such an adjustment would have advantaged the Unionists, and the fears of Scottish Liberals were confirmed when they learned that the Scottish commissioners included Lord Dundas and Sir James MacDougall (*Hansard*, 93: 1613), in addition to the chairman, James Lowther (the Speaker), Walter Jerred, a civil servant, as secretary, and Colonel Charles Close of the Ordnance Survey (*PP* 1917–18, Vol. XXV, cmnd. 8585). It was inevitable, therefore, that some Scottish MPs sought to ensure that a minimum number of constituencies were retained north of the border. The commissioners, however, were already at work before the terms of their appointment had been ratified by parliament, operating on the following principles:-

(1) That the number of seats in Great Britain remain substantially the same.

(2) That constituencies with populations below 50,000 should be liberated.

(3) That a burgh with a population over 70,000 should become a parliamentary burgh if it had not yet achieved such a status.

(4) That no two-member burgh with a population above 120,000 should lose a member.

(5) That no two-member burgh currently undivided should be divided.

(6) That a burgh should receive a member for every 70,000 of its population, and one for any remainder over 50,000.

(7) That constituencies should relate to recognised administrative areas.

(8) That divided counties should seek to separate industrial and rural areas.

(9) That burgh districts be reorganised to ensure that all burghs in any district were in the same county.

(10) That where an ancient burgh fell into a county, the new county division should bear the burgh's name (*PP* 1917-18, Vol. XXV, cmnd. 8585).[3]

The application of these proposals were likely to prove exceptionally disadvantageous to the Highlands and Islands, where most seats would have fallen under the 50,000 population rule, and even some joint counties would have failed to approach the 70,000 mark required for the creation of new constituencies. The excessive rigidity imposed on the reapportionment process by these rules were recognised by all the parties in Scotland, and it was a Unionist, Sir George Younger (Ayr Burghs), who urged special consideration be given to the Highlands and Islands, despite their leanings to Radicalism (*Hansard*, 94: 644-47). Consequently, an amendment adding a further instruction allowing a margin of flexibility where strict adherence to the rules would 'result in the formation of constituencies of inconvenient size and character' (*Hansard*, 94: 668-9), moved by the member for Windsor, James Mason, was accepted by the government and passed without a division.

More contentious was an amendment tabled by Eugene Wason (Liberal, Clackmannan), that 'the number of members for Scotland shall be retained as at present' (*Hansard*, 94: 862), because he had heard Scotland stood to lose nine seats. Unable to argue his case on democratic grounds, he stated his case in nationalistic terms. Wason warned that Scottish members were increasingly rebuked for not forming an independent party like the Irish and, by implication, that a reduction of seats would only fuel a sense of national neglect. His seconder, Adamson (West Fife), who a week earlier had led a delegation of Scottish Labour politicians and trade unionists to the home secretary on the subject, claimed that the proposal was backed by nearly all important bodies within Scotland, and should be accepted in recognition of his nation's contribution to the United Kingdom. The most nationalistic intervention, however, came from James Hogge (Liberal, Edinburgh East), who questioned the integrity of the boundary commissioners, arguing that if Scotland's representation were reduced it should be accompanied by the establishment of a Scottish parliament, and (or at least) the elimination of university seats. In response, Sir George Cave, the home secretary, refused to accept the amendment because it violated 'the principle of equality of votes' (*Hansard*, 94: 865) on which the bill was based, and pointed out that Scotland's special circumstances were recognised by the additional instruction to the boundary commission. He was supported by Sir George Younger, whose opposition in principle was reinforced by his view that Scotland, in fact, would not lose any members at all. Given the opposition of the government and English backbenchers, Wason did not press his amendment to a division.

As in the nineteenth century, the future of the burgh districts continued to be a source of contention, particularly as the same-county rule threatened several constituencies which currently satisfied the 50,000 population stipulation. Sir George Younger, for example, whose own seat was spread between Ayrshire and Argyll, moved that 'the Commissioners shall have the power, when regrouping boroughs [sic] to extend such groupings of boroughs in contiguous counties' (*Hansard*, 94: 877). Not only did he hope thereby to preserve such districts as the Hawick Burghs, but to provide a means for extending the district system and preventing liberated burghs – e.g. Perth, which could be placed in the Stirling Burghs – from falling into their counties. His amendment appealed not only to Unionists wishing to keep burgh electors out of the counties, but also to Liberal burgh district members such as Arthur Ponsonby (Stirling Burghs). A major critic was Adamson, who saw the proposal as an attempt to reduce the representation of industrial areas, and both Liberal and Unionist members – especially English MPs, whose single burghs, though larger than many in the Scottish groups, were marked for liberation – expressed reservations. Nevertheless, the government accepted Sir George's proposal, which was added to the amended instructions.

The Scottish boundary commissioners, aided by assistant commissioners drawn from the ranks of sheriffs, completed their work by the end of September 1917 (*PP* 1917-1918, Vol. XIV, cmnd 8759). Their report proposed the most far-reaching restructuring of the constituency system since 1707, because democratisation enforced a fundamental redistribution which had been largely avoided in 1832, 1868, and 1885 through the acquisition of additional seats. The fears of the nationalists were allayed as the number of seats rose from 70 to 71; but the commissioners did not permit the liberalisation of their instructions to compromise the integrity of their scheme. Reducing burgh groupings from thirteen to six, they resisted the temptation at the heart of Younger's amendment to gerrymander on behalf of rural interests, and in only one case, the Montrose District, were burghs in a grouping located in more than one county. Where new parliamentary burghs were plucked out of counties and added to a grouping it was compatible with democratic objectives, and betrayed no evidence of partisanship. Such was the austerity and rectitude of the commissioners that they produced the most equitable relationship between seats and votes that Scotland ever experienced before 1983.

Rural regions, predictably, suffered most at the hands of the Boundary Commission, although they remained the most favoured.

In Highland, both the Wick and Inverness Burghs were identified for liberation, and Campbeltown, Inveraray and Oban, constituents of Ayr Burghs, marked for ejection into Argyll. The commissioners also announced the banns for Caithness and Sutherland, whose union had been mooted and resisted ever since 1832. More positively, having failed to find sufficient favour in 1885, a new seat of Western Isles, carved out of Inverness and Ross and Cromarty, was proposed, 'having regard to...the character of the constituency and pursuits of the islanders' (*PP* 1917-1918, Vol. XIV, cmnd 8759: 6). As a result, the number of Highland seats were to be reduced from eight to six. Nevertheless, the population of Caithness and Sutherland, Ross and Cromarty and the Western Isles were each below 50,000, and Orkney and Shetland just met the general survival standard.

Although its representation was also to fall, the rural East also received benign consideration. Predictably, Perth and the burghs of St Andrews and Elgin were identified for liberation, whilst Nairn and Forres, components of the defunct Inverness Burghs, were to be added to Moray and Nairn. The diminutive county of Kincardine was to be added to Aberdeenshire, and the joint counties, reinforced by elements of the Elgin Burghs, were to form three constituencies: Aberdeenshire Central, Aberdeenshire East, and Kincardine and West Aberdeenshire. The Montrose Burghs were to be saved through the addition of Kirriemuir, pushing its population over the 50,000 mark. (Without Younger's amendment this seat would have fallen, because the loss of Inverbervie in Kincardineshire would have reduced its size below the critical level.) Perth was not to be associated with the Stirling Burghs, as Sir George had hoped, but was to be thrown into its county which, through an amalgamation with Kinross (freed from Clackmannan), was divided into Perth and Kinross and Western. The commissioners further recommended that Elgin and Nairn be renamed Moray and Nairn out of deference to local opinion, and that East Fife be known as the St Andrews division, in accordance with their general instructions. It was a measure of the considerable generosity accorded to this region, that only Banffshire, the new county seat of St Andrews, the two Perthshire divisions, and Montrose Burghs, had populations in excess of 50,000, and the commissioners themselves admitted that Kincardineshire and Aberdeenshire were only entitled to two seats 'on a strict application of the rules' (*PP* 1917-1918, Vol. XIV, cmnd, 8759: 5). Nevertheless, under their proposals, the East was still to emerge with between three and four fewer seats than before the war.

In contrast to the East and Highlands, retrenchment in the Borders, which had a long history of over-representation was particularly severe, because the commissioners chose to strictly impose the 50,000 and 70,000 population rules by associating this predominantly rural region with the Lothian coalfield. They recommended the liberation of the Hawick and Dumfries burgh districts, and the amalgamation of Wigtown and Kirkcudbright in a new constituency, Galloway, so-called 'in deference to local sentiment, supported by representations of the councils of both counties' (*PP* 1917–1918, Vol. XIV, cmnd, 8759:6). Berwickshire was to be associated with the larger mining county of Haddington, and Peebles, detached from Selkirk, was to be swallowed by South Midlothian, leaving Selkirk to be annexed by Roxburgh. Thus, the Borders were reduced to three constituencies: Galloway, Dumfries, and Roxburgh and Selkirk, each with populations approaching 70,000.

Although the number of constituencies in the Central region (including Ayrshire and Bute) only rose from 12.4 to 14, there were considerable changes occasioned in part by the loss of Kinross to Perthshire and the acquisition of Peebles and Berwick. West Fife, the only county division to survive, was to lose electors to a reorganised burgh district system. Buckhaven, together with Methil and Innerleven, were to be added to an expanded Kirkcaldy Burghs (Kirkcaldy, Burntisland, Dysart and Kinghorn); while Dunfermline was to head a new burgh district including a fellow refugee from the Stirling Burghs, Inverkeithing, reinforced by Cowdenbeath and Lochgelly, both newly elevated to parliamentary burgh status. Culross and Queensferry were also to be ejected from the Stirling Burghs, being thrown respectively into West Fife and Linlithgowshire; and with the Falkirk Burghs losing Linlithgow, Airdrie, Hamilton and Lanark to their counties, a reconstituted burgh district of Stirling and Falkirk, in association with a new parliamentary burgh, Grangemouth, was created. The newly amalgamated counties of Stirling and Clackmannan, and Midlothian and Peebles, were to be divided into East Stirling and Clackmannan, West Stirling, North Midlothian, and South Midlothian and Peebles. To the west, the Commissioners recommended the ending of separate representation for Bute and its union with Ayrshire, and, following the abolition of the Kilmarnock Burghs, the creation of three joint-county divisions: Bute and Northern, Kilmarnock, and Southern. Ayr Burghs was to be compensated for the loss of its Argyllshire burghs through the acquisition of Ardrossan, Prestwick, Saltcoats and Troon, forming a new group of nearly 70,000 inhabitants. Of the fourteen seats planned for this region, only South Midlothian and Peebles had fewer than 50,000 inhabitants, and more than 80,000 lived in Linlithgow.

The major beneficiaries of the commission's scheme were Glasgow and Clydeside, where there was a substantial reorganisation of representation due to the municipal expansion of Glasgow, the restructuring of the burgh district system, and the addition of nine extra constituencies.

In Lanarkshire all the parliamentary burghs – Airdrie, Hamilton and Lanark from the Falkirk group, and Rutherglen from the defunct Kilmarnock District – were to fall into the county, and Renfrewshire was to receive Renfrew and Port Glasgow from the Kilmarnock Burghs. North of the Clyde, however, a new burgh district, Dumbarton Burghs, was to be created out of the county town (formerly in the Kilmarnock group), and Clydebank, a new parliamentary burgh. In consequence, Dunbartonshire was to remain undivided. Renfrewshire was to retain two seats (though reconstituted), but Lanarkshire, reinforced by its burghs, was to have its county divisions increased from six to seven, despite the loss of Govan, Partick and other territory to Glasgow. Paisley and Greenock were each to retain the status granted in 1832. Thus, despite the encroachment of Glasgow on its neighbouring counties, the commissioners still recommended an increase from 12.3 to 13 in the number of Clydeside constituencies.

The central feature of the new reapportionment was an increase from seven to fifteen divisions in an expanded Glasgow, giving the metropolis just over a fifth of all the seats in Scotland. Even that allocation was not over-generous because eight of its divisions had populations over 70,000, rising to more than 90,000 in Gorbals.

Edinburgh/Leith was also to be reorganised, with Portobello and Musselburgh (still an independent municipal burgh) being detached from Leith Burghs and placed in Edinburgh East, so that the number of Edinburgh divisions increased from four to five. Leith, still outside the capital, was to become a single burgh constituency with more than 80,000 inhabitants. Dundee was to remain an undivided two-member seat, but enlarged to include Broughty Ferry, a middle class suburb previously included in Forfarshire. Similarly, Aberdeen was expanded to include the Kincardineshire fishing community of Torry, which had been part of the municipality from 1892, and a redivision of the two constituencies produced a homogeneous working class seat of Aberdeen North.[4] In all, the commissioners' proposals increased the number of MPs from the big cities (including Leith) to 25, some 35 per cent of the national total.

The drastic nature of the scheme inevitably aroused criticism during its progress through the Commons. Harmsworth objected that the commissioners had visited neither his own constituency, Sutherland, nor Caithness, and moved that the two counties remain separated, though including Dornoch and Wick.[5] John Bryce (Inverness Burghs) sought to save his seat on the grounds that its dismemberment would leave no parliamentary burgh north of a line from Dumbarton on the Clyde to Aberdeen. John Gulland protested strongly over the severe treatment of the Borders, and sought to maintain his constituency, Dumfries Burghs, through the addition of Maxwelltown, Annan, Hawick, Galashiels and Selkirk. The agricultural interest in Renfrewshire was represented by Sir George Younger, who moved the creation of a Renfrew Burgh district, including Port Glasgow, Gourock, Johnstone, Barrhead and Renfrew, together with bits of Govan parish outside Glasgow. None of these amendments was pressed to a formal division, even when they found a seconder, and elicited little sympathy from the Scottish secretary, Robert Munro, whose own seat, Wick Burghs, was marked for extinction.

It was a measure of backbench apathy and impotence that a number of MPs concentrated their energies on constituency nomenclature rather than on substantive modifications to the proposed scheme. Vernon-Harcourt, for example, wanted to change his seat's designation from Montrose Burghs to Angus Burghs (though it included Inverbervie in Kincardineshire); George Currie (Leith Burghs) sought to rename the Edinburgh constituencies Castle, Holyrood, Broughton, Merchiston and St Cuthberts; Colonel Stirling (West Perthshire) proposed Kinross and Western Perthshire be renamed West Perthshire and Kinross; and Macallum Scott (Glasgow Bridgeton) wanted Stirling and Falkirk Burghs to be called Falkirk and Stirling Burghs. All these and most similar proposals were rejected.

The only amendment accepted on constituency composition affected the Montrose Burghs, where the Commissioners' proposal to add the Small Burgh of Kirriemuir (pop. 3,500), thereby pushing the existing group over 50,000 in population, was rejected, following local opposition, which preferred the existing association with Forfar, whose MP, John Falconer, successfully pleaded their case. Of the few changes of nomenclature accepted – such as the decision to call Southern Ayrshire South Ayrshire instead – the most notable was Asquith's successful opposition to his East Fife division being re-designated as St Andrews. It is tempting to see this slight on the ancient university town, whose electors were to join his constituency, as a factor securing Asquith's defeat in the subsequent general election.

The democratic spirit of the reform was consolidated by the new registration provisions, which removed the rating and poor law restrictions, and reduced the residential qualification to six months. Furthermore, the stipulation that registration officers, burgh and county clerks, were enjoined 'to cause a house to house or other sufficient inquiry to be made' (*P.G. Stat* 1918, ch.64, 1st sched., cl.6) before compiling a twice-yearly list of voters, shifted the previous bias of under-registration to one of over-registration.

As with most British reforms, the 1918 Representation of the People Act was a compromise with the past. The survival of FPTP, a central feature of the electoral system, is a particular case in point. The retention of a qualifying period was also part of the inheritance, as was the survival of plural voting; and restrictions on the female franchise reflected the caution that had accompanied concession to principle in earlier franchise extensions. The retention of undivided two-member burgh constituencies created in 1868 was somewhat eccentric, as was the survival, indeed renewal, of the burgh district system. Nevertheless, by earlier standards the changes in 1918 were exceptionally dramatic. Not only was universal manhood suffrage realised and a generous female franchise established, but redistribution, which had been hitherto employed to frustrate the consequences of increasing the electorate, was placed at the disposal of democratising forces. As a result, the Fourth Reform Act stands apart from its predecessors, and deserves a status at least equal to the legislation of 1832.

1918–1928

The major deficiency of the 1918 Act had been its failure to enfranchise women on the same basis as men. As early as 1919, Adamson, Chairman of the Parliamentary Labour Party, introduced a private member's bill aimed at achieving universal adult suffrage (Butler: 15-38). The attempt failed, as did similar bills in 1920, 1923 and 1924. In the general election of 1924, however, Stanley Baldwin pledged himself (if not his party) to equalise the franchise before a subsequent election if the Unionists were returned. Lack of unity within the cabinet delayed the introduction of the relevant legislation, but pressure from the opposition and Unionist advocates, such as Lady Astor, forced Baldwin and Joynson-Hicks, the home secretary, to honour the prime minister's election pledge.

The bill introduced in 1928 conceded the vote to all adults 21 years or over fulfilling a three months' residential requirement. Both men and women could claim an extra vote on a spouse's business qualification, though no person was permitted to vote more than twice in any one general election, and no more than one vote could be cast in any constituency. Joynson-Hicks regarded the bill as the conclusion of the reform process begun in 1832, and the prime minister expressed the view that the bill had transformed enfranchisement from a privilege into a right.

Although Labour members objected to the extension of the business vote, the maintenance of a residential qualification, and the continued representation of the universities, the bill was carried on second reading by 387 votes to 10. The dissidents were Tory backwoodsmen such as Colonel Appin, who opposed female suffrage on the ground that as the United Kingdom governed the largest Mohammedan empire in the world, it would be offensive to Indian Muslims to be ruled by a predominantly female electorate (*Hansard*, 215: 1391).

The consensus behind the reform did not prevent Sir Alexander Sprot (Unionist, North Lanark), moving a motion to raise the age qualification from 21 to 25. He claimed not only strong contemporary support for his amendment, but also Biblical underpinning in the parable of the Prodigal Son (Luke 15: 11-32), arguing that the profligate, having wasted his inheritance on achieving his majority, had become 'as good a citizen as his stay-at-home brother' by the age of twenty five (*Hansard*, 216: 223). Such doubtful exegesis, however, only commended his arguments to those inherently opposed to female suffrage, and Sprot's amendment was defeated by 359 votes to 16. Attempts by Labour members to alter the bill in conformity with their second reading criticisms fell on stony ground, so that the equalisation of the franchise was introduced on terms outlined by the home secretary.

The System

The Franchise

By 1921 the Scottish electorate had grown from 760,000 in 1910 to more than 2.2 million, with the male electorate increasing to a little over 1.3 million, and enfranchised females, zero in 1910, numbering 911,000. Assuming a voting life of 50 years, it is estimated that fewer than 30 per cent of the electors in 1922 had been eligible to vote in the general election of December 1910. The degree of change, however, varied from one constituency to another depending on the demographic distribution of females and the uneven consequences of the removal of registration qualifications that had been particularly prejudicial to the enfranchisement of the industrial working class.

The Female Franchise. In contrast to England and Wales, the female franchise was not based on the local government franchise. Instead it was extended to women 30 years or over who were themselves, or their husbands, occupiers as owners or tenants of lands or premises in the constituency in which they claimed the vote. In the case of a dwelling house it was a householder suffrage without an annual rental limitation, but in the case of non-domestic premises the property had to be of a yearly value of not less than £5. Unfurnished lodgers were classified as tenants, as were 'service voters', although in the latter case those living in the same premises as their employer were specifically excluded from the franchise, reflecting the terms of the 1884 legislation. Joint occupancy was restricted to two persons for enfranchisement purposes, except where they were 'bona fide engaged as partners, carrying out their profession, trade, or business on the premises' (*P.G. Stat* 1918, ch.43, (1) iv). In the case of joint occupancy, the aggregate annual value of the premises could be 'not less than the amount produced by multiplying five pounds by the number of joint occupiers'

(*P.G. Stat* 1918, ch.43, (4) vi). A woman could also be registered if her husband was a local government elector, because the local government franchise in Scotland was more stringent than the provisions outlined above.

By 1921, some 79.2 per cent of Scottish females 30 years or more held the vote, more or less the same as the 79.5 per cent that did so in England and Wales. The major exclusions within the age limit were living-in domestic servants, and non-householder spinsters.

Table 6.1: The Electorate 1921*

	Females 30+ Enfranchised	Females as Percentage of Electorate	Estimated increase in male electors 1910–1921	Estimated increase in all electors 1910-1921
	%	%	%	%
Aberdeen	82.0	41.5	77	203
Dundee	78.1	44.9	84	252
Edinburgh/Leith	85.4	44.7	57	184
Glasgow	89.6	40.3	109	251
Highland	67.9	39.4	84	203
East	74.5	43.7	47	161
Central	75.8	39.8	65	174
Clydeside	80.8	40.6	72	192
Borders	69.7	42.9	40	146
All	**79.2**	**40.5**	**72**	**192**

***Source:* *1921 Census.*

The proportion of females with the ballot varied considerably from one constituency to another, with urban/industrial areas exhibiting higher levels than rural regions (Table 6.1). In Glasgow, for example, almost 90 per cent of age-eligible women were registered, as were more than 80 per cent in Aberdeen, Edinburgh/Leith, and the Clydeside counties. The highest proportion in any constituency was 93.3 per cent in Lanarkshire Hamilton. By contrast, fewer than 70 per cent of age-eligible women were enrolled in the Borders and Highland, where Argyll, with only 60.9 per cent registered, was the lowest in Scotland. The urban/rural dichotomy was particularly evident in the East, where, for example 83 per cent of age-eligible females in East Aberdeenshire, dominated by the Small Burghs of Peterhead and Fraserburgh, were enrolled, as against only 66.7 per cent in Kincardine and West Aberdeenshire, a much more rural constituency. Similarly, whereas 74.3 per cent of age-eligible women in the Perth division of Perthshire – which included the county town – were enfranchised, only 63.4 per cent enjoyed the privilege in Kinross and Western.

Overall, females constituted 40.5 per cent of the Scottish electorate in 1921, ranging from 51.5 per cent in Montrose Burghs (the only seat in which they comprised more than half the electors), to 35.5 per cent in Linlithgow. Regionally, women were more dominant in Edinburgh/Leith, Dundee, the East and Borders, than in Glasgow, Clydeside, Central and Highland (Table 6.1). Within the cities there was a tendency for the more middle class constituencies to be the more female. In Glasgow, whilst Hillhead and Partick were 45.5 per cent and 44.1 per cent female, respectively, women were only 38.5 per cent of the electorate in Govan and 38.8 per cent of the roll in Tradeston. Similarly, whereas in working class Edinburgh East females were only 42.1 per cent of the electorate, in salubrious Edinburgh South women electors were only five fewer than the men; and whilst douce Aberdeen South was 43 per cent female, women were only 39.8 per cent of the roll in the more industrial Aberdeen North.

There was no association, however, between the proportion of age-eligible females enfranchised in a constituency and women as a proportion of the electorate ($r = -0.1$). For example, although females were a substantially greater proportion of the electoral roll in the Montrose Burghs than in Linlithgow, a somewhat smaller proportion of age-eligible females were enfranchised in the former (85.8 per cent) than in the latter (86.2 per cent). In Lanarkshire Hamilton, where there was virtual universal adult suffrage, women accounted for a mere 40.6 per cent of the voters (and the constituency was only the 36th most female seat), whereas although Kinross and Western had one of the least favourable levels of female enfranchisement, 44.7 per cent of its electors were female (the seventh highest in Scotland). An important variable accounting for this apparent paradox is that, in constituencies based on heavy industry and mining, there were few employment opportunities for females. Consequently, in such seats there were relatively fewer single working class females aged 30 or over than elsewhere, and those that remained were more likely to be married, hence eligible to vote. By contrast, textile seats such as Montrose Burghs, Paisley, and Dundee,[6] although more female due to the nature of the local economy had a smaller proportion of age-eligible females enfranchised, because the electoral system worked against the enrolment of single working class women. Similarly, working class female resident domestic servants in middle class constituencies remained explicitly unenfranchised.

Unfortunately, due to the absence of opinion polls, it is impossible to estimate the impact the female franchise had on electoral outcomes, 1918–1924. Later evidence suggests that holding other variables constant females have been more generally right-wing than males. In the four elections before 1929, however, it is more important to stress the class composition rather than the distinctively gender aspect of the female electorate, because it was particularly biased against single working class women. That bias was clearly more important in seats where the proportion of age-eligible females with the vote was relatively low. It seems, therefore, not unreasonable to hypothesise that the female franchise somewhat deepened the natural Unionist bias of suburban and rural seats, but had a much more marginal impact in predominantly working class constituencies.

The election in which females had the most potential influence, 1918–1924, was that of 1918 due to the effective disfranchisement of most servicemen. Excluding servicemen, who accounted for 30.7 per cent of the male register in 1918, and the 389 female military electors, women constituted 42.7 per cent of the Scottish electorate, 48.4 per cent in the burghs and 45.9 per cent in the counties (*PP* 1918, Vol. XIX: 925). In all there were perhaps 16 constituencies in which females effectively outnumbered men in 1918, including Dundee, Aberdeen (2), and each of the divisions of Edinburgh/Leith. By contrast, males undoubtedly dominated throughout Glasgow and Clydeside, as in all constituencies characterised by reserved trades. There is, however, little evidence that the greater maleness of the Clydeside electorate greatly assisted the left in 1918, and with the Labour surge of 1922 coming in those areas where returning servicemen were a lesser influence than elsewhere, the significance of gender is impossible to detect.

Between 1924 and 1929, the number of Scottish electors grew by just under 660,000, a rise of 29 per cent. Butler estimates that around 16.5 per cent of the expansion between 1928 and 1929 was due to the Act, and the rest to growth in the population and increasing accuracy of the register (Butler: 145). Translating his calculations into the Scottish context, the equalisation of the franchise added around 420,000 women to the roll, increasing their number rather more than 60 per cent. In any event, with Scotswomen comprising 53 per cent of the register in 1929, a predominantly female electorate had emerged for the first time (see Table 6.2).

Table 6.2: Women as a Proportion of the Electorate in 1929 by Region

Aberdn. %	Dund. %	Edinb. %	Glasg. %	Highlnd %	East %	Clyde. %	Centrl %	Bordrs %	All %
55.6	57.6	55.6	52.7	50.2	54.5	51.5	51.6	54.8	53.0

Burghs: 53.9 per cent *Counties: 52.1 per cent.*

Females were marginally more predominant in the burghs (53.9 per cent) than counties (52.1 per cent), particularly so in middle class constituencies like Edinburgh South (63.0 per cent) and West (56.3 per cent), Glasgow Hillhead (60.4 per cent), Pollok (57.8 per cent) and Cathcart (55.8 per cent), and Aberdeen South (58.5 per cent). Women were also strongly represented in the textile seats of Dundee (57.8 per cent), Paisley (55.0 per cent), and Roxburgh and Selkirk (56.2 per cent). Females were also strong in the East, particularly in Fife East and Perthshire. There remained, however, 13 constituencies in which men remained more than half the electorate, although in South Ayrshire, the most male of Scotland's seats, women still constituted 47.5 per cent of the registration. Eight of the mostly male divisions were in the coalfields, South Ayrshire, Fife West, Linlithgow, and five of the seven Lanarkshire divisions (Rutherglen and rural Lanark, being the exceptions). Two others included the heavy engineering seat of Dumbarton Burghs, and Glasgow Central, where it would appear the wives of businessmen had failed to apply for a second vote. Men also predominated in three of the six Highland seats, though only just so in Caithness and Sutherland.[6] As in the earlier period, it is impossible to assess the impact of the revised female franchise on voting parameters, though it is noteworthy that the change in electoral support for the major parties, 1924–1929, was not great, especially in Labour's case. It is, nevertheless, tempting to suggest that the strength of Unionism, 1931–1964, was assisted by the continuing influence of the 1931 crisis on a relatively new female electorate. The evidence, however, is less than circumstantial.

The Male Franchise. Although less numerically dramatic than the female franchise, the 72 per cent increase in the male electorate between 1910 and 1921 is more helpful as a guide to the socio–political impact of the post-war electorate.

Inevitably, given the uneven consequences of the 1884 legislation, the degree of change varied significantly from region to region (Table 6.1), and from one constituency to another (Table 6.3). The greatest changes were recorded in working class burghs. In Greenock, where at least since 1868 there had been a particularly low level of registration, more than two and a half times as many men were enrolled in 1921 than in the last election before the war,[7] and the male electorate more than doubled in Aberdeen North, across Glasgow, and in the burgh districts of Dunfermline, Dumbarton, and Stirling and Falkirk. In Dundee, too, there were almost twice as many men on the roll in 1921 as in December 1910. By contrast, in middle class Aberdeen South and Edinburgh/ Leith the number of male voters increased by little more than half, leading one to suspect that had it been possible to differentiate Glasgow's seats sharp contrasts would have been revealed between its working class and middle class divisions.

In the industrial counties and other burghs, the pattern was also varied. On Clydeside the male electorate increased by more than 80 per cent in Dunbartonshire and Paisley, falling to 61 per cent in Renfrewshire and only 50 per cent in semi-rural Lanarkshire Lanark. In the remaining Lanarkshire divisions, which had lost areas of low registration to Glasgow, the increases were around the national median of 67 per cent. Growth in the Central Region ranged from over 80 per cent in Fife West and Linlithgow to a modest 60 per cent in Midlothian and Peebles, slipping away to 48 per cent in Berwick and Haddington, and 36 per cent across the two divisions of Stirlingshire and Clackmannan.

Reflecting a proportionately high enfranchisement under the Third Reform Act, the increased male electorate in the rural/small town regions of East (+47 per cent) and Borders (+40 per cent) was particularly modest. In Fife East the expansion was less than a third. The Highlands (+84 per cent), which along with Dundee had the highest regional growth after Glasgow, presented a more varied picture. In the three divisions of Ross and Cromarty and Inverness (+112 per cent) the increase was marginally greater than in Glasgow, and Orkney and Shetland's male electorate grew by +87 per cent, but the expansion in Caithness and Sutherland (+56 per cent) and Argyll (+51 per cent) was well below the national mean.

It was a measure of the impact of the 1918 franchise, that even in the region of least change (Borders) there were two and a half times as many voters (male and female) in 1921 than in 1910 (see Table 6.1). In Glasgow and Dundee, where there were three and a half times as many, it is probable that only around 20 per cent of the 1922 electorate had been enrolled twelve years earlier.

Table 6.3: Estimated Percentage Increase in the Male Electorate, December 1910–1921

	Increase %		Increase %
Greenock	165	Lanarkshire/ Bothwell	65
Dunfermline Burghs	120	Coatbridge/ Northern	
Dumbarton Burghs	120	Motherwell	
Inverness/Ross and	112	Renfrewshire (2	61
Cromarty (3)		Ayrshire (3))	61
Stirling & Falkirk Burghs	112	Kirkcaldy Burghs	60
Aberdeen North	111	Midlothian & Peebles (2)	60
Glasgow (15)	109	Caithness & Sutherland	56
Dundee (2)	94	Edinburgh (5)	55
Orkney & Shetland	87	Aberdeen & Kincardine (3)	55
Linlithgow	85	Aberdeen South	54
Paisley	83	Argyll	51
Dunbartonshire	83	Lanarkshire Lanark	50
Fife West	81	Berwick & Haddington	48
Lanarkshire Hamilton/		Roxburgh & Selkirk	43
Rutherglen	71	Perth & Kinross (2)	43
		Dumfries	42
Ayr Burghs	70	Forfar	42
		Montrose	40
Moray & Nairn	70	Stirling & Clackmannan (2)	36
Leith	67	Galloway	35
Banffshire	67	Fife East	31

brackets denote the number of seats

Similarly, in Aberdeen and Highland, where the electorates trebled, only one in four of those registered in 1922 could have cast a ballot in the last pre-war contest. Thus, the parties were faced with having to mobilise a large number of new voters if they were to succeed in the new political environment. It was to the advantage of Labour that most of the new electorate, both men and women, were working class, and particularly disadvantageous to the Liberals that they had to make their appeal with a divided and discredited leadership.

The Business Vote (*P.P.* 1944-45, Vol. X, 109). The business vote was not a significant feature of the Scottish franchise. In 1945 (the only occasion on which a return of the post-1918 Scottish business vote was made), there were as few as 8,437 such electors across the whole of Scotland, of whom 3,387 were in Glasgow Central, where they constituted 9.5 per cent of the roll, followed by 864 in Edinburgh North, where they were less than two per cent of the register. It has been estimated (Butler: 147), that the Unionists won Glasgow Central through the added influence of such electors four times – presumably 1922, 1923, 1929 and 1945 – but a more cautious prediction would perhaps restrict its decisive influence to 1923 and 1929.

Seats and Electors. A major feature of the 1918 reforms was that redistribution recognised for the first time the principle that electors should be equally represented,[8] though the rules for liberation (50,000 pop.) and creation (70,000 pop.) were somewhat at variance. The reduction of burgh districts from thirteen to six ended their function as a break to the just representation of the larger burghs and the artificial protection of agricultural interests in the counties, and the amalgamation of smaller counties with larger neighbours further reduced the increasing over-representation of rural societies. Industrial areas, Glasgow in particular, received the justice they had been so long denied. As a result, the coefficient of variation between all constituencies – Dundee being divided into two for this exercise – was reduced from 0.49 in December 1910 to 0.16 in 1921. Amongst burgh constituencies the variation coefficient fell from 0.45 to 0.14, and in the counties from 0.51 to 0.16.

Table 6.4: The Regional Distribution of Seats and Electors, 1921

	Electors	Seats	Seat Change 1885-Post 1918	'Fair' Seat Distribution based on 1921 Electorate	Actual minus 'Fair' Seat Distribution
Aberdeen	77,587	2	0.0	2.5	–0.5
Dundee	78,435	2	0.0	2.5	–0.5
Edinburgh/ Leith	197,659	6	+1.0	6.3	–0.3
Glasgow	509,684	15	+8.0	16.3	–1.3
Highland	155,960	6	–2.0	5.0	+1.0
East	274,409	10	–3.3	8.8	+1.2
Central	434,292	14	+1.6	13.9	+0.1
Clydeside	403,269	13	+0.7	12.9	+0.1
Borders	94,042	3	–5.0	3.0	0.0
All	**2,225,337**	**71**	**+1.0**	**71.2**	

For the first time, regions enjoyed representation broadly in conformity with the size of their electorates (Table 6.4), though it could be argued that between the Moray Firth and Fife, the rural/small town East enjoyed an extra seat at the collective expense of Aberdeen and Dundee, and that the new Western Isles seat might more appropriately have gone to Glasgow.

The under-representation of Aberdeen, Dundee and Edinburgh/Leith, however, was less a function of perfidy than the constraints imposed by local government boundaries, though the inclusion of Musselburgh in Edinburgh was an anomaly because the Small Burgh was linked to Midlothian for local government purposes.

Variations within regions were also much reduced. The three Border constituencies, for example, were very similar in size. On Clydeside, apart from Paisley (elect. 38,076), where burgh boundaries were a barrier to parity, the range of the electorates in 1921 was between 27,098 in Lanarkshire Hamilton and 34,053 in Dunbartonshire. Nevertheless, in some areas wide (but much reduced) variations remained. In Highland, where Argyll and Inverness were above the national average of 31,342 per seat, the Western Isles had barely 20,000 electors, and there were fewer than 25,000 electors in Inverness, Ross and Cromarty, Caithness and Sutherland, and Orkney and Shetland. Similarly, in the East, whereas the Perth Division of Perthshire and East Fife were above the national mean, half the constituencies had fewer than 25,000 electors. Over-representation in this region was due to the survival of the Montrose Burghs, which ought to have fallen under the 50,000 rule, following the decision not to add Kirriemuir. In Central, there was a contrast between North Ayrshire and Bute (40,536) and Linlithgow (36,484) on the one hand, and South Midlothian and Peebles (23,203), North Midlothian (24,751), and West Stirling (22,179), on the other.

Table 6.5: Estimated Consequences of Redistribution on Party Fortunesin General Elections, 1922–1929

	Seats 1922			*Seats 1923*		
	Actual	**Est. on 1885–1918 Distrib.**	**Gain Post-1918**	**Actual**	**Est. on 1885–1918 Distrib.**	**Gain Post-1918**
Unionist	13	10.5	+2.5	14	13.5	+0.5
Nat. Liberal	12	15.1	-3.1			
Liberal	15	20.4	-5.4	22	28.7	-6.7
Labour	29	22.2	+6.8	34	26.7	+7.3
Other	2	1.9	+0.1	1	1.0	-
Total	71	70.1	+1.1	71	69.9	+1.1

	Seats 1924			*Seats 1929*		
	Actual	**Est. on 1885–1918 Distrib.**	**Gain Post-1918**	**Actual**	**Est. on 1885–1918 Distrib.**	**Gain Post-1918**
Unionist	36	39.0	-3.0	20	23.2	-3.2
Liberal	8	9.7	-1.7	13	16.4	-3.4
Labour	26	20.3	+5.7	37*	29.3	+7.7
Other	1	1.0	-	1	1.0	-
Total	71	70.1	+1.0	71	69.9	+1.1

* *Including Maclean who was technically Independent Labour*

Redistribution had important consequences for the political parties, especially for the Liberals and Labour, because it reduced the weight of rural/small town regions in favour of the central belt. Particularly illustrative of the change was the effective transfer of seven burgh district seats to Glasgow, thereby shifting representation from an area of particular Liberal strength in the pre-war period to one of exceptional weakness. Table 6.5 compares the number of seats won by the parties, 1922–1929, with what might have been the outcome had the constituency system, 1885–1918, been retained.[9]

The main beneficiary of redistribution was clearly the Labour Party, which, but for reapportionment, might well have had seven or more fewer seats in 1922, 1923 and 1929, and six fewer in 1924. But for redistribution, Labour would have had two fewer seats than the Liberals in 1923, the gap between themselves and the Unionists would have been twice as large in 1924, and their lead over the Unionists in 1929 reduced from seventeen to six. The Liberals were heavily disadvantaged by the reduced influence of the rural regions, and but for reapportionment might well have been the largest single party in 1923, enjoying more than twice the representation of the Unionists. The impact of redistribution on the Unionists was mixed. In 1922, the reallocation of seats was worth an extra 2.5 seats to their cause, but following their breakthrough in the rural regions, they would have held three more seats under the old dispensation in 1924 and 1929.

Conclusion

Despite its warts, the Fourth Reform Act represented a genuine attempt to democratise an important part of the political process, and in so doing brought a fundamental change to the electoral system. Not only was the principle of manhood suffrage conceded, but earlier registration provisions which had compromised the generosity of previous franchises were largely swept away, as was the gerrymandered constituency system that hitherto had vitiated the concept of one vote:one value.

Female enfranchisement in 1918 also marked a fundamental break with the past – though some women were already local government electors – helping to swell the electorate three-fold. The higher age limit and other restrictions, however, marred its status as a democratic franchise, thereby tarnishing the democratic credentials of the legislation as a whole, although with four-fifths of age-eligible women enrolled a significantly higher proportion were enfranchised than men before 1918. Not until the Equalisation of the Franchise in 1928 was a democratic female electorate established.

As consequential as the reforms themselves was the decision to retain FPTP, a survivor of the pre-reform (i.e. pre-1832) system. The rejection of AV in the British context represented a major Unionist victory over the Liberals – and to a lesser extent Labour – as was, in retrospect, the defeat of STV. The retention of FPTP sealed the fate of the Liberals, and opened the door to a more class-polarised political conflict. Prospectively, the divisions over STV and AV indicated that the question of proportional representation had replaced the franchise as the most contentious aspect of the electoral system. With the rise of party, especially third parties, an electoral system based on equal electoral districts in the context of FPTP was to become less acceptable as a sufficient condition for the realisation of one vote one value than hitherto, and it is in this matter that the democratic credentials of the post-1918 system remains most open to challenge.

From a Scottish perspective, the 1918 Act marks the highest point in the assimilation of its electoral system within the United Kingdom. Already in 1884 the franchise had been made virtually the same as in England and Wales, but in 1918 registration practices were also standardised, and no concessions were made to Scotland's national claims in the distribution of seats. The lack of preferential treatment over reapportionment was a relief from earlier negative discrimination, but was in marked contrast to the continued toleration of severe over-representation in Ireland. To the extent that peripheral areas within Scotland were generously treated, it arose from their peculiar geographical circumstances as sparsely-populated areas. Later redistributions, however, were to recognise the strength of national sensibilities, beginning a process of increasing over-representation, and thereby reducing the standardisation achieved in 1918.

In more parochial terms, the most distinctive feature of the Fourth Reform Act was its introduction of the first major Scottish reapportionment since 1707, because the accumulation of 25 extra seats, 1832–1885, had ameliorated injustices without removing anomalies. The acquisition of only one more seat in 1918 and the arithmetical imperatives of the redistribution scheme made substantial changes inevitable. The disappearance of Bute and Sutherland as separate constituencies and the liberation of most of the burgh districts was a resolution which had evaded the intentions of reformers ever since 1832, and the increased prominence given to Glasgow underlined the fundamental shift in electoral geography. Tardily following the population movements of the previous century, Scottish parliamentary representation had become concentrated in a narrow strip of land between Glasgow and Edinburgh, which returned 48 of the 71 MPs, creating an overwhelmingly urban and industrial polity. Thus, the evasion of reapportionment in the nineteenth century meant that the introduction of a one vote:one value redistribution in context of adult suffrage greatly compounded the degree of change.

In contrast to England, where the new electoral settlement left the political establishment undisturbed, the same factors which had sustained (if not enhanced) Unionist hegemony there revolutionised the party system in Scotland by ending almost 90 years of Liberal suzerainty. The vastly expanded electorate found the Liberals no longer able to withstand the claims of Labour on the left and ill-equipped to mobilise the anti-socialist right; and redistribution, eliminating most of the burgh districts and reducing the number of county seats, diminished the Liberal heartland, while the increased importance of greater Clydeside, the focal point of religious prejudice and class antagonism, promoted the interests of Unionism and Socialism. The new electoral system, therefore, was as hostile to Liberalism as that of the previous century had proved particularly favourable. Thus, the increasing similarity between the party systems in Scotland and England, which reached its peak in the early 1950s, was greatly facilitated by the Fourth Reform Act.

Notes

1. This followed a decision to ensure an even balance between supporters and opponents of female suffrage (Pugh: 73).
2. The decision was only unanimous because three opponents – Lord Salisbury, Sir Frederick Banbury and Colonel James Craig – had resigned over the issue (Pugh:

84).

3. Excluded from these instructions are those relating to PR, which were dropped from the original instructions after their consideration by parliament.
4. In fact Aberdeen North was misnamed because it included Torry, south of the Dee. Essentially, it was Aberdeen East, incorporating nearly all the working class electorate in the city. Aberdeen South was really Aberdeen South West, a wedge of middle class inner suburbs.
5. For the consideration of amendments to the Scottish redistribution proposals see *Hansard,* 98: 2199-2242 and 99: 2399-2410.
6. The other mostly-male Highland constituencies in 1929 were Inverness and Ross and Cromarty
7. The task of calculating the increase involves estimating the 1910 electorate in the post-1918 constituencies. This is by no means possible in every case (see Table 6.3).
8. Though in 1918 population size had to be used as the measure in the absence of a register including all adult males and females 30+.
9. The estimate is calculated by taking the proportion of seats won in each region, 1922-1929, and reallocating them by the same proportions according to the number of seats in each region, 1885-1918. (For example, 10 seats won in Glasgow [67 per cent], would have counted as 4.3 out of 7 before the war.)

References

Butler, DE, *The Electoral System in Britain Since 1918*, Oxford, 1963.

Census (Scotland) 1911.

Census (Scotland) 1921.

Craig, FWS, *British Parliamentary Election Results, 1918-1949*, Glasgow, 1969.

Hansard (5th Series)

Parliamentary Paper, 1917-18, Vol. XXV, cmnd. 8463, *Letter from Mr. Speaker to the Prime Minister.*

Parliamentary Paper, 1917-18, Vol. XXV, cmnd. 8585, *Boundary Commission (Scotland) Appointment of Commissioners.*

Parliamentary Paper, 1917-18, Vol. XIV, cmnd. 8759, *Report of the Boundary Commission (Scotland).*

Parliamentary Paper, 1918, Vol. IIX, (925), *Parliamentary and Local Government Electors (United Kingdom).*

Parliamentary Papers, 1944-45, Vol. X(313), *Parliamentary Constituencies (Electors) (Scotland).*

Pugh, M, *Electoral Reform in War and Peace, 1906-18,* London, 1978.

Representation of the People Act, 1918, (8 Geo. 5, Ch. 64).

Representation of the People (Equal Franchise) Act, 1928, (18 & 19 Geo. 5, Ch.12).

7 *The Operation of the System, 1918–1929*

The democratisation of the electoral system had a profound effect on Scottish politics because it upset the social and geographical balance that had lain at the heart of the pre-war constitution. The new electorate was dominated by working class men and women, and redistribution heavily weighted representation towards the central belt, reducing the rural regions to a rump of nineteen constituencies. These factors alone would have made it difficult for the Liberals to reconstitute a broadly based national appeal – as they had achieved with increasing difficulty following previous reform acts – but combined with the crisis in the party following the formation of Lloyd George's government in 1916, the task proved impossible. As a result, Scottish politics became more fragmented, losing the consensual aspect which had most characterised its nineteenth century representation.

Although performing poorly in 1918, the pace of change was set by the Labour Party, whose overtly sectional appeal to the industrial working class enabled it to win more seats than either the Liberals or Unionists in 1922 and 1923 and carry just over half of all the Scottish constituencies in 1929. Labour also commanded more votes than any single party from 1922–1929. Even so, fewer than a third of the registered electorate supported Labour in any election, 1918–1929, and the party had little standing in the rural regions. In no sense, therefore, did Labour represent the national will as had the Liberals before 1918. The major consequence of the electoral breakthrough of Labour for the evolving party system, therefore, was to create an alignment on the left, balancing that of the Unionists, and narrowing the centre ground occupied by the Liberals.

Labour's success was in part a function of confusion and division on the centre-right, because the traditional anti-Conservatism of the Scottish electorate, including significant sections of the middle class, inhibited the consolidation of an anti-Labour coalition. In 1923, for example, in an election fought in defense of free trade, the Liberals recorded their highest vote ever in Scotland, and came within 50,000 votes of the Unionists. As late as 1929 Liberal candidates outpolled the Unionists in Edinburgh, Highland and Borders, and were a creditable second in the East. The behaviour of the centre vote had a critical influence on the outcome of elections, for although it was reluctant to swing to the left, its unwillingness to coalesce behind the Unionists in 1923 and 1929, and its division in 1922 played an important role in securing Labour success.

The Unionists, still smarting from the elections of 1910 and mindful that their victory in 1900 had depended on a broader base than Conservatism alone could provide, proceeded cautiously, deprecating their Conservative roots in favour of a strategy that continued to admit the importance of the Scottish Liberal tradition. Their decision not to follow the English party in describing themselves as Conservatives from 1925 (Warner: 191), recognised the critical importance to their alignment of working class Unionism centred on Orange Presbyterianism in the West, and the desirability of an accommodation with continuing

Liberalism elsewhere. The division of the party into two largely autonomous federations (East and West), coupled with a high degree of independence enjoyed by the constituency associations, facilitated flexibility in adapting to local political circumstances. The benefits to the Scottish right of coalitionism were particularly evident in 1918 and 1924, as were the disadvantages of detachment from the centre in 1923 and 1929.

The uneven geographical distribution of party support inevitably fragmented the nature of electoral competition. Urban and industrial constituencies were mostly dominated by the socially polarised struggle between Labour and Unionists, although in the smaller burghs the anti-socialist standard was frequently carried by Liberals and National Liberals. In rural/small town seats adjustment to the post-war political system proved particularly difficult, and the choices presented to the electors varied by region and from one contest to the next. In the East and Borders, for example, where Labour was weak, the modal return in 1918 was one of unopposed Coalition Liberals; in 1922 the struggle was dominated by a confrontation between Liberals and National Liberals; in 1923 most seats were subjected to straight fights between Liberals and Unionists; and in 1924 and 1929, following Labour interventions, the majority of contests were three-cornered. In the Highlands, however, where both the Unionists and Labour had little standing, elections were dominated by various sorts of Liberals, with the Highland Land League presenting as many candidates in 1918 as did the Unionists in 1923, 1924, and 1929.

The System

The Distribution of Candidates (Tables 7.1 and 7.2)

Although the Labour Party had been reorganised in 1918, its capacity to mount constituency election campaigns in Scotland remained heavily dependent on its federated components, the Independent Labour Party (ILP), the Co-operative Party, trades councils, and lodges of the miners' union (Hutchison: Ch. 9). Consequently, of the 43 Labour candidates who stood in 1918, only two appeared in the five divisions of Edinburgh, and none at all in the rural/small town peripheries, apart from Roxburgh and Selkirk and the Montrose Burghs, whose electorates included a significant number of textile workers. By contrast, all 17 seats in the West were fought, together with 11 of the 15 constituencies in Glasgow. Additionally, unofficial Labour aspirants ran in Aberdeen North, Dunfermline Burghs, Glasgow Central and Kelvingrove, and the intervention of a British Socialist in Tradeston ensured that Pollok was the only Glasgow constituency failing to present a left-wing choice.

The 1918 pattern was repeated in 1922 and 1923, although in both Lanarkshire Motherwell and Greenock, Communist candidates were preferred by local trade union interests, effectively barring Labour from standing. In 1924, however, a determined effort produced thirteen Labour candidates in the rural/small town seats, so that with 63 aspirants in the field Labour offered a wider choice than any other party. A further improvement in 1929 found Labour presenting candidates in all but five constituencies. The exceptions included Dundee, where Labour ran in harness with Scrymgeour the Prohibitionist, Glasgow Govan, in which Maclean, the member since 1918, had lost the endorsement of the ILP[1] and Orkney and Shetland, Caithness and Sutherland, and Kincardine and West Aberdeenshire, in which Labour never intervened before its demise in 1950. Although the foray into the rural peripheries was hardly evidence of a greatly expanded electoral appeal, it did, nevertheless, reflect Labour's pretensions and organisational capacity to present itself as a national party.

Table 7.1: The Distribution of Candidates in Urban/Industrial Constituencies
(51 Constituencies: 52 Seats)

	1918		1922	1923	1924	1929
Co. Union	31	Unionist	30	39	42	49
Co. Liberal	14	Nat. Liberal	20			
Liberal	26		31	40	17	27
Labour	39		41	45	50	50
Other	21		8	7	3	15
All	131		130	131	112	141

Table 7.2: The Distribution of Candidates in Rural/Small Town Constituencies
(19 Constituencies).

	1918		1922	1923	1924	1929
Co.Union	3	Unionist	6	13	14	16
Co. Liberal	14	Nat. Liberal	13			
Liberal	7		17	19	17	18
Labour	2		2	3	13	16
Other	8		-	1	–	1
All	34		38	36	44	51

In certain respects the distribution of Unionist candidates followed a similar pattern to that of Labour. Although the absence of Unionists from rural constituencies in 1918 and 1922 largely reflected understandings with Coalition Liberals[2] and Coalition/National Liberals, it also emphasised the roots of Unionism in Glasgow and the industrial counties of the West. Thus, of the 34 Coalition Unionists who stood in 1918 only three were in the periphery – Central Aberdeenshire, Dumfries and Kinross and West Perthshire – although they were more than adequately supported by independent Unionists in East Fife and Forfar, where none of the candidates had the coupon. Unionists also deferred to Liberal Coalitionists in the burgh districts – apart from the Ayr Burghs, where George Younger was defending a seat he had held since 1906 – and gave a free run to Godfrey Collins, an independent Liberal in Greenock, who subsequently took the Coalition whip. The willingness of Unionists to recognise Coalition Liberals, however, was not always undisputed. In Glasgow Cathcart, for example, the Unionists adopted Sir Archibald Shaw, an ironmaster and former lord provost of Glasgow, as their candidate in May, 1918, and it was not until the end of November that the Liberals adopted John Pratt, the retiring member for Linlithgow, who received the Lloyd George coupon. The Unionists refused instructions from their Glasgow headquarters to support Pratt, and it was only on 5 December that a telegram from Bonar Law finally persuaded Shaw to stand aside. Following the election a sharp letter was sent from the Cathcart Unionists to Sir George Younger, the party chairman, complaining of their maltreatment (Young: 7-10). Nevertheless, the Coalition Unionists, with eleven candidates in Glasgow, eighteen in the central belt, and four in Edinburgh/Leith, had established themselves as the main opposition to the Labour threat.

Despite the collapse of the Coalition on the eve of the 1922 election, the Scottish Unionist MPs did not favour the break with Lloyd George, and that was reflected by their Eastern Division, who decided not to oppose incumbent National (Coalition) Liberals (Cook: 17). The National Liberals reciprocated in like manner, so that both parties contested more or less the same constituencies as in 1918, although a Unionist decision to fight Greenock almost led to the seat being won by a Communist. The three additional Unionists on the periphery included the 1918 non-coupon Unionist victors in Fife East and Forfar.

Even in 1923 there were still strong pressures amongst Scottish Unionists, led by Sir George Younger, for an anti-socialist pact with the reunited Liberal Party. Conversations to that end were held between Younger and James Hogge, the radical home ruler who sat for Edinburgh East, but the issue of tariff reform prevented any general arrangement (Cook: 131). Consequently, the Unionists increased their candidates to 52, sixteen more than in the previous year. Having previously stood aside in the Highlands, three Unionists came forward in 1923, so that with their candidates in the East doubling to eight, their party contested most rural constituencies for the first time since 1910. Extending their influence, the Unionists also made their initial interventions in Glasgow Bridgeton, Gorbals and Partick, Renfrew West, Lanarkshire Rutherglen, and Dumbarton Burghs, following the defeat of National Liberal incumbents in 1922. A Unionist also stood for the first time in Ayrshire Kilmarnock, where an Asquithian Liberal had enjoyed a successful straight run against Labour the previous year. Similarly, Berwick and Haddington and Roxburgh and Selkirk, both carried by National Liberals in 1922, were exposed to Unionist interventions, and Unionists replaced National Liberal candidates in Edinburgh East, Aberdeen North, and Dundee (1), as standard-bearers of the right. On the other hand, local understandings found Unionists standing down in favour of Liberals in East Stirling and Clackmannan and Glasgow Tradeston (two seats Coalition Unionists had won in 1918), Leith, Greenock, Galloway, and Lanarkshire Hamilton. Unionists also permitted the Liberals to continue unmolested against Labour opposition in the burgh districts of Montrose, Kirkcaldy, Dunfermline and Stirling and Falkirk.

With only four more Unionists standing in 1924, the distribution of candidates was very similar to 1923. An improved bargaining position *vis-à-vis* the Liberals, however, enabled the Unionists to secure a pact with them whereby, in return for a decision not to oppose a vulnerable Asquith in Paisley or contest Glasgow St Rollox, the Liberals in the west agreed to withdraw from nineteen constituencies they had fought in 1923 (Cook: 288). As a result, not only did the Unionists field 18 more candidates than the Liberals throughout Scotland, but their nominations outstripped them 42:17 in the urban/industrial heart-lands. In

1929, the only seats uncontested by the Unionists were Ross and Cromarty, Inverness, Aberdeen North, Dundee (1), Leith, and the Montrose Burghs, where they never opposed the Liberals. Thus, by 1924, the Unionists had emerged as the clear champions of anti-Labourism in the central belt, having pushed the Liberals to the periphery, and although the Liberals increased their candidates in industrial/urban seats to 27 in 1929, they were substantially fewer than the 49 defending the Unionist cause.

Despite the national split between Lloyd George and Asquith, the distribution of Coalition and independent Liberals in 1918 minimised conflict at the local level, when only in Berwick and Haddington, Caithness and Sutherland and the Western Isles did both factions present candidates. (In the two Highland cases, no other party was represented.) Consequently, Liberals of one sort or the other stood in 39 of the industrial/urban seats and throughout the rural periphery. By 1922, however, the close association between the Coalition Liberals (National Liberals) and the Unionists was more apparent, so in that election there were no fewer than seventeen constituencies in which the two Liberal factions were opposed. In all six Highland constituencies there were straight fights between Liberals and National Liberals, as there were in Roxburgh and Selkirk and the Eastern rural seats of Moray and Nairn, Aberdeenshire East, and Kincardine and West Aberdeenshire, whilst their internecine battle in the Perth division of Perthshire was complicated by the presence of the Unionists and Labour. In urban/industrial constituencies, opposing Liberals appeared in Aberdeen North, Glasgow Gorbals, Lanarkshire Mother-well, and Berwick and East Lothian, and monopolised the contests in Glasgow Partick and Edinburgh East. Somewhat confusingly, a Liberal and National Liberal ran in tandem against Labour and a Prohibitionist in Dundee.

Perhaps the most remarkable feature of the break between the National Liberals and Unionists in Scotland was that despite a close affinity which had extended beyond the collapse of the coalition at the British level, none of the Scottish National Liberal MPs deserted to the Unionists in 1923. Not that the reunion of Liberalism was altogether painless, especially where National Liberals and Liberals had been in opposition in 1922. In Ross and Cromarty, Argyll, and Moray and Nairn, many Asquithians were noisily (if not mutinously) irreconciled to the adoption of National Liberals who had defeated their own candidates less than a year previously. Neither was there great love between the two factions in Roxburgh and Selkirk (Cook: 288). Nevertheless, despite these differences, the united party presented 59 candidates in contesting all but twelve seats – five in Glasgow, five in the West, Dundee (1) and West Fife – fighting more constituencies than either Labour or the Unionists. The results of the election, however, indicated that outside the periphery and Edinburgh/Leith there was no concentrated support for the party, which hastened its demoralisation and a massive retreat in 1924.

By contesting only 34 seats in 1924, the Liberals had relinquished any pretension of representing most of the Scottish people. The pact with the Unionists in the west was not simply a last desperate attempt to shore-up Asquith, but also a less than convincing smokescreen to cover a massive retreat from industrial constituencies. Only five Liberals contested the 32 seats in Glasgow and the West, and it was a measure of their dependency on the Unionists that only one of them opposed a Unionist. Similarly, of the six Liberals standing in Central, four had a straight run against Labour, the exceptions being the part-rural seats of Berwick and Haddington and South Midlothian and Peebles. In Glasgow Bridgeton and Partick and Lanarkshire Hamilton the Liberal Associations 'called upon their members to vote Conservative [Unionist]' (Cook: 288). The movement of Liberalism to the right was particularly evident in Dundee. In 1910, and to an ambivalent extent in 1918, there had been a local agreement between the Liberals and Labour to present only one candidate in the two-member seat. In 1923, however, the Liberals combined with the Unionists to resist Labour, now in a tacit alliance with the Prohibitionist, Edwin Scrymgeour (Walker 1970; 1979). Half the Liberal candidates in 1924 were confined to the rural East, Borders and Highland, and a further five to Edinburgh/Leith. Only where Labour was weak were the Liberals well represented. The Liberals, therefore, had ceased to constitute a credible independent force throughout the central lowlands, with the possible exception of Greenock and Edinburgh/Leith. In 1929, the collapse of the regional pact (though not necessarily local arrangements) with the Unionists on Clydeside increased the number of Liberals standing in Glasgow and the West to fourteen, but did nothing to fundamentally alter the settlement of 1924.

Despite pressures towards bi-polarisation, there were more candidates per constituency in 1929 (2.7) than in 1918 (2.3). Even in urban/industrial seats, where the number of aspirants had fallen from a steady 2.5 in previous contests to 2.2 in 1924, the refusal of the Liberals to die pushed the figure to a record 2.8 five years later, whilst in the rural periphery there was an expansion from less than two candidates per seat in 1918 and 1923 to 2.3 in 1924 and 2.7 in 1929, as both the Unionists and Labour increased their challenges to Liberal monopoly. Labour benefited most from a higher number of candidates in the urban/industrial seats because they gained from disunity on the centre-right, whilst the Unionist gained from Labour intervention on the periphery. Labour also benefited from having established a settled pattern of intervention by 1918, thereby offering its clientele a consistent choice over five elections. Labour's opponents to the right, however, presented a menu that not only varied from one election to the next, but from one constituency to another depending on local circumstances and understandings.

Participation

The democratisation of the electoral system was accompanied by a drop in turnout from an average per constituency of 79 per cent, 1885–1910, to 68 per cent, 1918–1929 (Table 7.3). There were, however, significant regional variations. Excluding the exceptional case of 1918, turnout increased two per cent on average in Dundee, and fell by only three per cent in Glasgow and Central, and by six per cent in the West and Borders. On the other hand, the decline in both Aberdeen and Edinburgh was nine per cent, eleven per cent in the East, and twenty per cent in Highland. Thus, the regions in which the electorate grew most (excepting Highland), were also the areas in which participation was at its highest. It would appear, therefore, that the Labour Party and its allies in the unions had succeeded in mobilising the new working class voters to levels of participation almost comparable with those of the pre-war electorate. Similarly, in areas where they were historically strong (Glasgow, the West and Borders), the Unionists also succeeded in extending their coalition amongst anti-Labour electors across the social classes.

Table 7.3: Average Percentage Turnout per Constituency in General Elections, 1918–1929 (by Region)*

	1918	1922	1923	1924	1929	All 1918–1929
	%	%	%	%	%	%
Aberdeen	40	57	57	67	65	57 (61)
Dundee	47	81	73	84	83	73 (80)
Edinburgh	53	69	65	75	74	67(70)
Glasgow	57	77	69	78	75	71 (75)
Highland	47	50	45	52	55	50 (51)
East	48	58	64	67	70	63 (65)
Central	54	74	72	78	76	71 (75)
West	63	75	72	79	77	73 (76)
Borders	56	71	76	79	80	73 (76)
All	**55**	**70**	**68**	**75**	**73**	**68 (71)**

* *Brackets excludes 1918*

Lower turnouts were associated with the more Liberal areas, as if underlining the generally confused status of Liberalism in the new political climate. The exceptionally low turnout in Highland, for example, reflected a region in which both Labour and the Unionists had a very weak base, and the rural East was one in which Labour was equally limited and the Unionists were only slowly establishing a new foothold. Similarly, the rather moderate level of participation in Edinburgh was in a city where the working class movement was less well established than elsewhere in the central belt, and residual Liberalism continued to hold Unionism at bay. The particularly low turnouts in Aberdeen, more characteristic of its rural hinterland than industrial Scotland, are somewhat more difficult to explain, though the relatively small-scale nature of its industrial enterprises may have been a factor inhibiting the political mobilisation of manual workers.

It appears, therefore, that the activation of the new electorate rested heavily on the popularity and organisational capacities of the Labour Party and its trade union allies, supplemented in some measure by the institutions of popular Unionism on the right. Where Labour was weak, the Liberals found it more difficult to attract the new electors than following previous extensions of the franchise. Consequently, in rural areas, particularly in the East and Highland, the post-1918 electorate was weakly incorporated into the reconstituted electoral system, emphasising their peripheral status in a polity which had marginalised the influence of primary producers.

The General Election 1918 (Table 7.4)

The election of 1918 was a triumph for the Coalition largely because it was better able than the left in mobilising its potential voters (Table 7.4). With the support of less than three in ten of the registered electors, 53 Coalitionists were returned; whilst the left, backed by a mere 16.4 per cent of the electorate captured only eight seats. Although the Asquithian Liberals also secured eight MPs, it was with only 15 per cent of the votes cast, indicating not only the unpopularity of their leader, but a fundamental change in the nature of political opinion.

The Coalition was at its strongest in the Borders and Glasgow, where it polled 37.7 per cent and 32.8 per cent of the electorate respectively, and at its weakest in Dundee (17.5 per cent), the East (17.7 per cent), Central (21.0 per cent) and Aberdeen (23.0 per cent). The combined left proved most popular in Dundee (29.1 per cent) and across the central belt, Glasgow (21.0 per cent), the West (20.9 per cent), and Central (19.1 per cent), with the independent Liberals significantly stronger than elsewhere in Edinburgh (18.4 per cent) and the East (16.4 per cent).

In Glasgow, the Coalition Unionists were clearly at their strongest, their candidates averaging 61 per cent of the poll in mostly three-cornered fights, and winning two thirds of the seats, including working class Roman Catholic constituencies in the eastern part of the city, such as Shettleston, St Rollox, Springburn and Tradeston. Unionist successes in Bonar Law's commercial division, Central, and Hillhead, Kelvingrove and Pollok, established an electoral base, which broadly lasted beyond 1950. Official Labour, enjoying barely half the support afforded to the Coalition, was restricted to a single victory in the working class Protestant and shipbuilding division of Govan, home of Glasgow Rangers football team, where Neil Maclean won on a minority vote. It was, however, a measure of Labour's appeal across the sectarian divide that the Irish-born Catholic leader, John Wheatley, carrying a larger share of the registered electors than Maclean, was only narrowly defeated in Shettleston, centred on Celtic Park.

Labour's difficulties in winning the support of an essentially patriotic working class undoubtedly reflected suspicions concerning the ambivalence of its leadership towards the war. That incoherence was well exemplified by the contest in Glasgow Gorbals: one of the poorest parts of the city, the election was essentially an open primary between George Barnes, the former Labour member for Blackfriars and Hutchesontown – who had served in Lloyd George's wartime administration as the minister for pensions – and John Maclean, the official Labour candidate with strong left-wing credentials as a Clydeside agitator. Barnes, in the absence of a Coalitionist, won the seat by a two to one margin.

Labour's problems in Glasgow, however, were minor to those of the Liberals whose seven candidates, five of them retiring MPs, averaged only 10 per cent of the poll, representing a derisory 2.8 per cent of the electorate across the city. Thomas Wood, a former Scottish secretary and chancellor of the Duchy of Lancaster, won barely eight per cent of the ballot in St Rollox. The best Liberal performance was in Tradeston, where Dundas White, seeking re-election, won only 17.4 per cent of the votes, and came third behind the British Socialist Party.[3]

Table 7.4
Support for the Parties at the General Election, 1918, expressed as a percentage of the registered electorate.*

	Aber.	Dund.	Edin./Leith	Glas.	High.	East	Cent.	West	Bord.	All
	%	%	%	%	%	%	%	%	%	%
Co.Unionist	14.8 (1)	–	21.7 (3)	24.8 (10)	–	8.7 (1)	15.0 (4)	17.6 (8)	19.1 (1)	16.9 (28)
Co. Liberal	8.2	17.5 (1)	3.4	8.0 (3)	32.7 (5)	8.8 (6)	6.0 (3)	11.6 (5)	18.6 (2)	10.6 (25)
Co. NDP	–	–	2.6	–	–	–	–	1.4	–	0.7
All Coalition	*23.0*	*17.5*	*27.7*	*32.8*	*32.7*	*17.5*	*21.0*	*30.6*	*37.7*	*28.2*
Unionist	–	–	–	–	–	9.4 (2)	–	–	–	0.7 (2)
Independent	4.0	–		0.2	–	3.2	3.2	2.8	–	1.6
Liberal	4.9	–	18.4 (2)	2.8	6.6 (1)	16.4 (1)	10.5 (2)	7.7 (2)	10.8	8.2 (8)
Labour	–	5.0	7.0 (1)	15.4 (1)	–	1.9	17.1 (1)	20.5 (2)	8.0	12.9 (5)
HLL	–	–	–	–	7.4	–	–	–	–	0.4
Other Left	8.5 (1)	24.1 (1)	–	5.6 (1)	–	–	2.0	0.4	–	3.1 (3)
All Left	*8.5*	*29.1*	*7.0*	*21.0*	*7.4*	*1.9*	*19.1*	*20.9*	*8.0*	*16.4*
Total	**40.4**	**46.6**	**53.1**	**56.8**	**46.7**	**48.4**	**53.8**	**62.0**	**56.5**	**55.1**
Coalition Lead over Left	*+14.5*	*–11.6*	*+20.7*	*+11.8*	*+25.3*	*+15.6*	*+1.9*	*+9.7*	*+29.7*	*+11.8*

* Seats won in brackets. Co. NDP = New Democratic Party HLL = Highland Land League

The distribution of support between the left and right in the West was similar to that in Glasgow, although the Liberals, partly reflecting a five per cent higher turnout, did rather better. The seven Coalition Unionists in Lanarkshire failed to emulate their colleagues' appeal in the working class constituencies of Glasgow, but Lt. Colonel Arthur Buchanan won almost two thirds of the vote in Catholic Coatbridge, and Bothwell was narrowly carried in a straight fight with Labour. Motherwell fell to Robert Nelson, a Coalition Unionist, despite Hugh Ferguson, a local auctioneer and burgh councillor with strong Orange connections, capturing a tenth of the votes as an Independent Unionist, in a four-cornered fight. The meandering Northern division also went to a Coalition Union-ist on a four-way split; and Lanark, which included the more rural and conserv-ative parts of the former Southern division, and had been recaptured by the Unionists in a 1913 by-election, elected a new member, Walter Elliot, with almost 70 per cent of the poll. Dunbartonshire was carried by the Coalition Unionists with over half the votes in a three-cornered fight, and their Liberal allies won both Renfrewshire seats. In Ayrshire, Sir Aylmer Hunter-Weston, returned for North Ayrshire in 1916, predictably won North Ayrshire and Bute; Kilmarnock was carried by Alexander Shaw, former Liberal member for the Kilmarnock Burghs, as a Coalitionist; and Ayr Burghs were comfortably retained by Sir George Younger.

Labour and the independent Liberals were restricted to a total four out of seventeen seats in the West. Significantly, both Labour victories went to 'war patriots':[4] Duncan Graham, the local Miners' County General Secretary, whose victory in Lanarkshire Hamilton was assisted by an administrative error which had temporarily conferred the coupon on both his Unionist (who retained it) and New Democratic Party opponents, and James Brown, another miners' union official, who beat a Coalition Unionist by less than 900 votes in South Ayrshire. Confusion in the Coalitionist ranks was also a feature of the contest in Greeenock, where Samuel Chapman, the Unionist, resuming his challenge to Godfrey Collins, was initially in receipt of the coupon. That support, however, was later withdrawn because the government whips had intended that Collins, although an independent Liberal, should not be opposed (Donald), which contributed to Chapman's defeat. Collin's success was further assisted by a local Labour movement divided between the trades council, which leant towards the Communist Party, and the Irish working class, who, under the promptings the Nationalist, TP O'Connor, favoured Labour. The Liberals also won in Paisley, where Sir John McCallum won with 34 per cent of the ballot in a very close race with Labour and the Coalition-endorsed New Democratic Party.

Although the coalition seemingly performed less well in the ten constituencies of the Central region than to the west and south, it disguised the fact that the two privy council Asquithian Liberals who prevailed, Donald Maclean (South Midlothian and Peebles) and John Macdonald (Stirling and Falkirk Burghs), each cornered three fifths of the vote against Labour in the absence of a Coalitionist. In that sense they were no more independent of the right than were the Liberal Unionist victors in Dunfermline and Kirkcaldy. More indicative of the true Liberal position was the result in Berwick and Haddington, where a former Scottish secretary, Harold Tennant, won only 16 per cent of the ballot, while the Liberal Coalitionist carried the seat with more than half the votes. Elsewhere, apart from West Fife, where Adamson carried the constituency for

Labour with more than 70 per cent of the poll, Coalition Unionists held sway. North Midlothian, which intruded on suburban Edinburgh, was easily retained by Sir John Hope, who had captured the undivided county from the Liberals in 1912; and Kidd crushed 'Manny' Shinwell in the adjacent mining county of Linlithgow by a six to four margin. Harry Hope, the former member for Bute, beat Labour and Liberal opposition without difficulty in West Stirling, whilst the mining seat of East Stirling and Clackmannan also fell to the Unionists, though with a lesser share of the vote.

The chronic position of post-war independent Liberalism was hardly more evident than in Aberdeen and Dundee, neither of which had remotely threatened to return a Conservative or Unionist since before 1832. In a reconstituted Aberdeen South, Frederick Thomson, a Coalition Unionist, had a 40 per cent majority over the defending Liberal, Sir James Fleming, a former lord provost, partly due to a decision of the Aberdeen Liberal Association to support coalitionists (Hutchison: 309-10); while in the North division no Asquithian stood, and Duncan Pirie had the distinction of being the only Liberal Coalitionist seeking re-election to be defeated, falling to Frank Rose, an unendorsed pro-war Labour nominee. In Dundee no independent Liberal stood, and only one Coalition Liberal, Winston Churchill, was a candidate. In a somewhat confusing contest, where the unendorsed Labour incumbent, Wilkie, advised voters to support Churchill rather than the other Labour candidate, Brown, who was effectively running in tandem with a Prohibitionist, the electors endorsed the decision of 1910 (Walker 1970; 1979).[5]

Edinburgh/Leith was the least Labour of the big cities, less Unionist than Glasgow, and more Liberal than any other region in 1918. In part this reflected the number of candidates advanced by the parties, but that in itself indicated their relative organisational and voting strengths. Nevertheless, Coalition Unionists were the largest faction, winning the three seats they fought, the South division falling to Charles Murray with three quarters of the votes. Labour stood in three constituencies, including Edinburgh Central, where William Graham, a future president of the board of trade defeated a Coalition Liberal. The Liberals were more ubiquitous, and James Hogge, the incumbent member, successfully retained Edinburgh East, in the absence of Labour, against a Coalition New Democratic Party candidate. The most impressive Liberal result, however, was in Leith, where Wedgwood Benn, despite a Labour intervention, removed a Coalition Conservative, C Currie, who had won the seat at a by-election in 1914. In many respects this was the best Liberal result in the 1918 election, because it was carried without reliance on tacit (or otherwise) support from other parties. By the same token it highlighted the weakness of the party almost everywhere else.

In the East and Borders the 1918 election was general low-key largely due to the Coalitionist orientation of incumbent Liberals and the weakness of Labour. In Galloway, Moray and Nairn, Banff, Kincardine and West Aberdeen, and the Perth division of Perthshire, former members were returned unopposed as Coalition Liberals. In Roxburgh and Selkirk and Montrose Burghs there was only Labour opposition to Coalition Liberals, and there was only Independent Liberal (non-Asquithian) opposition to Sir William Cowan seeking re-election as a Coalition Liberal in Aberdeenshire East. Only in Aberdeenshire Central, Kinross and West Perthshire and Dumfries did Liberals face Coalition candidates, a Unionist in each case. Deference towards Liberal Coalitionists was not to the liking of many local Unionists, and while they maintained a reluctant discipline in Aberdeenshire East, they intervened, without the coupon, against Falconer and Asquith, independent Liberals tacitly supported by the coalition government, in Forfar and East Fife, carrying both constituencies (Bull). With Aberdeenshire Central also falling to a (Coalition) Unionist, it was clear that the East was losing its pristine Liberalism, as was cruelly underlined by the rapid defection of the single Liberal victor, James Gardiner (Kinross and West Perthshire) to the National government. Similarly, the result in Dumfries – where a former Liberal chief whip, John Gulland, fell to a Coalition Unionist in the only seat they contested in the region – suggested that the Borders were ripe for a return to Unionism.

Representation in the Highlands was dominated by Coalition Liberals (four of them incumbents), who carried five of the six seats. The Liberals contested Caithness and Sutherland without success, but narrowly prevailed in the newly-created Western Isles, the only other seat they fought. The most significant feature of the election was the heavy defeat of the four Highland Land League candidates, because it indicated that rural radicalism in the region was largely a spent force, even when allied to a franchise that had significantly increased the number of electors. In the Western Isles, perhaps the poorest constituency in Scotland, the Land Leaguer won barely 800 votes. As in the East and Borders, politics in the Highlands was moving to the right.

Despite the somewhat confused character of the 1918 general election, the new political parameters were already emerging. In an electoral system which favoured bi-polarity, Labour, although performing poorly, had established itself as the major force on the left in industrial constituencies, pushing the Liberals firmly towards the centre and right. The Unionists found not only had there been a substantial move towards them amongst the middle class electors of the large cities, but they had succeeded in consolidating and extending their pre-war popular constituency amongst conservative artisans. There was also strong evidence that they were poised to make substantial gains in the countryside. By contrast, the Liberals, having lost to Labour the left-wing working class electorate, found it difficult to adapt to the mass politics of the post-war dispensation, particularly in urban/industrial constituencies outside Edinburgh. Not only were the Coalition Liberals demonstrably reliant on Unionist support, but so, too, were the Asquithian Liberals in at least half their seats. Only in rural Scotland and most of Edinburgh, where Labour was weak, did Liberalism appear to have a future as an independent progressive alliance.

The General Election of 1922 (Table 7.5)

Between 1918 and 1922 Labour's popularity with the electorate increased as the issues of the war receded and domestic matters came to the fore. In a country where in 31 constituencies more than half the population lived in dwellings of less than three rooms, housing was a particularly relevant issue. Already before 1914 the Scottish Miners' Federation had been instrumental in securing the establishment of a Royal Commission into the provision of working class accommodation (*PP* 1917–18, Vol. XIV, cmnd. 8731, esp. para 1991), which, together with the *Commission of Inquiry into the Industrial Unrest* during the war, had concluded that state action was needed because the housing problem 'appears too great for private enterprise to meet' (*PP* 1917–18, Vol. XIV, cmnd. 8669: para 8). Furthermore, rent strikes, in which women had played an important role during 1915, were resumed with encouragement from the ILP in Glasgow between 1919 and 1922, as war-time controls were relaxed.[6] The demand for rent control played an important part in the 1922 election in working class constituencies throughout Scotland, and once elected the Labour MPs pledged themselves to 'urge without ceasing the need for houses suitable to enshrine the spirit of home'(Middlemas: 112). Issues such as these and unemployment (Hutchison: 284) enabled Labour to make a broadly-based class appeal which cut across the religious-sectarian divide and the status distinctions within the working class between skilled and unskilled workers. Furthermore, the return of servicemen, who had been effectively debarred from voting in 1918, and the settlement of Irish independence, which enabled the Nationalist electorate to swing unequivocally behind Labour, produced an electorate structurally more favourable to the left in 1922 than on the previous occasion.

In 1922, 70.4 per cent of the electorate voted, compared to only 55.1 per cent in 1918 (see Table 7.5). The combined share of the right (Unionists and National Liberals) was 1.9 per cent higher than that cast for the Coalition four years previously, but its effects were more than negated by a rise of 8.3 per cent on the left and a 6.9 per cent improvement in Liberal fortunes (Table 7.5). Although across Scotland the right enjoyed a 5.4 per cent lead over the left, Labour alone outpolled the coalition across the coalfields of Central and the West, whilst the combined left outdistanced its opponents in Dundee and ran just behind the Unionists and National Liberals in Glasgow.

In Glasgow, Labour's share of the electorate more than doubled, matching the share of the Coalition Unionists and Liberals in 1918. National Liberals fell to Jimmy Maxton in the dockside seat of Bridgeton and John Wheatley in Shettleston; whilst the Unionists yielded Maryhill, Tradeston, Springburn, dominated by the railway workshop, to Keir Hardie's younger brother, George, and Camlachie to the Rev Campbell Stephen. In the seven divisions lost by the Coalition, its share of the poll fell from 57.6 per cent in 1918 to 38.6 per cent in 1922, not only due to a drop of just over a thousand votes per candidate, but a huge increase of more than 120 per cent (approaching 8,500), in the votes cast on average for each successful Labour aspirant. So vital was the increased turnout to Labour that had the election been confined to the voters of 1918, it is possible that only Shettleston would have changed its allegiance. Labour also retained Govan, and George Buchanan picked up Gorbals, vacated by Barnes, against the former Labour candidate, John Maclean, somewhat eccentrically coming forward as an Independent Communist. Labour also captured Cathcart, when Captain John Hay, a former Free Church overseas missionary, benefited from the refusal of the local Unionists to accept instructions from the Scottish Unionist Whip, Sir John Gilmour, to stand aside again in favour of a National Liberal (Young: 13-17). With Labour taking ten seats, and a National Liberal taking Partick in a straight fight against a Liberal, the Unionists were restricted to Central, Hillhead, Kelvingrove, and Pollok. The Liberals again performed poorly in Glasgow, their ten candidates averaging only 4,000 votes each, despite three of them having only one opponent.

Table 7.5
Support for the Parties at the General Election, 1922, expressed as a percentage of the registered electorate*

	Aber.	**Dund.**	**Edin./Leith**	**Glas.**	**High.**	**East**	**Cent.**	**West**	**Bord.**	**All**
	%	%	%	%	%	%	%	%	%	%
Unionist	17.8 (1)	–	24.4 (2)	23.2 (4)	–	15.7 (1)	14.3 (1)	19.2 (4)	22.6	17.7 (13)
Nat Liberal	8.9	27.9	8.2	11.5 (1)	27.5 (5)	11.9 (3)	15.4 (2)	7.9	10.8 (1)	12.4 (12)
The Right	*26.7*	*27.9*	*32.6*	*34.7*	*27.5*	*27.6*	*29.7*	*27.1*	*33.4*	*30.1*
Independent	–	–	–	–	–	–	1.3	1.3	–	0.5
Liberal	15.7	3.9	26.7 (3)	7.9	22.7 (1)	25.7 (6)	10.1	11.2 (3)	37.2 (2)	15.1 (15)
Labour	14.8 (1)	20.1 (1)	9.7 (1)	32.8 (10)	–	5.3	32.8 (7)	32.0 (9)	–	22.6 (29)
Communist	–	4.5	–	0.9	–	–	–	3.3 (1)	–	1.2 (1)
Other Left	–	24.1 (1)	–	–	–	–	–	–	–	0.9 (1)
The Left	*14.8*	*48.7*	*9.7*	*33.7*	0	*5.3*	*32.8*	*35.3*	*0*	*24.7*
Total	**57.2**	**80.5**	**69.0**	**76.3**	**50.2**	**58.6**	**73.9**	**74.9**	**70.5**	**70.4**
Right Lead over Left	*+11.9*	*–20.8*	*+22.9*	*+1.0*	*+27.5*	*+22.3*	*–3.1*	*–8.2*	*+33.4*	*+5.4*

* seats won in brackets

Labour also made progress in the West outside Glasgow, where the right, in contrast to Glasgow fell back on 1918 (-3.5 per cent), as the left established an 8.2 per cent lead over its Unionist and National Liberal opponents. In the seven seats which Labour gained from the government's supporters, the Coalition vote fell on average by 1,500 in each seat and its share of the poll slipped from 57.7 per cent to 39.1 per cent, whilst Labour's vote rose on average by almost 5,000. Due to a more even political spread of the electors than in the city, only one of Labour's MPs, David Kirkwood, who won Dumbarton Burghs from the National Liberals and held the constituency until its suppression in 1950, was elected with more than 60 per cent of the poll, and Labour's five Lanarkshire seats were carried with an average of only 52.3 per cent of the votes. The sixth Lanarkshire seat, Motherwell, went to John Newbold, the former Labour candidate standing unopposed on the left as a Communist supported by the local Trades Council (Hutchison: 290-1). Labour also triumphed in both the Renfrewshire seats, assisted by a Liberal intervention in the East division.

Godfrey Collins narrowly retained Greenock as a Liberal against a Unionist and another Communist enjoying trades council backing, Alexander Geddes, who came within 750 votes of victory (Donald); and a second Liberal, Asquith, having been returned at a by-election in 1920, retained his Paisley seat with a majority of little more than 300 as the standard-bearer of the right against Labour. In yet another example of mainstream Liberalism's dependence on Unionism, the Liberals were permitted a successful free run against Labour in Ayrshire Kilmarnock. So generous were the Unionists and so capricious the electoral system, that with almost twice the support of the Liberals in the region they still held only one more seat (Lanarkshire Lanark, Dunbartonshire, North Ayrshire and Bute, and Ayr Burghs). Perhaps the most revealing result for the right was in Lanarkshire Motherwell, where Ferguson, standing as an Independent Unionist backed by the Orange Lodges, substantially outpolled the National Liberal.

Although Labour's strength in the Central Region was virtually the same as in Glasgow and the West, an improved performance by the right (+8.7 per cent), restricted the left to a lead of 3.1 per cent. Nevertheless, Labour made six gains. A static Unionist vote in East Stirling and Clackmannan was insufficient to resist a 4,559 rise in Labour support, and in West Stirling, where the Liberals stood down, Sir Harry Hope's extra 1,211 electors were not enough to offset a gain of 5,110 by the editor of *Forward,* Tom Johnston. In neighbouring Linlithgow, the intervention of a Liberal accompanied a reduction of 3,905 in the Unionist vote, ensuring a victory for Emanuel Shinwell, whose supporters rose by 5,342. Both the burgh districts of Dunfermline and Stirling and Falkirk fell to Labour miners, each experiencing the benefit of 6,000 more electors in their party's tally. The enhancement was particularly necessary in Dunfermline because Wallace, the incumbent National Liberal, had boosted his vote by 4,565. The sixth Labour win was in South Midlothian and Peebles, where the defending Liberal, Sir Donald Maclean, was narrowly pushed to the bottom of the poll, Westwood carrying the seat with 36 per cent of the ballot. The Coalition rot in Central was only just stopped in North Midlothian, when a new candidate, George Hutchison, held on with only two fifths of the votes; while in Berwick and Haddington, a National Liberal, Walter Waring, the former Liberal member for Banffshire, held the seat for his party with only 31 per cent of the ballot. The only Labour set-back was in the Kirkcaldy Burghs, where Tom Kennedy lost to the National Liberal, Sir Robert Hutchison, the seat he had captured at a by-election in 1921. In this highly marginal region, only Fife West could be considered a safe seat.

Labour consolidated its position in Aberdeen North, but it was in Dundee that the left made a major advance following the retiral of Wilkie and the polarisation of the left-right battle, with Churchill harnessed to a second National Liberal, and Morel (Labour) in alliance with Scrymgeour (Prohibitionist). The defeat of Churchill, who ran behind his colleague with 5,322 votes fewer than in 1918, was most emphatic (Walker); and with almost half the registered voters leaning to the left, Dundee was clearly the most radical of the cities. The Asquithian Liberals were outpolled by the Communists in Dundee, but in Aberdeen South, where there was no Labour candidate, Sir Charles Mallet secured 42 per cent of the poll against a Unionist.

Predictably, Liberal candidates performed creditably in Edinburgh, where they benefited from the absence of Labour candidates in the East, North, South and West divisions. Nevertheless, whilst the Liberals increased their share of the electorate by 8.3 per cent, the Coalition also made gains of 4.9 per cent to remain the dominant alignment in the capital. The Liberals easily retained Edinburgh East against National Liberal opposition, and Wedgwood Benn won more than half the poll against both Labour and Unionist candidates in Leith. The most encouraging Liberal result was the victory of Henry Phillips, a protégé of Asquith, who added more than 6,000 votes to the Liberal tally of 1918 in taking the West division despite an increase in the Unionist vote of 2,517; but the Unionists easily retained Edinburgh North and South.

The Liberal recovery was particularly marked in the East and Borders, where they won eight seats, as against four to the National Liberals and one to the Unionists. In the three Border constituencies they outpolled the right. Liberals prevailed in a block of constituencies extending from Banffshire to East Fife. In Banffshire, a former Coalition Liberal, Sir Charles Barrie, was returned unopposed, and a second turncoat, Alexander Murray, in Kincardine and West Aberdeen, won re-election against a National Liberal. Sir William Cowan, a National Liberal incumbent, lost East Aberdeenshire to a local Liberal journalist, Frederick Martin; while in Central Aberdeenshire, Murdoch Wood, who had regained the seat from the Coalition Unionists in a 1919 by-election, overwhelmed his Unionist opponent. The Liberals also won back Forfarshire, where John Falconer recaptured his former seat from the Unionists; and in East Fife, James Millar, who had represented part of the division as the member for St Andrews Burghs, January to December 1910, won back the constituency from his leader's nemesis, Sir Alexander Sprot. The National Liberals, however, held on in Moray and Nairn to link with successes in the Highlands; retained the Montrose Burghs in a straight fight with Labour; and gained Kinross and West Perthshire, where James Gardiner, having defected to the National Liberals, was returned unopposed. The single Unionist success came in the Perth Division of Perthshire, with Archibald Skelton gaining the seat against Liberal, National Liberal, and Labour opponents, following the retiral of the incumbent National Liberal. In the Borders, the former Coalition Liberal stood down in Galloway, allowing the seat to be captured by a Liberal, Cecil Dudgeon, against a Unionist opponent; and a second Liberal, Dr William Chapple, having failed to retain

Stirlingshire in 1918, was returned in Dumfries. A third Liberal, however, was successfully repulsed by Sir Thomas Hetherington, National Liberal, in a straight fight in Roxburgh and Selkirk.

The dispute between the two Liberal factions for the allegiance of rural areas was no more clearly joined than in the Highlands, where all six contests were monopolised by the intra-party conflict. Only in Orkney and Shetland, however, where Sir Robert Hamilton defeated the incumbent, Sir Malcolm Smith, did the Asquithian prevail. Robert Harmsworth, supporter of the coalition in 1918, but coming forward as an independent Liberal in 1922, fell to a local laird, Sir Archibald Sinclair, in Caithness and Sutherland; and even in the Western Isles the incumbent Liberal, Dr Murray, was outpolled by his National opponent, Sir William Cotts, whom he had previously defeated. The preference of the Highlands for the National Liberals was clearly at variance with the East and Borders, but was quite consistent with the region's historic ambivalence towards mainstream Liberalism, especially its religious disestablishmentarianism. It was also the case that in many respects the National Liberals were more collectivist than the Liberals, which may well have been an important factor in a region heavily dependent on government intervention. Archibald Sinclair, for example, identified with the political approach of Lloyd George, and gained the bulk of his votes in the more radical towns (De Groot: 50-53). The difference between the factions, however, should not be exaggerated, as was observed in Caithness and Sutherland: 'On issues important to the constituency the two candidates were not far apart: both were Liberal Free Traders who supported land redistribution, aid to the fishing industry and improvement of harbours' (De Groot: 52).

The election of 1922 had been dominated by the breakthrough of the Labour Party, its near monopoly of the left, and its capture of 29 seats. Although the Unionists lost 17 of the 30 constituencies they had taken in 1918, they had consolidated their position as the main defence against socialism in urban/industrial areas. By contrast, nine of the fifteen Liberals sat for rural/small town seats, as did nine of the twelve National Liberals. Thus, the improvement in the Liberal position had not been in politically significant regions, and in the central lowlands outside Edinburgh/Leith both wings of the party were becoming increasingly dependent on open or tacit Unionist support. It was clear that they had become a peripheral party in most senses of the term, but even on the periphery they had yet to be fully tested by the Unionists.

The General Election of 1923 (Table 7.6)

The 1923 general election was less notable for a modest improvement on the left (+2.5 per cent), or an increase in the number of Labour MPs to 34, than the consequences of the break-up of the Coalition in Scotland, occasioned by Baldwin's break with free trade, which alienated the National Liberals and helped reunify the Liberal Party. So strongly did the free trade issue resonate north of the border, that the revived Liberals won 22 seats, against only fourteen held by the Unionists, although their share of the electorate was only 4.1 per cent higher than that of the Asquithians the previous year. With the defection of the National Liberals, support for the right fell by 8.7 per cent on 1922, but the

Unionists gained strength (+3.7 per cent) and, more importantly, were no longer inhibited by doubtful allies in extending their appeal on the rural periphery.

In Glasgow, Labour outdistanced the right for the first time, and took Partick, formerly held by the National Liberals, at the first time of asking, as the Unionists, also making an initial intervention, pushed the Liberal to the foot of the poll. In Cathcart, however, where the right was reunited, Baillie MacDonald, a Unionist piano manufacturer, captured the constituency from Labour. All ten Liberal candidates performed poorly, averaging a mere 5,000 votes each.

A drop in turnout in the West left Labour (though not the left), slightly weaker than in 1922 (-2.0 per cent). Labour, however, took two seats from the Unionists: Lanarkshire Lanark in a straight fight, in one of the few seats where its vote actually rose, and Dunbartonshire, where a Liberal intervention hardly affected the outcome. By contrast, a Unionist intervention in Liberal-held Ayrshire Kilmarnock enabled Labour to seize the constituency from Sir Donald Maclean, a new Liberal candidate. The Liberals, however, held on in Greenock in a straight fight against a Communist, who won 38.7 per cent of the poll; and Asquith's defence of Paisley succeeded due to a split in the socialist vote following the refusal of the ILP to endorse the official Co-operative (Labour) nominee, Biggar, because he was a rent collector (Hutchison: 290). The sole Unionist gain (adding to the retention of Ayr Burghs and Bute and North Ayrshire), was Lanarkshire Motherwell, where the Orangeman, Ferguson, now recognised as an official Unionist, displaced the incumbent Communist Newbold, who had hoped to benefit from the continued absence of Labour opposition.

With nine candidates in Central, the Liberals (21.6 per cent) easily outpolled the five Unionist nominees (12.0 per cent), but where both parties stood the Unionists won more votes, and neither approached Labour's performance, whose 36 per cent share of the electorate was its best result outside Dundee. Appropriately, Labour made three gains: North Midlothian was taken from Unionists in a three-cornered fight; Kirkcaldy Burghs was recaptured from the Liberals in a straight fight; and a nine per cent increase in turnout propelled Labour to the top of the poll in Berwick and East Lothian, pushing the former National Liberal incumbent to the foot of the poll. The only Liberal seat remaining in the region was Stirling and Falkirk, won by Sir George McRae (MP for Edinburgh East from 1899–1909), removing Hugh Murnin in a straight fight that went against the trend. It was a measure of the leftward shift of political opinion in this region that in West Fife there was a straight fight between Labour and the Communists.

The intervention of a Unionist in Aberdeen North and a Labour candidate in Aberdeen South forced the Liberals to the bottom of the poll in both constituencies, but in Dundee the Liberal candidate came with 314 votes of Morel. Significantly, the first Unionist intervention in Dundee since the war followed a local electoral pact with the Liberals to run their candidates in tandem against Labour and the Prohibitionists.

Table 7.6
Support for the Parties at the General Election, 1923, expressed as a percentage of the registered electorate*

	Aber.	**Dund.**	**Edin./Leith**	**Glas.**	**High.**	**East**	**Cent.**	**West**	**Bord.**	**All**
	%	%	%	%	%	%	%	%	%	%
Unionist	21.9 (1)	14.3	18.3 (1)	23.4 (5)	14.0	27.5 (3)	12.0	24.1 (3)	33.8 (1)	21.4 (14)
Liberal	13.3	16.0	32.7 (4)	10.2	25.0 (6)	33.8 (7)	21.6 (1)	13.5 (2)	31.6 (2)	19.2 (22)
Labour	21.9 (1)	16.0 (1)	13.8 (1)	33.5 (10)	4.9	2.9	36.0 (9)	30.0 (12)	10.2	24.3 (34)
Communist	–	6.8	–	2.0	–	–	–	3.4	–	1.9
Other Left	–	19.7 (1)	–	–	1.8	–	2.2	0.7	–	1.0 (1)
The Left	*21.9*	*42.5*	*13.8*	*33.5*	*7.7*	*2.9*	*38.2*	*34.1*	*10.2*	*27.2*
Total	**57.1**	**72.8**	**64.8**	**69.1**	**45.7**	**64.2**	**71.8**	**71.7**	**75.6**	**67.8**
Unionist Lead over Left	*0*	*–28.2*	*+4.5*	*–12.1*	*+6.3*	*+24.6*	*+26.2*	*–10.0*	*+23.6*	*–5.8*

* seats won in brackets

The Liberal revival was most clearly evident in Edinburgh/Leith, where their six candidates won the allegiance of 32.7 per cent of the electorate and took four seats, easily outstripping the Unionists (18.3 per cent), standing in four seats, and Labour (13.8 per cent), contesting only half the constituencies. The movement to the Liberals was particularly evident in Edinburgh North, where, on virtually the same turnout as in 1922, there was a swing of 17.5 per cent to Peter Raffan, giving him a clear victory of the defending Unionist, Patrick Ford, in a straight fight. Similarly, a swing of 10.0 per cent to the Liberals in the South Division substantially reduced the majority of Sir Samuel Chapman. Henry Phillipps comfortably retained the Edinburgh West despite the intervention of a Labour candidate who won a quarter of the votes; and James Hogge won nearly 70 per cent of the ballot in Edinburgh East against the Unionists, who were contesting the constituency for the first time. Leith was easily retained by Wedgwood Benn in a straight fight with Labour, although he did not appear to benefit greatly from the absence of a Unionist interest. Edinburgh Central was held comfortably for Labour by Graham, his majority doubling in a straight fight with a Liberal.

Following their reunification, the Liberals found themselves in a defensive posture on the periphery, where they held eighteen of the nineteen seats. They were assisted in their task by the luxury of unopposed returns in Caithness and Sutherland, Ross and Cromarty, Banffshire and Galloway, and the absence of Labour candidates in all but four constituencies: Roxburgh and Selkirk and Western Isles, where they provoked three-cornered contests, and Montrose Burghs and Inverness, where they provided the only opposition.

Despite the break-up of their alliance with the National Liberals, the Unionists standing alone were as well supported as the Coalition in 1922, and took three seats from the Liberals: James Stuart, son of the 17th Earl of Moray, captured Moray and Nairn; Barclay-Harvey, a Deeside Laird, somewhat surprisingly won Kincardine and West Aberdeenshire; and Kinross and West Perthshire fell to Scotland's first female MP, the 'Red' Duchess of Atholl, a former opponent of female suffrage, who had been encouraged to stand by Haldane and a former Liberal MP for the constituency (Hetherington: 98). It was evidence of a latent Unionist vote in Moray and Nairn and Kincardine and West Aberdeenshire, that the intervention of Unionist candidates raised turnout respectively by 11.3 per cent and 9.5 per cent on 1922, so that the Liberal incumbents increased their vote while losing their seats. Similarly, in Kinross and West Perthshire the defeated Liberal polled more than the Liberal victor in 1918.

Ominously, the intervention of a Labour candidate in the Borders constituency of Roxburgh and Selkirk enabled the Earl of Dalkeith to beat the former National Liberal, Sir Thomas Henderson, with 43.1 per cent of the votes; and the Liberal recapture of the Perth division of Perthshire was greatly assisted by the withdrawal of Labour, whose candidate had won 18.9 per cent of the ballot in 1922. Clearly a substantial Labour intervention threatened the Liberals in seats they carried in straight fights against Unionists, especially as most of the seats which the Liberals had won in the East and Borders in 1923 were vulnerable to swings of less than 3.5 per cent.

Liberals continued to represent all the Highland divisions, with narrow wins in Argyll and Orkney and Shetland. It was, however, a measure of the confusing nature of rural politics at this time that Bob Boothby, in winning a creditable

45.7 per cent of the vote standing as the Unionist in Orkney and Shetland, described Gladstone as 'the greatest statesman the country has ever produced,' and the old Liberal party as 'the greatest Party the country has ever known' (James: 50-2). The Liberals retained the Western Isles with less than 40 per cent of the ballot in a three-cornered contest; and only in Inverness, where the incumbent, Sir Murdoch Macdonald, buried his Labour adversary, was the Liberal win emphatic. Thus, whilst the Liberals retained fifteen of the rural seats, they were far from constituting a secure base, especially as there remained a very large number of registered voters, particularly in the Highlands, who had yet no settled party allegiance.

The election of 1923 confirmed the initiative which Labour had seized the previous year as the party consolidated its position in the central lowlands; and the reunited Liberal Party staged a revival in Edinburgh and dominated representation in rural/small town constituencies. In many respects, however, the Liberal position was vulnerable, depending on Unionist support for the odd seat in the central belt outside the capital and the absence of Labour candidates on the periphery. Although the Unionists held only 14 constituencies they had established themselves as the main challengers to Labour, and were poised to make major gains from both Labour and the Liberals should circumstances prove more propitious.

The General Election of 1924 (Table 7.7)

The refusal of the Labour government to prosecute the Communist, Campbell, for his article in the *Workers' Weekly* calling on soldiers not to fire on striking workers, precipitated defeat in parliament, following the desertion of the Liberals, and a *Red Scare* election which polarised public opinion. In Scotland, as elsewhere, both the Unionists and Labour increased their share of the registered electorate, +9.1 per cent and +6.6 per cent respectively, as the Liberal share diminished 6.7 per cent. Scottish Liberal parliamentary strength fell from 22 to eight, and Labour MPs were reduced from 34 to 26, as the Unionists won just over half the seats. It was arguably the best Conservative/Unionist result since before 1832, the triumph of 1900 notwithstanding, because in knocking out the Liberals it made possible the emergence of a unified centre-right coalition almost equal to that of the left (Table 7.7).

Ten of the seats won by the Unionists from Labour – Glasgow Maryhill and Partick, Renfrew East and West, Dunbartonshire, Lanarkshire North, Ayrshire Kilmarnock, North Midlothian, Linlithgow and West Stirling – were constituencies which the Liberals had fought in 1923 but stood down in a year later. It was quite appropriate, therefore, that in Ayrshire Kilmarnock, a seat in which his party had been third in 1923, that the victorious Unionist, Major Charles MacAndrew, thanked both 'Unionists and Liberals who had supported him...(and) subsequently attended the Conservative and Liberal clubs' (Shedden: 63). The absence of Liberal candidates, however, was only one factor contributing to Unionist success, for while the aggregate Liberal vote in the former Labour seats had been only a little over 43,000 in 1923, the Unionist vote grew by over 58,000 between 1923 and 1924, and Labour's by rather more than 10,500. Thus, even if it is assumed the Unionists inherited the lion's share of former Liberal support, it would appear that at least half their advance came from increased turnout. Indeed, the likelihood that most, if not all, these constituencies (apart from Ayrshire Kilmarnock), would have been gained even if the Liberals had stood, would seem supported by the outcome in Lanarkshire Lanark, where – despite a Liberal intervention in what had been a straight fight in 1923 – the Unionists, adding 1,560 to their vote, took the seat from Labour, who only lost 42 electors. Similarly, in Berwick and Haddington, three-cornered in 1923 and 1924, the Unionists captured the constituency from Labour, increasing their vote 3,237 as Labour's grew by 306, and the Liberal vote fell by 1,098. The only Unionist loss was Lanarkshire Motherwell, which the victorious Labour Party was contesting for the first time since 1918, following pressure on the Communist, Newbold, to withdraw his candidature (Donnachie et.al.: 41).

Whilst there were swings to the right in seats where Unionists stood against Labour, there were mostly swings to the left where Labour faced Liberal opposition only, because Unionist electors were unwilling to vote for a party that had backed the Labour government.[7] Consequently, Paisley finally fell to Labour in a straight fight, marking the end of Asquith's association with Scotland, and in losing Stirling and Falkirk (again to Labour), the Liberals lost their foothold in the burgh districts. Godfrey Collins, however, the beneficiary of a continuing dispute between the Greenock Branch of the ILP and the Communist-dominated trades council, who each entered a candidate, survived the general slaughter.

The results in Edinburgh, where their share of the electorate fell by 10.3 per cent on 1923, were calamitous for the Liberals, as they were outpolled by Labour, leaving the Unionists as the biggest faction. In Edinburgh West, Phillipp's proportion of the poll fell by 11 per cent, pushing him into third place behind Labour, and enabled the Unionist, MacIntyre, to carry the seat; and in Edinburgh North, Peter Raffan also came third as a consequence of Labour intervention, with his percentage of the poll collapsing by no less than 33 per cent on 1923, to produce another Unionist gain. Even more dramatic was the outcome in Edinburgh East, which Labour carried the first time of asking from Hogge, landing him in third place, his share of the vote tumbling from 68.3 per cent to 26.7 per cent between 1923 and 1924. The one Liberal consolation in the conurbation was Wedgwood Benn's easy win as the leader of an anti-socialist coalition in Leith, despite a five per cent swing to Labour.

Whereas Unionist progress in the central lowlands was eased by the demise of Liberal candidatures, on the periphery it was seemingly facilitated by the intrusion of Labour. In six counties – Argyll, Dumfries, Aberdeenshire East and Central, Perth Perthshire and Forfar – which were the object of a two-party battle in 1923 but were exposed to Labour attentions in 1924, the Liberal share of the poll fell between the two elections from an average of 53.8 per cent to 31.2 per cent, while the Unionist proportion (46.4 per cent in 1923 and 46.2 per cent in 1924), hardly changed. Significantly, the Unionists also won seats without the assistance of Labour. East Fife was captured by the Unionists on an 8.5 per cent swing from the Liberals, while Galloway, held unopposed by Cecil Dudgeon for the Liberals in 1923, fell to the Tories on a 7.1 per cent swing since 1922.

Table 7.7
Support for the Parties at the General Election, 1924, expressed as a percentage of the registered electorate*

	Aber.	Dund.	Edin./Leith	Glas.	High.	East	Cent.	West	Bord.	All
	%	%	%	%	%	%	%	%	%	%
Unionist	33.8 (1)	16.5	27.0 (3)	35.5 (7)	13.3 (1)	32.2 (9)	20.0 (4)	34.8 (8)	38.1 (3)	30.5 (36)
Liberal	–	18.2	22.4 (1)	4.2	25.5 (5)	20.9 (1)	18.3	5.3 (1)	27.4	12.5 (8)
Labour	32.9 (1)	22.9 (1)	25.1 (2)	37.5 (8)	14.7	14.0	39.2 (6)	37.1 (8)	13.8	30.9 (26)
Communist	–	5.4	–	–	–	–	–	1.4	–	0.5
Other Left	–	20.8 (1)	–	–	–	–	–	–	–	0.7 (1)
The Left	*32.9*	*49.1*	*25.1*	*37.5*	*14.7*	*14.0*	*39.2*	*38.5*	*13.8*	*32.1*
Total	**66.7**	**83.8**	**74.5**	**77.2**	**53.5**	**67.1**	**77.5**	**78.6**	**79.3**	**75.1**
Unionist Lead over Left	*+0.9*	*–32.6*	*+1.9*	*–2.0*	*–1.4*	*+18.2*	*–19.2*	*-3.7*	*+24.3*	*–1.6*

* seats won in brackets

It is, therefore, a measure of Unionist success that in all likelihood they would have made all their gains without Labour intervention. With Banffshire returning its first Unionist/Conservative since 1835 in its first contested election since January 1910, the only Liberal seat in the East and Borders was Montrose Burghs, which the Unionists did not contest.

The Liberals were forced back into their Highland fastnesses, where they retained Orkney and Shetland, Caithness and Sutherland and Ross and Cromarty without opposition, though in Caithness and Sutherland, following the decision of Unionists not to contest, a number of Liberals, angered by Sinclair's support for the Labour government, considered finding a candidate more to their taste (De Groot: 66). Inverness was easily held against Labour, and the Western Isles was distinguished as the only Liberal seat held against candidates of both major parties.

In common with their English counterparts, the Scottish elecorate in 1924 deserted the Liberals in large numbers, exposing the fragility of their successes the previous year, polarising electoral politics between left and right, and ending Liberalism as a major political force. The unwillingness of the right to vote Liberal even where only they opposed Labour demonstrated how discredited they had become. With a substantial vote in all regions outside the Highlands and almost as many seats as Labour in the urban/industrial heartland, the Unionists were emerging as a truly national party in both a social and geographical sense. On the other hand, with Labour continuing to poll more votes than the Unionists, it was clear that the struggle for supremacy was far from resolved.

The General Election of 1929 (Table 7.8)

The general election of 1929 was an *annus mirabilis* for the Scottish Labour Party, when it returned 36 MPs. Labour's share of the electorate, however, was only 0.2 per cent greater than in 1924. The main development had been a drop of 4.1 per cent in Unionist support, leading to a loss of sixteen seats. Although the Liberals increased their popularity by 0.8 per cent in carrying thirteen constituencies, their minority status was confirmed. The stability of the voting pattern was quite remarkable given the the turbulence of the general strike, the equalisation of the franchise, and the economic problems of the late 1920s.

The main development in the evolving structure of electoral competition took place in the Central region, where the Unionists contested all the seats for the first time, whilst Liberal candidates, who had hitherto represented anti-Labour coalitions, stood down in the burgh districts of Stirling and Falkirk, Kirkcaldy, and Dunfermline. Consequently, the Unionist share of the electorate in Central grew by 5.2 per cent, although it was insufficient to prevent the loss of Berwick and Haddington (probably due to Liberal intervention), Linlithgow, and West Stirling, to Labour.

The recession in the Unionist vote was varied. In Glasgow, where Maryhill and Partick were retaken by Labour, it fell by only 3.0 per cent. In the West, however, it declined by 6.4 per cent, resulting in the loss of Ayrshire Kilmarnock, Dunbartonshire, West Renfrew, Lanarkshire North, and Lanark.

Table 7.8
Support for the Parties at the General Election, 1929, expressed as a percentage of the registered electorate

	Aber.	**Dund.**	**Edin./Leith**	**Glas.**	**High.**	**East**	**Cent.**	**West**	**Bord.**	**All**
	%	%	%	%	%	%	%	%	%	%
Unionist	21.6 (1)	16.7	20.9 (2)	32.5 (5)	11.1 (1)	28.0 (6)	25.2 (1)	28.4 (3)	30.9 (1)	26.4 (20)
Independent	–	–	–	–	–	–	1.8	–	–	0.2
Liberal	9.8	16.2	24.4 (1)	2.4	29.3 (5)	25.3 (4)	8.4	7.9 (1)	32.5 (2)	13.3 (13)
N.P.S	–	–	–	0.3	–	–	–	0.2	–	0.1
Labour	31.8 (1)	22.3 (1)	28.2 (3)	36.7 (9)	13.9	16.6	38.3 (9)	38.6 (13)	16.6	31.1 (36)
Communist	1.7	3.6	–	0.1	–	–	2.0	1.5	–	0.8
Other Left	–	22.3 (1)	–	2.7 (1)	0.9	–	–	–	–	1.5 (1)
The Left	*33.5*	*49.6*	*28.2*	*39.5*	*14.8*	*16.6*	*40.3*	*40.1*	*16.6*	*33.4*
Total	**64.9**	**82.5**	**73.5**	**74.7**	**55.2**	**69.9**	**75.7**	**76.7**	**80.0**	**73.4**
Unionist Lead over Left	*–11.9*	*–32.9*	*–7.3*	*–7.0*	*–3.7*	*+11.4*	*–15.1*	*–11.7*	*+14.3*	*–7.0*

* seats won in brackets

A similar movement in Edinburgh/Leith (-6.1 per cent), led to a Labour gain in Edinburgh West. The Unionists lost substantial ground in Aberdeen, though this was because a Liberal replaced a Unionist as the standard-bearer of the right in the North division. In Dundee, where the balance between left and right hardly changed, both alignments increased their strength.

In the Borders, the Unionist share of the electorate fell by 7.2 per cent, which allowed the Liberals, increasing their strength by 5.1 per cent, to become the strongest party in this diminutive region and recapture Galloway and Dumfries. There was also a revival of Liberal fortunes in the East (+4.4 per cent) and a similar recession in the Unionist position (-4.2 per cent), that facilitated the Liberal recapture of Banff, Kincardine and West Aberdeenshire, and Fife East.

Remarkably, the Liberals failed to oppose Bob Boothby in East Aberdeenshire, which enabled him to defeat a Church of Scotland minister – standing for Labour – by 13,354:10,110, following a campaign punctuated by rowdy meetings in Peterhead and Fraserburgh (James: 98-9).

The Liberals continued to hold five of the Highland constituencies, though they failed to retake Argyll. Labour, however, doubled its strength in the Western Isles – a seat it was to take in 1935 – and captured more than 40 per cent of the votes in Inverness and Ross and Cromarty. Charles Oman, a tea planter on holiday from the Malay States, contested Caithness and Sutherland as an unofficial Labour candidate, though both he and a Unionist, who likened the Liberal Party to the German fleet at Scapa Flow, were easily defeated by Archibald Sinclair (De Groot:72-3).

Table 7.9: Ranking of Support for the Various Alignments by Region
as a percentage of the registered electorate

Left (mostly Labour)		**Centre (Liberal)**		**Right (Unionist)**	
Dundee	49.6	**Borders**	32.5	**Glasgow**	32.5
Central	40.3	**Highland**	29.3	**Borders**	30.9
West	40.1	**East**	25.3	**West**	28.4
Glasgow	39.5	**Edinburgh**	24.4	**East**	28.0
Aberdeen	33.5	**Dundee**	16.2	*(All Scotland)*	*(26.4)*
(All Scotland)	*(33.4)*	*(All Scotland)*	*(13.3)*	**Central**	25.2
Edinburgh	28.2	**Aberdeen**	9.8	**Aberdeen**	21.6
Borders	16.6	**Central**	8.4	**Edinburgh**	20.9
East	16.6	**West**	7.9	**Dundee**	16.7
Highland	14.8	**Glasgow**	2.4	**Highland**	11.1

The distribution of party support which emerged in 1929 found the left – supported by 33.4 per cent of the electorate – as the dominant alignment, facing the Unionist right, commanding 26.4 per cent of the enrolled, and an unstable Liberal centre backed by 13.3 per cent of the electorate (Table 7.9).

In regional terms, the left was clearly at its strongest in industrial areas, especially in Dundee, where it attracted almost half the electorate. A steady two fifths of the enfranchised supported the left in Central, the West and Glasgow, followed by a third of the enrolment in Aberdeen. Even in Edinburgh/Leith

Labour was the leading party, despite running below its overall national share. In the Borders, East and Highland, however, only one in six of the electorate favoured the left, though it was more popular than the Unionists in Highland.

The Unionists were at their most appealing in Glasgow, closely followed by the Borders, the West and East, effecting an alliance between the more prosperous agricultural regions and the suburbanites and Orangemen of greater Clydeside. The right, however, ran behind both the centre and left in Edinburgh/Leith, relied on Liberal support in Dundee, and was below its national electoral strength in Central and Aberdeen. It was in Highland, though, where barely one in ten of the electorate supported the Unionists, that the right was at its weakest in 1929.

It was a measure of the Liberal retreat that by 1929 fewer than three out of every hundred electors voted for the party in Glasgow, and fewer than one in ten did so in Aberdeen, Central and the West. Only in Edinburgh/Leith, where there was a reluctance by the middle class establishment finally to desert the traditional party of bourgeois Scotland, did there appear to be an independent urban Liberal vote. Even so, as the election of 1924 had demonstrated, that support in the capital had become vulnerable. Only on the rural peripheries did the centre look secure, but even there the Liberals failed to outpoll the Unionists in the East, as they had done in 1923, and led the right by the narrowest of margins in the Borders. Consequently, only the Highlands afforded a position of relative security, although even there a smaller proportion of its electorate had cast a Liberal ballot than in the Borders.

Conclusion

After 1918 Scotland developed two quite distinct systems of electoral competition. The first, characteristic of most urban/industrial constituencies, was one in which a dominant Labour Party faced anti-socialist alliances increasingly monopolised by Unionists. The second, mostly characteristic of rural/small town constituencies, was one in which the Labour Party was weak and a dwindling band of Liberals sought to withstand the intrusion of Unionism. These basic patterns, however, were complicated by a few seats, especially in Edinburgh/Leith, where a genuine three-party system was sustained throughout the 1920s, and by intra-Liberal rivalry in the Highlands.

Perhaps the most critical feature of the new dispensation was the severed link between urban and rural radicalism that had sustained pre-war Liberal dominance, so that only the right continued to transcend the cultural divide. Thus, while Labour was the largest party, only the Unionists had a national constituency. Consequently, with the collapse of Liberalism under the weight of the greatly expanded electorate, Scotland was a less distinct political community than hitherto.

The urban electoral alignment was divided along two main axes – class and religion. Using census data on the size of dwellings as a robust indicator of social class, it is found, for example, that in 1924 Labour carried sixteen of the twenty constituencies in which more than 60 per cent of the inhabitants lived in dwellings of one or two rooms,[8] and held only four seats – Aberdeen North, Edinburgh East, Dunfermline Burghs and Kirkcaldy Burghs (all of them working class constituencies) – where more than half the population lived in households with three rooms or more. Similarly, the Unionist also benefited from the increased importance of class-based politics, enhanced by a redistribution scheme which had consolidated its base in the middle class suburbs of the larger conurbations, particularly greater Glasgow.

While Labour's vote was clearly class-based, by no means did all the working class vote for the party, whose performance, however impressive compared to that in England, appears modest in relation to the social structure and condition of the Scottish electorate. Labour never secured half the votes of electorally registered manual workers and their wives across nation as a whole, and even in regions of particular strength the party was by no means indisputably dominant, as the capacity of the Unionists to win industrial constituencies demonstrated. As elswhere in the United Kingdom, Labour was less a party of the working class than of the organised working class, and its collectivism was at odds with individualistic values inherited from a century of Liberalism. In the Scottish context, the strength of the Protestant work ethic and the wider Calvinistic virtues permeated not only the world-view of the Presbyterian lower middle class, on which Unionism was based, but also had a strong appeal for many native working-class Scots, amongst them not a few Labour leaders. At a fundamental level, the Labour movement with its demands for 'more money [and] more leisure' (STUC Annual Report, 1924: 68) represented a subversive counter culture. Unionism, therefore, emerged not simply as a class interest, but as the guardian of post-Reformation Scotland and the values of nineteenth century Liberalism against the improvident fecklesness of socialism, and was recognised as such by voters in all social classes.

Religion continued to play an important secondary role, particularly in greater Clydeside, despite the loosening of formal links between the Orange Order and Unionism in protest against the Irish Treaty (Hutchison: 288, 323-4). It was a measure of Unionism's appeal to the non-Catholic working class that in Lanarkshire Coatbridge, a constituency in which three-quarters of its inhabitants lived in dwellings of less than three rooms and an estimated three in ten of the population was Roman Catholic,[9] Labour had a majority of only 57 in 1924.

Particularly illustrative of the importance of religion were the activities of Councillor Ferguson in the coal-mining and steel-making division of Lanarkshire Motherwell, where 73.9 per cent of the population lived in two rooms or less and a quarter of the inhabitants were Roman Catholic. Supported by the Orange Order, Ferguson won eleven per cent of the poll as an Independent Unionist in 1918, and in 1922, under the same label, pushed the National Liberal to the bottom of the poll, coming second to a Communist. Unable to deny his success, he was officially adopted by the Unionists in 1923, against the opposition of Lord Belhaven and Provost Keith (Hutchison: 324), and carried the seat with a record number of votes. While an MP he used his influence with the chief constable of Lanarkshire to prohibit the Corpus Christi procession in Carfin, a Lithuanian mining village near Motherwell, as it contravened the Roman Catholic Relief Act, 1829 (McGhee). Although in 1924 he lost the seat to the Reverend James Barr, a United Presbyterian Minister wisely advanced by Labour, the repercussions of the Carfin crisis continued, precipitating the introduction of a Roman Catholic Relief Bill in 1926. Significantly, an unsuccessful attempt to have Scotland excluded from the bill's provisions was moved by two Clydeside Unionist MPs, Sir Alexander Sprot (Lanarkshire

North) and MacInnes Shaw (Renfrew East). No Unionist from the West of Scotland supported the measure, and nor did Sir Godfrey Collins, the Liberal MP for Greenock (*Hansard,* 200: 1562-1642). By contrast, Labour, respecting its electorate, was constrained to give the measure vociferous backing.

Estimating the precise impact of religion on the distribution of party support, however, is elusive, because it cannot be isolated from other variables, especially social class. In regional terms, Labour's absolute strength in 1929 was hardly different in Glasgow and the West, where sectarianism was strong, than in Central (Lothians and Fife), where it was weaker (Table 7.9). On the other hand, the Unionists had more support in Glasgow and the West than in Central. Comparing the seven Lanarkshire constituencies with working class Fife,[10] in an attempt to remove middle class suburbanites from the equation, it is found that in 1929 the electorate favoured Labour to the Unionists by 42.9 per cent to 27.7 per cent in the former, and by 42.7 per cent to 22.6 per cent in the latter. It would seem, therefore, that while the sectarian factor had a broadly neutral influence on the net Labour vote,[11] anti-Catholicism was a positive benefit to the Unionists in the West.

On the rural periphery, a mixture of unopposed returns, a varying menu of candidates, and the uncertain political orientation of Liberals candidates inhibited the establishment of clear voting parameters between the parties, and was responsible for relatively low levels of participation by the electorate in the East and Highland.

The content of the Liberal/Unionist confrontation on the periphery is not easy to determine. In some respects it was a ritualistic re-enactment of the nineteenth century struggle between the professional/shopkeeper-dominated Liberal establishment in the burghs against the Whig/Tory-led hierarchy in the countryside. In a number of constituencies that confrontation was sharpened in 1918 because the suppression of the burgh districts increased small urban influence in some county seats. Traditional divisions within Presbyterianism also continued to play their part, with the United Presbyterian voluntaries providing the organisational backbone of independent Liberalism, the Auld Kirk fortifying Unionism, and the Highland Free Presbyterians challenging both.

Outside the Highlands, however, the ending of the conflict between landowners and tenant farmers, their common dislike of employer contributions to national insurance, their fear of land nationalisation, and the attraction of agricultural subsidies and tariffs, had weakened rural radicalism, enabling the Unionists to build a broad-based alignment that transcended traditional sociopolitical divisions, thereby undermining the Liberal coalition. Even a high status Liberal landowner, Archibald Sinclair, found it increasingly difficult to mobilise voters in the rural areas (De Groot: 53, 58). Above all, Liberal support for Labour governments at Westminster did not sit well in areas where antisocialism was part of the general consensus.

In most respects the disputes between between the Liberal and Unionist leaderships in the rural/small town constituencies were minimal because the objectives of Liberal land reform had been largely realised by 1914. Furthermore, the tradition of non-partisanship in local politics had meant that Liberals and Unionists had frequently worked together in municipal government, and the restructuring of county government in 1889 had brought together the burgh and rural leaders in a similarly consensual relationship. Thus, by the 1920s, the

Liberal and Unionist elites were largely integrated both politically and economically, and neither had any reason to raise the political consciousness of the new working class electorate. For the traditional élites, the politics of rural parliamentary representation had ceased to be less focused on local issues, which had divided them, than on the need for a common defense against the wider political system, because redistribution had weakened the influence of primary producers, and the democratised franchise raised the spectre of socialism. Nowhere was that more evident than in East Aberdeenshire, where, in 1929 the Liberals 'saved the day for Boothby' by 'declaring their respect for him,' and allowed the tyro Unionist a straight fight against Labour (James: 99).[12] The Liberal/Conservative battle only survived on the periphery because in most seats Labour was so weak there were no pressing reasons for the old party leaders and voters to coalesce. East Aberdeenshire, with a significant Labour vote in Peterhead and Fraserburgh, was the exception which proved the rule.

The disorientation of politics on the periphery after 1918 helps to explain why the Liberal collapse elsewhere was so complete. Since at least the middle of the nineteenth century urban Liberal and Conservative (Unionist) leaders had been part of a unified social and economic establishment, though divided politically by religion. Religious Dissenters had defined urban Liberalism and made its supporters sympathetic to all kinds of institutional reform from the kirk to education to Ireland and the Constitution, thereby attracting the support of left-leaning working class voters. Local politics, however, was non-partisan, permitting a level of friendly association in politics between Liberal and Conservative (Unionist) politicians not evident in the struggle to determine representation at Westminster. In contrast to the periphery, however, Labour and other socialists from the 1880s began to challenge the power of the bi-partisan middle class leadership at the local level, latterly forcing Liberals and Unionists to form loose coalitions of Independents for electoral purposes. Electoral reform in 1918 made such arrangements also necessary for the conduct of national elections if Labour was to be resisted, but in this it was necessary that the anti-socialist candidate should adopt a recognised national party label. It was to the Unionists that the responsibility fell because with the passing of the Fourth Reform Act and the rise of Labour, and the creation of the Irish Free State, Liberalism's disparate coalition began to disintegrate, whereas the Unionists with their Orange allies constituted a broadly-based popular alignment against the left. Thus viewed, the collapse of Liberalism was almost the last step in a process whereby the Scottish middle class was finally reintegrated following the crisis of the 1843 Presbyterian Disruption. The last step was the unification of the main Free Churches with the Church of Scotland in 1929, followed by the grand Unionist and National Liberal coalition of 1931 that was to dominate Scotland for a generation.

Notes

1. Maclean had lost the ILP nomination to another candidate, but when he announced his decision to stand on an Independent Labour ticket, the ILP nominee stood down. (Craig: 590).
2. Coalition candidates being those whose nomination received the 'Coupon' in 1918 as recognition of their endorsement by the leaders of the National Government.

3. White subsequently joined the ILP (Hutchison: 280).
4. Labour 'War Patriots' (after Hutchison) included Adamson (West Fife), Barnes (Ind. Labour, Glasgow Gorbals), Brown (South Ayrshire), Graham (Hamilton) Rose (Ind. Labour, Aberdeen North), and Wilkie (Ind. Labour, Dundee).
5. 20,752 electors voted for both Churchill and Wilkie; 4,625 voted for both Brown and Scrymgeour (Prohibitionist); and 1,885 for both Wilkie and Brown. For full details see Craig (p. 715).
6. See McLean (1983) for a thorough account of the various reasons for Labour's electoral rise on Clydeside
7. Cook suggests that in Paisley 'local Conservatives [Unionists] were hostile to the pact and may even have voted Labour to oust the Liberal' (p. 312)
8. The remaining four being Unionist-held Ayrshire Kilmarnock, Lanarkshire North, and Linlithgow, and Liberal-held Greenock.
9. Estimate Number of Roman Catholics = Total Catholics in Diocese/Proportion of Diocesan Baptisms in the Constituency.
10. West Fife, Dunfermline Burghs and Kirkcaldy Burghs.
11. It would appear, therefore, that the greater Unionism of non-Catholic electors was counterbalanced by the greater Labourness of Catholics.
12. Nor did the Liberals contest the seat again until after Boothby's retiral from the Commons.

References

Bull, SR, 'Asquith's Decline and the General Election of 1918,' *Scottish Historical Review,* Vol. 49, 1970.

The Catholic Directory and Clergy and Laity, 1923, Edinburgh, 1923.

Census (Scotland) 1921.

Cook, C, *The Age of Alignment, Electoral Politics in Britain, 1922-1929*, London, 1975.

Craig, FWS, *British Parliamentary Election Results, 1918-1949*, Glasgow, 1969.

De Groot, GJ, *Liberal Crusader: The Life of Sir Archibald Sinclair,* London, 1993

Donald, J, *Past Elections in Greenock*, Greenock, 1933.

Donnachie, I, (edit.) et.al., *Forward! Labour Politics in Scotland, 1888-1988*, Edinburgh, 1989.

Hetherington, S, *Katharine Atholl, 1874-1960: Against the Tide,* Aberdeen, 1989

Hutchison, IGC, *A Political History of Scotland, 1832-1924*, Edinburgh, 1986.

James, RR, *Bob Boothby*, London, 1988.

McGhee, S, 'Carfin and the Roman Catholic Relief Act of 1926,' *Innes Review*, Vol. XVI, 1965.

McLean, I, *The Legend of Red Clydeside*, Edinburgh, 1983.

Middlemas, RKO, *The Clydesiders*, London, 1965.

Parliamentary Paper, Session 1917-18, Vol. XIV, cmnd. 8669, *Commission of Inquiry into the Industrial Unrest.*

Parliamentary Paper, Session 1917-18, Vol. XIV, cmnd. 8760, 345, *Report on the Housing of the Industrial Population of Scotland, Rural and Urban, 1917-18.*

Scottish Trades Union Congress (STUC), *27th Annual Report*, Glasgow, 1924.

Shedden, Sir Lewis, *The Parliamentary History of Kilmarnock*, Kilmarnock, 1929.

Walker, W, 'Dundee's Disenchantment with Churchill,' *Scottish Historical Review,* Vol. 49, 1970.

Walker, W, *Juteopolis*, Edinburgh, 1979

Warner, G, *The Scottish Tory Party*, London, 1988.

Young, JH, *A History of the Cathcart Conservative and Unionist Association, 1918-1993*, Glasgow, 1994.

8 *The Members 1923 and 1924*

Of the seventy MPs *in situ* at the dissolution of 1918, only half were returned at the general election; only thirteen, including four Liberals who came back after defeat in 1918, remained at the end of 1922; and a mere six survived the contest of 1924. The changes were in part a consequence of redistribution, but more importantly of the widening of the franchise and changed political circumstances that had eroded the credibility of the Liberal Party.

Despite the large turnover in personnel and the wholesale reconstruction of the constituency map, only fifteen incumbent MPs – twelve Liberals and three Unionists – failed to contest the election of 1918. Incumbents undoubtedly benefited from the timing of the election so close to the end of the war, because it speeded-up the process of candidate selection, and with most of the new constituency associations hardly formed, the ready availability of sitting MPs made them obvious choices, even when they had little connection with their new seats.

In the burghs the reduction in the number of districts almost inevitably occasioned a number of retirals. John Barran, the Leeds textile manufacturer, failed to find a seat following the suppression of the Hawick grouping,[1] while a combination of liberation and old age led to the withdrawal of Anstruther-Gray (St Andrews Burghs) and John Bryce (Inverness Burghs). Similarly, the disappearance of Perth Burgh constituency occasioned the retirement of Alexander Whyte, who never sought re-election, despite being under forty years of age. Charles Price, in his sixty third year, stood down on the redistricting of Edinburgh Central. Least explicable was the decision of a youthful Vernon-Harcourt to quit the little-changed Montrose District, despite his chances of success.[2]

Redistribution in the counties enforced retirement on Molteno (Dumfriesshire) and Waring (Banffshire). Percy Molteno passed his seat to Gulland, whose Dumfries District had been thrown into the county; and Waring was ousted by Charles Barrie, recently elected to represent the doomed Elgin Burghs, which included Banff and Cullen, transferred to a reconstructed Banffshire in 1918. Waring tried without success to capture the English seat of Blaydon in 1918, but was returned in 1922 as a National Liberal in Berwick and East Lothian. Following defeat the following year, he drifted away from Liberalism and concluded his parliamentary ambitions as the losing Conservative candidate at Wallsend in 1929. Molteno, a Perthshire landowner, was to be beaten narrowly by the Duchess of Atholl in 1923, in an attempt to win Kinross and West Perthshire.

The combination of Caithness and Sutherland occasioned the departure of an elderly Alphaeus Morton (Sutherland), sweetened with a knighthood, in favour of a newly-created baronet, Sir Robert Harmsworth, the MP for Caithness. On the amalgamation of Roxburgh and Selkirk, Sir John Jardine stepped aside for a younger Robert Monro, refugee from the extinguished Wick Burghs. Similarly, the dismemberment of Clackmannan and Kinross confirmed the decision of the septuagenarian, Eugene Wason, to retire, leaving the way for the new division of East Stirling and Clackmannan to be contested by Dr Chapple, the former MP for Stirlingshire. The retirals of John Ainsworth (Argyll) and William Beale (Ayr South) were also unequivocally a function of age. Somewhat surprisingly, the union of Wigtown and Kirkcudbright found Viscount Dalrymple, first elected as a Unionist for Wigtown in 1915, leaving the field to Gilbert McMicking (Kirkcudbright), standing as a Coalition Liberal. William Watson, a Unionist elected to Lanark South in 1913 also retired and, after failing in Galloway in 1922 and Carlisle in 1923, came back to represent Carlisle in the parliament of 1924 to 1929.

Finding a seat proved less difficult for the Liberals than attracting the favours of the new electorate, and sixteen former Liberal MPs who remained loyal to Asquith were defeated in 1918. So, too, was Duncan Pirie standing as a National Liberal in North Aberdeen; and in Leith, a Unionist, George Currie, who had captured the old burgh district at a by-election in 1914, fell to a newly-arrived English Liberal, Wedgwood Benn. Ironically, both Currie and Benn subsequently defected to Labour, the former to serve as a London county councillor and president of Chelsea Labour Party, the latter to become MP for North Aberdeen in 1929,

The process of exceptional change was by no means completed in 1918. In 1922, Labour's Scottish Westminster contingent increased from six to 29, the Unionists advanced from fourteen seats in 1923 to 36 in 1924, while the Liberals (including the National Liberals) fell from 27 in 1922 to 8 two years later. Even two of the three pre-war Labour members had retired by 1922. Consequently, after the 1924 election, only three Unionists – Hunter-Weston (Bute and North Ayrshire), John Gilmour (Pollok), Harry Hope (MP for Forfar, having lost West Stirlingshire) – two Liberals, Godfrey Collins (Greenock) and James Macpherson (Ross and Cromarty), together with William Adamson (Fife West), Labour, remained of those sitting in the pre-war parliament.

It is not easy to pinpoint a particular election for the purposes of examining what impact electoral change had on the social characteristics of Scottish parliamentary representation. 1918 was clearly atypical; in 1922 the Liberals remained divided; in 1922 and 1923 the Unionists had still to reveal their underlying strength; and in 1924 the Liberals were too few to offer a useful picture of their new persona. For comparative purposes, therefore, the Labour and Unionist MPs returned in 1924 will be examined, because they reflect the social polarisation of politics resulting from electoral reform, together with the 22 Liberals elected in 1923.

The 1923 Liberals

The Liberals elected in 1923 were characteristic of those returned in December, 1910. Seven (almost a third) were lawyers; an equal number (including three publishers) were businessmen; five were journalists or authors; and a couple were landowners (see Tables 8.1 and 8.2). Broadly, they were divided on the one hand between the upper middle class – who had strong educational links with English public schools and the ancient English universities, and had professional connections with the London legal and commercial establishment –

and on the other by a group of men with diverse social backgrounds connected in various ways with publishing, writing, journalism, and support for worthy causes, both political and moral, which exercised the minds of well-meaning Liberals at the turn of the century. Although the dichotomy can hardly be rigid – the latter group, for example, included some establishment figures – it is worth making because what most distinguished Liberal MPs from Unionist MPs was their association with the printed word.

The eight burgh Liberals were led by Asquith (Paisley), following his humiliation in East Fife, supported by his former PPS, Henry Phillipps (Edinburgh West). Phillipps, another public school Englishman (Charterhouse, Heidelberg, and Caius), had been called to the bar at Lincoln's Inn in 1907, and before his election in West Edinburgh had sought a seat in Blackpool (1906), Maidstone (January and December 1910), and Rochdale (1918). His claim to a Scottish division rested on a period of twelve years as a schoolmaster at Fettes (1893–1905), and an Edinburgh-born wife.

Five of the remaining burgh Liberals elected in 1923 were connected with journalism and publishing: Sir Godfrey Collins (Greenock), was managing director of AG Collins, the Glasgow and London publishers; Peter Raffan (Edinburgh North), an Aberdonian, was both editor and proprietor of *The South Wales Gazette*; Wedgwood Benn (Leith), a nonconformist Englishman married to a Scotswoman, was associated with his family's publishing business; and John Sturrock (Montrose Burghs) had an interest in John Leng, newspaper proprietors of Dundee. They were joined by James Hogge (Edinburgh East), at various times United Free Church Minister, social investigator, journalist and author. The most notable of the group was Collins, although as a member of the Scottish commercial establishment he was the least radical, serving as a junior treasury minister in the post-war administration of Lloyd George, and from 1931 as Scottish secretary in the National Government. By contrast, Raffan, president of the English League for the Taxation of Land Values, wrote pamphlets on the land question, and James Hogge, a strong home ruler, authored such volumes as *Facts on Gambling*, *Scotland Insured*, and *War Pensions Allowances*. Hogge, Raffan and Benn also associated themselves with good causes: Hogge as president of the National Federation of Discharged and Demobilised Sailors and Soldiers; Raffan, in addition to the aforementioned league, as chairman of the South Wales Workers' Education Association and secretary of the Band of Hope Union; and Benn as chairman of the National Relief Fund. Raffan had also been active in local politics as chairman of Monmouth County Council, 1909–1910. One might also include in their number Sir George McCrae (Stirling and Falkirk) for his lecturing on finance and income tax, old age pensions and land values. On the other hand, this merchant had more solid credentials as vice-president of the Scottish Local Government Board (1909–1919), and as chairman of the Scottish Board of Health (1919–1922). He had previously sat for East Edinburgh (1899–1909), but had resigned on his appointment to the Local Government Board. Like Raffan, he had served in local government, and was Edinburgh City Treasurer in 1891.

The fourteen county Liberals were somewhat more conservative than those from the burghs, being characterised by men like Sir Robert Hamilton (Orkney and Shetland), James Macpherson (Ross and Cromarty) and James Millar (East Fife), each of whom was a member of a London Inn of Court. Despite his name,

Hamilton had little connection with Scotland. After his education at St. Paul's and Trinity College, Cambridge, he was called to the Inner Temple before entering the colonial service, becoming principle judge and chief justice in the East African Protectorate, 1905–1920. His claim to the islands' seat rested on his marriage to a native of Kirkwall. James Macpherson as the son of an Inverness JP had stronger Highland connections, but he had been educated outside the region at George Watson's and Edinburgh University prior to practising law at the Middle Temple. A resident of south-east England, he concluded his working life as the Recorder of Southend. The route south was also followed by James Millar, the son of an Edinburgh doctor, who went to school locally and graduated from Edinburgh University, but within a year of his call to the Scottish bar had repaired to the Middle Temple. However, a fourth lawyer, Robert Mitchell (Perth, Perthshire), was rather more parochial. The son of a Perth solicitor, he proceeded from the local academy to St Andrews and Edinburgh Universities before returning to the family firm. Subsequently, he served on Perth Burgh Council, and was instrumental in the creation of the Scottish County Cricket Championship. People like him were the backbone of numerous Liberal associations, but they rarely aspired to enter parliament, and he himself only served for a year.

Table 8.1: Occupations of Scottish Liberal (1923), Unionist and Labour MPs (1924)

	Liberals			*Unionists*			*Labour*		
	Burgh	**County**	**All**	**Burgh**	**County**	**All**	**Burgh**	**County**	**All**
Scottish Lawyers	–	2	2	2	5	7	1	–	1
English Lawyers	1	3	4	–	2	2	–	–	–
Lawyer/Academic	1	–	1	–	–	–	–	–	–
Lawyer/Businessman	–	–	–	2	–	2	–	–	–
(All Lawyers)	(2)	(5)	(7)	(4)	(7)	(11)	(1)	(–)	(1)
Landowners	–	2	2	2	6	8	–	–	–
Gentlemen	–	–	–	–	1	1	–	–	–
Service Officers	–	–	–	1	8	9	–	–	–
Businessmen	1	3	4	4	1	5	–	–	–
(All Businessmen)	(1)	(3)	(4)	(6)	(1)	(7)	(–)	(–)	(–)
Publishers	3	–	3	–	–	–	1	–	1
Journalists/Authors/Propogandists	2	3	5	–	–	–	4	2	6
Doctors	–	1	1	1	–	1	–	–	–
Doctor/Photographer	–	–	–	–	–	–	1	–	1
Wood Turner	–	–	–	–	1	1	–	–	–
Miners	–	–	–	–	–	–	2	6	8
Engineers	–	–	–	–	–	–	3	–	3
Teachers	–	–	–	–	–	–	1	–	1
Ministers	–	–	–	–	–	–	1	1	2
Hairdresser	–	–	–	–	–	–	1	–	1
Carpenter	–	–	–	–	–	–	1	–	1
Patternmaker	–	–	–	–	–	–	1	–	1
Total	**8**	**14**	**22**	**12**	**24**	**36**	**17**	**9**	**26**

Table 8.2

Characteristics of Scottish Liberal (1923), Unionist and Labour MPs (1924)

	Liberals (n=22)			Unionists (n=36)			Labour (n=26)		
	Burgh	County	All	Burgh	County	All	Burgh	County	All
Scotsmen	5	12	17	12	18	30	14	8	22
Englishmen	3	–	3	–	3	3	1	1	2
Attended Scottish Schools	5	9	14	10	11	21	14	8	22
Attended English Schools	2	2	4	2	11	13	1	1	2
Attended Scottish University	1	7	8	7	7	14	4	1	5
Attended English University	4	2	6	4	6	10	1 (Ruskin)		1
Scottish Local Government Councillors (inc. School Boards)	1	2	3	3	4	7	10	5	15
English Local Government Councillors	2	–	2	–	–	–	–	–	–
Main location of Economic Interests.									
(1) Scotland	4	7	11	10	14		9	15	24
(2) England	3	7	10	–	2		–	2	2
(3) Other	1	7	7	–	8 (Soldiers)		–	–	
Represented an English Constituency	–	2	2	1	–	1	–	–	–
Atttempted to rep. an English Constituency	1	1	2	–	–	1	–	–	–
Sat in Parliament before 1918	6	4	10	1	2	3	–	1	1
Experience active war service	2	4	6	6	13	19	2	–	2
Mean Age	55	48	50	47	46	46	49	52	50
Median Age	52	46	48	49	47	48	50	57	51

There still remained, in 1923, two Liberal landowners: Sir Archibald Sinclair of Ulbster (Caithness and Sutherland), and Cecil Dudgeon (Galloway). Sinclair, 'whose castle dominated the little town of Thurso...[and whose] vast estate filled the surrounding horizon' (Butler & Rose: 229) was in the old Whig tradition: his family had been active in Caithness politics before the Union, and his factor doubled as his political agent (De Groot: 60). Following his grandfather, who had been forced out of the constituency in 1885 by the Land Leaguers, his presence in parliament attested to the ephemeral impact of the Crofters on representation in the region. Educated at Eton and Sandhurst, Sinclair had been personal military secretary to Churchill when secretary of state for war, following him to the colonial office, 1921–22, and on his election to parliament in 1923 was already lord lieutenant of his county. It was a measure of his local status that as late as 1966 some could still recall 'how people were astonished by the lack of respect when somebody had the temerity to question him at a political meeting in Bettyhill' (Butler & Rose: 229).[3] However much an anachronism he may have been,[4] Sinclair was to lead the Liberal Party for ten years following the general election of 1935. Cecil Dudgeon held land in Galloway, served on Kirkcudbright County Council after 1911, and became chairman of the Education Authority in 1922, the same year he was returned unopposed to parliament. Defeated in 1924, he was re-elected in 1929, only to suffer again in 1931, but this time as a candidate of Oswald Mosley's New Party.

Businessmen were represented by Alexander Livingstone (Western Isles), Sir Murdoch Macdonald (Inverness), and Sir Charles Barrie (Banff). Livingstone appropriately came from a west highland family, and his wife was from Skye. He, however, was head of an exporting firm based in London, where he was later to become a member of the Common Council of the City, and his first attempt to enter the Commons had been at Dover in 1918. His radicalism later led him to join the Labour Party after retiring from the Western Isles in 1929, but in 1931 he defected to National Labour. Similarly, Sir Murdo, although born and educated in Inverness later established himself as a London-based civil engineer; but Sir Charles Barrie, as a shipowner and merchant in Dundee, where his father had been lord provost, was Scots-based.

The journalists and propagandists were led by Sir William Sutherland (Argyll), a graduate of Glasgow High School and University. The author of such titles as *Old Age Pensions* (1907), *The Call of the Land* (1909), *The Land Question* (1910), and *Rural Regeneration of England* (1913), he was involved with the preparation of the pre-war old age pensions, national insurance and small landholders acts. During the war he was secretary to the cabinet committee on the supply of munitions, and chancellor of the Duchy of Lancaster for a brief period in 1922. Less exalted were Murdo Wood (Central Aberdeen), Frederick Martin (East Aberdeen) and William Chapple (Dumfries). Both Wood and Martin were natives of north east Scotland, and attended local secondary schools of no great status. Wood, however, progressed from Fordyce Academy near his home village of Cullen to Edinburgh University and the London School of Economics and Political Science, becoming a barrister at Gray's Inn. He was also a sub-editor on the *Daily Mail* prior to his war service in the Gordon Highlanders and on the staff of the Royal Flying Corps. Martin also joined the Gordon Highlanders in 1914, following his education in the fishing burgh of

Peterhead and a spell as a journalist on the *Aberdeen Press and Journal*. He was almost blinded in the war and spent some time at St Dunstans before his return in 1922. Following defeat in 1924 and an unsuccessful attempt to capture the Central division in 1929, he unsuccessfully contested his former seat as a Labour candidate in 1931 and 1935. Dr William Chapple, one of the few members to remain from 1910, clearly belongs to this group of propagandists, with his edifying works on *The Unfit* and *Alcohol Abuse*; so, too, does a second survivor, James Falconer (Forfar), the son of a farmer, who became founder of the Scottish Rural Workers' Society.

The 1924 Unionists

Although the Unionist MPs elected in 1924 included the first Scottish female MP – a consequence of the 1918 Act – the substantial increase in their numbers on 1910 did not greatly expand the base of their recruitment. Of the 36 returned in 1924, eleven were lawyers, eight landowners, nine service officers and only seven were businessmen (including two lawyers). Unionist members, however, remained, as in 1910, more firmly rooted in Scottish society than the Liberals. For example, whereas only one of the 1923 burgh Liberals had attended a Scottish University, seven of the twelve 1924 burgh Unionists had done so, and whereas only two out of seven legally qualified Liberals practised in Scotland, nine of the eleven 1924 Unionist lawyers were based in their native land. Again, although a number of the rural Unionists had been educated at English public schools and Oxford and Cambridge, their economic welfare and political influence were based on the ownership of property north of the border. Consequently, while half the Liberals depended for their livelihoods on interests outside Scotland, the same could be said of only two Unionists, excluding the peculiar case of service officers. Unionists were also distinguished from the Liberals and Labour in that more than half their number had fought in the First World War.

In 1924, there were twelve Unionist burgh MPs, of whom four had a legal background, four were businessmen, two were landowners, one a soldier, and one a doctor of medicine.

All the lawyers – Frederick Thomson (Aberdeen South), Sir Robert Horne (Glasgow Hillhead), Patrick Ford (Edinburgh North), and Ian MacIntyre (Edinburgh West) – received much of their education in Scotland. Indeed, all four had received their schooling in Edinburgh – Thomson and Ford at the Academy, Horne at George Watson's, and MacIntyre at Fettes – and Thomson, Ford and MacIntyre then passed through Edinburgh University, while Horne graduated from Glasgow University. Thomson and Ford, however, completed their university education at University College and New College, Oxford, respectively. Although Thomson had been called to the bar at the Inner Temple in 1904, all four practised in Scotland, and MacIntyre became a writer to the signet. Thomson and Horne were also substantial businessmen, the former as general manager of the British Linen Bank. Horne, sometime lecturer in philosophy at the University of North Wales and external examiner at Aberdeen University, and holder of several important cabinet posts under Lloyd George, including the chancellorship of the exchequer, had commercial interests as chairman of the Great Western Railway, and as a director of the Suez Canal Company, P & O, and Lloyd's Bank. MacIntyre's claim to an Edinburgh constituency was enhanced by a brief period on Edinburgh City Council, 1918–20, although there is no evidence that Unionists held local government experience to be an important qualification for holding a parliamentary seat.

Three of the businessmen – Robert MacDonald (Cathcart), Sir William Alexander (Central), and James Couper (Maryhill) – sat for Glasgow constituencies. The most substantial was probably Sir William, who inherited Bonar Law's business division. Educated at Kelvinside Academy and the universities of Glasgow and Göttingen, he became director of administration of explosive factories at the ministry of munitions, 1916–17, and held other similar posts until the end of the war. Couper and MacDonald, also born and raised in Glasgow, were particularly associated with the commercial and public life of their native city. A justice of the peace, Couper inherited a family shipping interest, and was a member of the Baltic Shipping Exchange, the Glasgow Royal Exchange and the Chamber of Commerce; while MacDonald, the son of a local engineer and spindlemaker, and himself a piano maker, served from 1914 to 1923 on the city council. The fourth businessman, Sir Samuel Chapman (Edinburgh South), was chairman of Messrs. Scott, Son & Company with interests in London, Edinburgh and Glasgow. He lived in Perthshire, where he was a JP and a member of the county education authority. An active Unionist, he held the chairmanship of the political committee of the Scottish Unionist Club.

Traditional Tory Unionism was reflected by Sir John Gilmour (Glasgow Pollok), and John Baird (Ayr Burghs). Gilmour belonged to a long-established Fifeshire landed family. Appropriately, he was educated at Glenalmond and Edinburgh University before polishing at Trinity Hall, Cambridge. He joined the Fife and Forfar Yeomanry, rising to the rank of lieutenant colonel, and experienced active service in the Boer War, and in Gallipoli, Egypt and Palestine during the Great War, winning the DSO. On returning to his estates, he became a director of the Caledonian Railway and the Royal Highland Agricultural Society. In the parliament of 1924–29 he was Scottish secretary, and in 1936 was appointed vice-lieutenant of his county. Similarly, John Baird, Eton and Christ Church, the son of a Kincardineshire landowner, whose family had introduced modern farming methods to the county, had strong local traditional roots further cemented in 1905 through his marriage to the daughter of the 10th Earl of Kintore. For a short time he pursued a diplomatic career, but from 1910 until his defeat in 1922 represented the English constituency of Rugby. He, too, secured a DSO, having served in the British Expeditionary Force as a major in the Scottish Horse. For a short time he served as PPS to Bonar Law, and as a junior minister after his death. In 1925 he became Baron Stonehaven and Governor General of Australia until 1930. From 1931 to 1936 he held the critical post of chairman of the Conservative and Unionist Party, and was made Viscount Stonehaven for his pains in 1938.

The two other Unionist burgh MPs, Walter Elliot (Kelvingrove) and George Broun-Lindsay (Partick), both represented Glasgow constituencies. A native of the city, Elliot was educated at Glasgow Academy and graduated in medicine from the local university. During the First World War he served in the Royal Scots Grays, and in 1918 was returned for the Lanark division of Lanarkshire. In 1923 he lost his seat, but moved successfully to Kelvingrove in 1924. He served in various ministries, rising to the post of secretary of state for Scotland, 1936–

38, when he became minister of health.[5] Broun-Lindsay, a native of East Lothian, experienced a typical soldier's training at Cheltenham and Sandhurst before being commissioned in 1909 in the King's Own Scottish Borderers. In 1921 he retired from the army with the rank of major, and in 1924 was elected to parliament at the first attempt, but retired from the fray following defeat in 1929.

At the social apex of county Unionist representation were the Duchess of Atholl (Kinross and West Perthshire), daughter of the 10th Earl of Banff and wife of the 8th Duke; the Earl of Dalkeith (Roxburgh and Selkirk), eldest son of the 7th Duke of Buccleuch and Queensberry; and James Stuart (Moray and Nairn), a son of the 17th Earl of Moray and son-in-law of the 9th Duke of Devonshire. Of the three, the duchess (whose husband, 'Bardie', had held West Perthshire, 1910–1917), was quite the most qualified to enter parliament for a Scottish constituency, for although educated in England at Wimbledon High School and the Royal College of Music, she had a distinguished record of public service in Scotland before arriving at Westminster.[6] From 1910–1912 she had been a member of a Commission of Inquiry into the Highlands and Islands Medical Services, and between 1920 and 1924 was Chairwoman of the Scottish Board of Health's Consultative Committee on the Highlands and Islands. Between 1918 and 1920 she had served on the Central Agricultural Wages Committee for Scotland, and from 1917–18 as a member of a departmental committee on Scottish teachers. On her election she had already served several years as a member of Perthshire's education authority.[7] It was quite appropriate that as parliamentary secretary to the board of education, 1924–29, she was to become the first Unionist female to hold government office. She was later to gain notoriety as the 'Red Duchess' for her defence of the Spanish Republic, which led to her loss of the party whip and defeat at a by-election she herself had precipitated. Predictably, Dalkeith and Stuart had similar careers before entering the House. The Earl attended Eton and Christ Church, before serving in the army, rising to the rank of lieutenant-colonel in the King's Own Scottish Borderers, and acting for a short time as ADC to the Governor General of Canada. Stuart also attended Eton, served as a captain in the Royal Scots, and was equerry to the Duke of York, 1920–21. As chief whip, 1942–45, he was described by Macmillan as 'the only man I think I have ever known who rather frightened Churchill' (Horne: 67). From 1951 Stuart was secretary of state for Scotland until removed by his brother-in-law, Harold Macmillan, on taking office as prime minister in 1957.

Below the aristocrats were a small group of gentry: Colin Barclay-Harvey (Kincardine and West Aberdeen), Sir Harry Hope (Forfar), and Charles MacAndrew (Ayrshire Kilmarnock). Barclay-Harvey (Eton and Christ Church), and MacAndrew (Uppingham and Trinity, Cambridge), in common with many members of their class, had received an English education, but Sir Harry had to be content with the Collegiate School and the University of Edinburgh. All three represented constituencies in their counties of residence, although Hope had previously sat for both Bute and West Stirling. It was evidence of their high social status that *noblesse oblige* required both Hope and Barclay-Harvey, whose house on the Dee at Dinnet almost rivalled Balmoral, to become county councillors after leaving parliament,[8] the former becoming convenor of Angus and president of the Scottish County Council's Association, 1940–42.

The soldiering fraternity were represented by Lieutenant-General Sir Aylmer Hunter-Weston (Bute and North Ayrshire), Colonel Archibald Shaw (Renfrew West), Colonel Chichester de W Crookshank (Berwick and Haddington), Colonel Sir Alexander Sprot (Lanark North), and Brigadier-General John Charteris (Dumfries); and naval officers by Commander Guy Fanshaw (West Stirling and Clackmannan), Commander Hon. Archibald Cochrane (Fife East), and Vice-Admiral Sir Arthur Henniker-Hugan (Galloway). Shaw, Hunter-Weston, de Crookshank and Fanshaw were themselves the sons of military officers of similar or even higher rank. Educationally, the servicemen had similar experiences to the landowners in that five had been to English public schools and only one, Charteris, had been to school in Scotland (Merchiston). Sprot (Harrow and Trinity, Cambridge) was the only one who went to university, the rest entering such institutions as the Royal Military Academy, Woolwich, or the appropriate Royal Navy training ship. As professional military men they had served the empire in many distant places from South Africa to China and Afghanistan, so that their local political involvement and connections were mostly less than those of the landowners. Shaw was exceptional in that he had served for a year on Glasgow City Council in 1921. Hunter-Weston and Henniker-Hugan had family and residential connections with the counties they represented, while the Englishman, de Crookshank, was linked by marriage to interests in his constituency. By contrast, Sprot, a native of Fife, had begun his political career by attempting unsuccessfully to capture Montrose Burghs in 1906, before defeating Asquith in East Fife in 1918. His inappropriate translation to Lanark North in 1923 followed his own defeat in East Fife the previous year. There appears even less to connect Fanshaw, an Englishman, with Stirling and Clackmannan, Cochrane from Aberdeenshire with Fife, and Charteris with Dumfries. Perhaps the essential point is that in the aftermath of the Great War, service officers had a particular appeal to Unionist selectors.

Seven county Unionists, all returned for the first time in 1924 – Alexander MacRobert (Renfrew East), David Fleming (Dunbartonshire), James Kidd (Linlithgow), George Hutchison (Midlothian South and Peebles), Frederick Macquisten (Argyll), Archibald Skelton (Perth, Perthshire), and Robert Smith (Central Aberdeen) – were members of the legal profession. In contrast to the landowners and servicemen they were strongly rooted in Scottish middle class culture. Six of them had attended Scottish secondary schools (high schools and grammar schools), and the seventh (Skelton) had been to Glenalmond. MacRobert and Fleming attended both Glasgow and Edinburgh Universities, Kidd and Hutchison were graduates of Edinburgh University, Maquisten of Glasgow University, while Skelton was at Edinburgh before extending his studies at Trinity, Oxford, and Smith went through Glasgow University to Trinity, Cambridge. Of the seven, only Smith (Inner Temple) and Maquisten (Gray's Inn) practised their profession in England.

The three remaining county Unionist MPs had little in common. Perhaps the most interesting was William Templeton because he was a manual worker, a wood turner. In 1909 he had become organising secretary of the Unionist Workers' League, and two years later he stood without success as the Liberal Unionist candidate in Ross and Cromarty. In 1924, however, was elected as the member for Banff, which hitherto had been a Liberal stronghold. The second, Stephen Mitchell, a director of the Imperial Tobacco Company, returned for

Lanarkshire Lanark in 1924, was distinguished as the only manufacturer to represent the Unionists in a county seat. His Scottish connections were almost as brief as his stay in parliament, which ended with his defeat in 1929, for despite his schooling at Loretto he completed his education at Jesus College, Cambridge, and resided in Gloucestershire, where he was to become high sheriff, 1945–46. Undoubtedly the most colourful, and perhaps the most liked of all Scottish Unionist MPs this century, was the old Etonian, Bob Boothby, born in Edinburgh the son of Sir Robert Boothby, manager of the Scottish Provident Association and a director of the Bank of Scotland. During the war he had served in the Scots Guards, and after failing to take Orkney and Shetland the previous year, snatched East Aberdeenshire from the Liberals in 1924,[9] and held the seat until he left the Commons in 1958.

The 1924 Labour MPs [10]

The Labour MPs of 1924 were very different from their Liberal and Unionist counterparts because they were predominantly working class – only nine of the twenty six, in 1924, were unequivocally middle class. Furthermore, whereas the nomination of their opponents mostly arose from a varying mixture of high social status, family connection, proven business acumen, and membership of a metropolitan professional elite, of barristers, City merchants and journalists, Labour members, mostly denied the benefits of a good education and respected social standing, constituted a novel source of parliamentary recruitment. Most of them were part of the socialist generation which had created the various working class institutions, both political and industrial, that in Scotland were uneasily co-operating within the tightening framework established by Henderson's new Labour Party Constitution.

The most distinct element were the miners, whose union, based on a federation of semi-autonomous county organisations, was uniquely placed to take advantage of the democratised electoral system, because their membership was territorially concentrated, (thus easily mobilised to maximum effect), and their industrial structures were readily adaptable to political purposes (Gregory: esp. ch. 9). The decentralised character of the union produced county executives from which MPs were readily found, and who were recognised by the voters as possessing leadership qualities. They were the working class equivalent of the landowners.

The second major group was the Clydeside-based ILP, a socially and politically heterogeneous collection of individuals, which associated middle class intellectuals, like Maxton, with small businessmen, such as Wheatley, skilled workmen, such as Kirkwood, and former Liberals, like Weir. Some of them had been industrially active on the Clyde during the war, but the focus of their activities tended to be Glasgow City Council, which has remained the main source of MP recruitment in the metropolis. Other strands were less significant, although the Social Democratic Federation, which had been strong in Aberdeen, did not go unrecognised, and nor did the Fabians in Edinburgh. The more radical elements of the dissenting Free Church tradition were represented by two United Free Church ministers, and the Union for Democratic Control, a means through which middle class Liberals had come to join the Labour Party, found particular recognition in Dundee, where Morel was the choice of the Jute

Workers' Union.

Although predominantly working class, Labour MPs almost inevitably possessed values and qualities which set them apart from many of their voters.[11] Practising the virtues of self-improvement, a number of them had extended their education beyond the narrow limits of their elementary schooling, strengthening their organisational capacities and propaganda skills as occasional authors and journalists. Several enjoyed a consequent measure of social mobility. Furthermore, nearly all (including the Miners) were teetotallers, some of them crusadingly so, reflecting the prohibitionist values of the ILP and the anti-drink stance of the STUC at this time. In one writer's view temperance was 'deeply embedded in [the] social consciousness' of Labour leaders and 'played the part that Methodism had for English Labour' (Knox: 22, 24). The early post-war Labour MPs were also pacifistic, most having been critical of the First World War for a variety of often confusing reasons (Knox: 46-52), which had particularly disadvantaged them in 1918. This 'hybrid moral eclecticism, associated with elitism, puritanism, and calvinism' (Knox: 52) was not too dissimilar from values and sentiments of more radical elements within the Liberal Party, whence a number of the Labour MPs themselves had come.

Eight of the seventeen Labour members from the burghs were returned in Glasgow, whose representation had a strong local flavour. Neil Maclean (Govan), James Maxton (Bridgeton), George Buchanan (Gorbals) and James Stewart (St Rollox) had been born in the city; John Wheatley, born at Waterford in Ireland, had lived in Glasgow since childhood; Thomas Henderson (Tradeston), a native of Fife, and George Hardie (Springburn), from Ayrshire and a brother of Keir Hardie, had lived there for some time before their adoption as parliamentary candidates; while Campbell Stephen (Camlachie), raised at Townhead, Renfrewshire, was a graduate of Glasgow University, Glasgow United Free Church College and the Royal Technical College. Buchanan, Stewart, Wheatley and Henderson had been members of Glasgow City Council before their election, and Maxton has served on the education authority.

The professional classes were represented in Glasgow by Maxton, a schoolteacher and graduate of Glasgow University, where he had been a member of the Unionist association and a volunteer in the 1st Lanarkshire Rifles, and Stephen, a Free Church minister at Ardrossan from 1911 to 1918, who was also a qualified schoolteacher and practised at the English bar from 1924. Both were members of the ILP and left the Labour Party in the crisis of 1931. Maxton, the most romantically remembered of the Clydesiders, had been organising secretary of the Glasgow Federation of the ILP and served on the National Executive Committee of the Labour Party, 1918–19. Following his election to parliament he served on the executive of the Parliamentary Labour Party, 1924–5, but after his appointment as chairman of the ILP in 1926 he played a critical role in increasing its estrangement from Labour, and was instrumental in the ILP's break with the larger movement after the collapse of the second MacDonald government. Maxton was never reconciled to the Labour Party, but following his death Campbell Stephen took the Labour Whip a few days before his own demise in October 1947.

Three of the Glaswegian MPs were skilled workers: Maclean, an engineer, Henderson, a carpenter, and Buchanan, a patternmaker. Maclean, however, 'an active member of the socialist movement from 1893' (Stenton & Lees: Vol. IV,

237), had ceased to work as a mechanic in 1912 to become an organiser for the Scottish Co-operative Wholesale Society. Similarly, Henderson, a carpenter in the shipyards of Belfast and the Clyde, was also active in the co-operative movement as a member of the Glasgow Board of Management. His greatest symbolic achievement was to be appointed Comptroller of the Royal Household in 1929. Buchanan, a member of the Boys' Brigade and Rechabites, was active within the United Patternmakers' Association, through which he became vice-chairman of the Clydeside Trades Council. He also gained a reputation as a street orator for the ILP, and as a strong opponent of the war. Between 1932 and 1948 he was chairman of the United Patternmakers' Society of Great Britain, and for a short time (1947–8) minister of pensions.

The three remaining members, Wheatley, Stewart and Hardie, were small businessmen, though two of them (Wheatley and Hardie) were ex-miners. Wheatley, a Roman Catholic teetotaller, publisher of religious and socialist tracts, and the most substantial of all the Clydesiders, cut his political teeth in the United Irish League before joining the ILP around 1907. As an influential member of the ILP he played a major role in reconciling the working class Catholic community to the Labour Party against hostility from their religious hierarchy (McLean). During the war he was intimately associated with the Clyde Workers' Committee, and later led the Glasgow rent strikes following post-war decontrol, which provided a springboard for his party's election successes in 1922. As minister of health in 1924 he laid the foundations of large-scale council house construction, and is often considered as the most successful minister in the first Labour administration. Stewart, the owner of two hairdressing shops, was a Fabian, founder member of the Scottish Labour Party, an original member of the ILP, and sometime leader of the Labour group on Glasgow City Council. He was closely associated with rent strikes during and after the war, and served as under-secretary of state for health at the Scottish Office in the 1924 government. Forced into the mines at the age of twelve, Hardie, a pacifist and temperance advocate, became active in the Scottish Labour Party and ILP, and later worked as a journalist on the *Miner* and *Labour Leader*. He also took evening classes, and after qualifying as an engineer established a small business. During the war he was active in the agitation against conscription, and assumed the chairmanship of the Glasgow ILP, 1917–18, following Dollan's imprisonment.

Four Labour members were elected in Edinburgh, Aberdeen and Dundee. Of these, three – William Graham (Edinburgh Central), Edmund Morel (Dundee) and Frank Rose (Aberdeen North) – were journalists or propagandists. Significantly, Rose and Graham, as supporters of the war, were amongst the few socialist returned in 1918.[12] The son of a master builder, Graham was a scholarship pupil at Heriots before joining the civil service as a clerk. Finding the career financially unrewarding, he became a journalist in the Borders, which enabled him to finance a brilliant career at Edinburgh University (1911–1917). An activist within the university Fabian Society, he was also elected to Edinburgh City Council in 1913. Reflecting his Calvinistic asceticism, (he was a teetotaller, non-smoker, and workaholic), it is recorded that his grandmother warned him to refrain from whistling: 'stop that noise, ye'll be greetin' afore nicht' (Donnachie et.al.: 46). An economist and close friend of Snowden, he became president of the board of trade in the Labour government, 1929–31.

Morel, a Frenchman, was a former Liberal, founder of the Congo Reform Association, and a leading member of the Union for Democratic Control through which he had been introduced to anti-war elements in the Labour movement, that led him, and Liberals like him, to join the ILP in 1918. Unlike Graham and Morel, Rose – a Londoner educated at an elementary school – had a distinctly working class background. After serving as an operative engineer, he became a journalist and wrote the official history of the Labour Party. He was the first of a small line of non-Scots to represent Aberdeen North. Like Graham, Shiels was also a member of the Fabian Society, Edinburgh City Council, and pro-war: indeed, he saw active service, and was awarded the Belgian Croix de Guerre. Having left school at the age of twelve, he had trained as a professional photographer, but following the war had taken the advantage of a government grant to qualify as a medical doctor from Edinburgh University in 1924. In the second Labour administration he was under-secretary of state for India.

By 1924, David Kirkwood (Dumbarton Burghs), William Watson (Dunfermline Burghs), Hugh Murnin (Stirling & Falkirk Burghs) and Thomas Kennedy (Kirkcaldy Burghs) had expelled the Liberals from four predominantly industrial burgh districts, and Rosslyn Mitchell had captured Paisley from Asquith. Both Murnin and Watson were miners. Murnin, who had entered the pit at the age of nine, was of Irish Roman Catholic extraction, and had been active in the United Irish League. A checkweighman, he became president of the National Union of Scottish Miners (NUSMW) in 1920, and later president of the Miners' Federation of Great Britain (MFGB). An alumnus of Donibristle elementary school, in his native Fife, Watson became a collier at the age of twelve. A militant teetotaller, he joined the ILP, and following two years at Ruskin College became a political organiser for the Scottish Miners from 1908 to his election in 1922, and served on Fife County Council from 1912 to 1930. David Kirkwood, a Glaswegian-born engineer, United Presbyterian and Good Templar, treasurer of the Clyde Workers' Committee (which landed him in prison during the war), and friend of Winston Churchill, who wrote the preface to his autobiography, was one of the more extrovert Red Clydesiders. For fifty years he was active in the Engineers' Union, served for a shorter period on Glasgow City Council, and spent twelve years as a member of the National Administrative Council of the ILP. In 1931 he broke with the Labour Party and took the ILP whip, but it was probably his trade union background that persuaded him to mend his fences with Labour in 1933. His *Life of Revolt* was crowned in 1951 when he joined the House of Lords.

The more Marxist tradition in British socialism was represented by Kennedy, the son of an Aberdeenshire gamekeeper and the son-in-law of an Aberdeen fish curer. As a member of the Social Democratic Federation, he spent seven years as a lecturer on socialism for *The Clarion*, became general secretary of the party, and contested Aberdeen North for the SDF in 1906 and January 1910. In 1912 he became active in the British Socialist Party (later leading its pro-war faction, the National Socialist Party), before joining the Royal Army Medical Corps as a volunteer in 1914. As a Labour MP (the NSP joined the Labour Party in 1918), he served as lord commissioner of the treasury in 1924, and as chief whip, 1927–31. The nemesis of Asquith, English-born Mitchell, was the son of an evangelical preacher, and a graduate of Hillhead High School and Glasgow University, where he organised a successful rectorial campaign on behalf of

Rosebery. From 1909 to 1925 (and from 1932) he was a member of Glasgow City Council, and in December 1910 was the Liberal parliamentary candidate in Bute. Sympathetic to Wheatley's housing policies, he drew close to the ILP, and defended rent strikers and Clydesiders prosecuted under the Defence of the Realm Act. In 1918 he joined the ILP, and unsuccessfully fought Bonar Law at the general election in Glasgow Central.

Six of the nine Labour county MPs elected in 1924 were miners – William Adamson (West Fife), James Brown (South Ayrshire), Duncan Graham (Lanarkshire Hamilton), John Robertson (Lanarkshire Bothwell), James Welsh (Lanarkshire Coatbridge), and Joseph Westwood (South Midlothian and Peebles). Adamson, 'respectable and dull-witted' (Webb *in* Pelling: 46) had represented his fellow Fifeshire miners since December, 1910. In 1917 he became chairman of the Parliamentary Labour Party and, 'as weak and ineffective as any man who ever held the post,'[13] leader from 1918 to 1921. Nevertheless, he served as Scottish secretary in the first two Labour governments. At the election of 1931, however, Adamson lost his seat to a Unionist because he divided the working class vote with Willie Gallacher, a Communist, who went on to win the seat in 1935. Brown, born in a mining village in Ayrshire, and Graham, a native of Airdrie, returned along with Adamson in 1918, both represented constituencies with which they had a life-long association. A collier since the age of twelve, Brown, a Good Templar, having held various posts in the Ayrshire Miners' Union, became secretary of the NUSMW from 1917 to 1936, and served on the executive of the MFGB. For fifty years he served as a Church of Scotland sunday school teacher, and in 1924 and 1929–31 was lord high commissioner to the General Assembly, the first commoner to hold the post for nearly 300 years. Graham, a checkweighman, and former Liberal activist who had joined the ILP in 1894, had been a political organiser of the Lanarkshire Miners from 1908 to 1918, when he became general secretary of the county union until his death in 1942. He also served on the executive of the NUSMW, 1928–1930, and of the MFGB in 1920 and 1929. Similarly, Robertson, a junior treasury minister in 1924, was active within the union and was sometime chairman of the NUSMW. The industrial-political character of the Miners' Union was underscored by the return of Shropshire-born Westwood, an active member of the Salvation Army, who was Fifeshire industrial organiser of the NUSMW from 1916 to 1929. Having begun his working career as a draper's apprentice and a messenger boy, he served as Scottish secretary from 1945 and 1947. A friend of Robert Smillie, Welsh, was yet another miners' agent to represent his native county and to rise within his union to become both vice-president of the Lanarkshire County Union and a member of the executive of the MFGB. He was also a director of the Douglas Water Co-operative Society, novelist, and poet. His maiden Commons speech was printed by the ILP as a pamphlet entitled *The King and the Miner: a contrast*.

The three non-miner county MPs were William Wright (Lanarkshire Rutherglen), Lauchlan Weir (East Stirling and Clackmannan), and the Rev James Barr (Lanarkshire Motherwell). Wright, an Englishman, Anglican lay reader, author and poet, had worked as an ILP organiser in South Wales, and at the time of his election was employed by the co-operative movement in Scotland. Son of a police constable, and grandson of a crofter evicted from Mull by the Duke of Argyll, Weir, journalist, actor, sailor and teacher, was a graduate of Milngavie

High School and Glasgow University. He founded the Glasgow Socialist Teachers' Society, and as 'Captain Swing' wrote a regular column for *Forward.* Although himself a native of Glasgow, his father came from Islay, and before joining the Labour Party Weir had stood on behalf of the Highland Land League in Argyll, 1918. From 1924 to 1931 he served as MacDonald's PPS, but following the formation of the National Government penned *The Tragedy of Ramsay MacDonald,* 'perhaps the most savage and derisory biography since the days of Swift' (Middlemas quoted *in* Knox: 269). James Barr, like Campbell Stephen, was a United Free Church Minister. Born in Ayrshire, he was educated at Kilmarnock Academy, Glasgow University and Glasgow Free Church College. A radical Liberal and pacifist, he opposed the Boer War and the Boy Scouts, supported Scottish nationalism (later becoming president of the Scottish Home Rule Association), and prohibition, and worked closely with ILP members on the Glasgow School Board. In 1913 he was made a life-long member of the Boilermakers' Society after he had supported them, as a minister in Govan, during a lock-out. During the Great War he was a member of the UDC, and despite his dissidence was appointed to the *Royal Commission on the Housing of the Industrial Population of Scotland.* In 1920 he joined the ILP. In 1927 he introduced a home rule Bill. Barr later became moderator of those United Presbyterians who refused to accept unification with the established kirk in 1929.

The Scottish Prohibitionist

The Scottish Prohibition Party was founded in 1901 by Edwin Scrymgeour, a Methodist and former ILPer, whose father had been both a Conservative and a Chartist. Born in Dundee and educated at its West End Academy, before becoming a clerk, he shared the representation of his native city from 1922 to 1931 with Labour. The Party had numerous small branches, and its organ, *The Scottish Prohibitionist,* described by Scrymgeour as 'The Torch of God' had a circulation of around 10,000. A burgh and parish councillor at various times over a 25-year period, his parliamentary ambitions were not only helped by his professed socialism but the strength of teetotalism within the Labour movement. Temperance was also popular with the new female electorate, so that while he failed to benefit from the second votes of Communist electors, which went overwhelmingly to Labour, he was compensated by the receipt of second votes from a significant minority of Liberals and Unionists. Scrymgeour was also very much in favour of home rule, which commended him to the Irish electorate, and, as a pacifist, had opposed the war, giving assistance to the No-Conscription Fellowship. It was singularly appropriate, therefore, that he should have run in tandem with Morel, in an unofficial pact with the Dundee Labour Party (Walker: 1970; 1979).

Conclusion

Although successful candidates for each of the parties continued to be drawn from the same sources as before the war, the collapse of the Liberals and the rise of the Unionists and Labour substantially changed the social characteristics of

Scottish parliamentary representation as a whole. The most obvious change, of course, was the emergence of working class MPs, a direct consequence of Labour's breakthrough following the new franchise. Indeed, consequently, the social class composition of Scottish representation in the 1920s was more representative of the electorate as a whole than at any time before or since. By contrast, the enfranchisement of females was followed by the early return of only one woman MP, and she had been an anti-suffragist. Although Jennie Lee was to join the duchess in 1929, her solitary status as the only female Scottish Labour MP, and brief sojourn in Lanarkshire Northern, only served to underline the male dominance of the socialist movement in Scotland.

Compared to 1910, Scottish MPs were also more clearly Scots in their background. Although the Unionists, like the Liberals, reflected in their education the anglicisation of the upper classes, they were much more likely than they to have economic interests north of the border, and seven of them had served as Scottish local government councillors, against only three 1923 Liberals. Labour MPs were even more parochial, in that most of them had been born, educated, and laboured in the places they represented, and just over half the burgh Labour members had been councillors. At the same time, however, most Labour MPs were already ambassadors for those localities in the political parties and trade unions which were integrating the British working class into a movement that transcended locality and Scotland itself. It was a paradox, therefore, that the most nationalised electorate, the Labour voters, were represented by locals, whereas the most parochial electorate, the unincorporated lower middle class Liberal voters, were (had been) represented by metropolitans.

Apart from social background, a distinctive feature of Unionist MPs was that nineteen of them had been on active service during the Great War, as against six Liberals and only two Labour MPs. In Labour's case, the poor military record was not accidental, indicating both opposition to the conflict and the possession of reserved occupational skills required in the pits and shipyards.

Although the departure of the Whigs to the Tories after 1885 sharply increased the differences in profile between Liberal and Unionist MPs, it was still the case that even in 1910 members of parliament in the major parties were more like each other than the disparate groups of voters who elected them. By 1924, however, the situation was reversed. The rise of Labour brought into parliament a group of Scottish MPs whose educational, social and political experiences were the polar opposite of the upper and middle class establishment, and they espoused variants of an ideology, socialism, so opposed to dominant values that they were almost certainly to the left of many of their supporters at the polls. At the same time, the Unionist breakthrough revived the traditional Conservative coalition of lawyers, landowners and service officers, which had been the dominant feature of representation in the mid-nineteenth century, and added a tranche of businessmen from the Liberal-capitalist camp. So deep were the social and ideological divisions between Labour and Unionist MPs that they could not even share wartime experiences as officers and men. Parliament, therefore, was less the place where political differences within Scotland were reconciled, than the public arena in which they were articulated and deepened.

Notes

1. His subsequent attempts to win Hull North West in 1922, 1923 and 1924 brought no success.
2. Most of the details regarding MPs in this chapter are derived from Stenton & Lees.
3. Bettyhill (named after Elizabeth, Duchess of Sutherland), was a dumping ground for crofters following the clearances in Strathnaver.
4. De Groot recounts 'Sometime in the early 1950s, Sinclair attended a party at the home of his younger son ... a studio manager at the BBC. Sinclair, who enjoyed himself immensely, nevertheless commented afterwards how surprising it was to find that almost everyone, even the women, had jobs' (239). As late as 1995, the Scottish Liberals (Liberal Democrats) still considered it worthwhile to put heavy pressure on a grand-daughter of Archibald Sinclair, Veronica Linklater, to stand in a Parliamentary by-election in Perth and Kinross.
5. Although a popular member, Elliot lost Kelvingrove in 1945. He represented the Scottish Universities, 1945-50; and was returned to represent Kelvingrove in 1950. An attempt by his wife to succeed him following his death in 1958 failed.
6. In 1920, she served on no fewer than 25 committees.
7. It is recounted that when meetings of the authority ran late, her train from Perth was delayed to suit her convenience (Hetherington: 86).
8. The present laird of Dinnet, the grandson of Barclay-Harvey, Marcus Humphrey, has also had a long almost unbroken stint as county councillor, regional councillor, and member of the new Aberdeenshire council elected in 1995. He was also selected to contest the seat, Kincardine and Deeside at a by-election in November 1991, which he lost to a Liberal Democrat. He subsequently lost his regional seat in 1994.
9. He got the nomination because 'Baillie Booth of Peterhead and his farmer friends,' were in Orkney on business during the 1923 election and were impressed by Boothby at one of his meetings (James: 53).
10. I am heavily indebted to William Knox (1984), from whose work most of this section is gleaned.
11. See particularly Knox (Introduction, 15-52).
12. Though Rose had not been an official Labour candidate.
13. 'He is a middle-aged Scottish miner, typical British proletarian in body and mind, with an instinctive suspicion of all intellectuals...In private conversation he painfully slow in speech, every word seems to need a deliberate effort. He is a total abstainer and is, I am told, domesticated and pious. He has neither wit, fervour, nor intellect; he is decidedly not a leader of men... Poor Old Sydney' (Cole: 142-3).

References

Butler DE, & Rose, R, *The British General Election, 1966*, London, 1966.
Cole, GDH (ed.), *Beatrice Webb Diaries, 1912-1924*, London, 1952.
De Groot, GJ, *Liberal Crusader: The Life of Sir Archibald Sinclair,* London, 1993
Gregory, R, *The Miners in British Politics, 1906-1914*, London, 1968.
Hetherington, S, *Katharine Atholl, 1874-1960: Against the Tide*, Aberdeen, 1989
Horne, A, *MacMillan, 1891-1945*, London, 1988.
James, RR, *Bob Boothby: A Portrait*, London, 1991.
Knox, W, *Scottish Labour Leaders, 1918-39: A Biographical Dictionary,* Edinburgh, 1984.
Lees, M, & Stenton, S, *Who's Who of British Members of Parliament, Vol. III, 1918-1945*, Sussex, 1979.
Lees, M, & Stenton, S, *Who's Who of British Members of Parliament, Vol. IV,* Sussex, 1981
McLean, I, *The Legend of Red Clydeside,* Edinburgh, 1983.
Pelling, H, *Short History of the Labour Party*, London, 1961.
Walker, W, 'Dundee's Disenchantment with Mr.Churchill,' *Scottish Historical Review, Vol. 49, 1970.*

9 *Conclusion*

As in the rest of the United Kingdom, the character of Scottish electoral politics changed dramatically following the passing of the Third Reform Act, because the diverse interests of the greatly swollen electorate could no longer be contained within the old structures. Thus, although contemporary events determined the details of the change, reform of the electoral system ensured that major developments of some sort were inevitable. In the burghs, the widening class base of the electorate broke the delicate socio-political consensus which the Liberals had nurtured over the previous half century, and assisted in the emergence of a Unionist coalition that ended their one-party character. A similar rationalisation of rural politics, based on the landlord-tenant conflict, ensured the emergence of a party system cutting across the urban-rural divide. The parallel institution of organised parties with responsibilities for nominating candidates and mobilising the new electorate replaced the informal control hitherto exercised by local notables, and increased the influence of national leaders. Thus, the equalisation of a generous franchise produced a measure of standardisation across a range of formal and informal aspects of the electoral process.

The introduction of manhood suffrage, as in other European countries, was associated with the rise of a socialist party, but the rejection of proportional representation meant that although democratisation increased standardisation through redistribution and general enfranchisement, the differences in political culture between industrial and agricultural regions became more diverse through Labour's inability to emerge as a credible force in the rural counties. It might, therefore, be argued that in the Scottish context the rural regions became peripheralised as the industrial areas became more completely integrated in the British political system.

These developments and their consequences can be summarised employing the categories adopted in the introductory chapter.

Formal Incorporation and Mobilisation. The equalisation of the franchise in 1884 incorporated just under three fifths of adult males across the country, the crucial additions being the rural peasantry and skilled artisans in the counties. There were, however, important variations to the overall pattern. In Glasgow, Dundee, Edinburgh/Leith, Clydeside, and Highland little more than half adult males were enfranchised, whereas in Aberdeen, and the counties and burghs of the rural/small town East and Borders it was around two thirds. As a result a greater proportion were enfranchised in the counties (58 per cent) than in the burghs (56 per cent). Apart from females, the industrial working class was most disadvantaged by the post-1884 system.

From 1885 the absolute number of voters increased substantially, not only because many more people were enfranchised, but also because the emergence of nationally-directed political parties ensured that uncontested elections became a feature of the past in all but a few exceptional cases. Consequently, in 1885, some 426,000 Scotsmen cast a ballot, rising to just under 645,000 in January 1910. The average turnout in burgh constituencies of 80 per cent, 1885–December 1910, was slightly higher than, 1868–1880, but fell four points to 79 per cent in the counties. The lowest turnouts were recorded in the Highland counties (70 per cent),[1] which had the rudiments of a popular franchise for the first time, and Aberdeen (70 per cent), whose level of participation was lower than that in the Eastern counties (72 per cent). The mobilisation of electors continued to be at its greatest in the Borders (89 per cent in the burghs and 86 per cent in the counties), closely followed by the industrial West (84 per cent in the burghs and 82 per cent in the counties). The interaction between formal incorporation and mobilisation of registered electors meant that in January 1910, participation of all adult males varied between just under two fifths in the Highland counties and 45 per cent in Glasgow to more than 55 per cent in the Borders as a whole (see Table 9.1).

Table 9.1: Formal Incorporation and Mobilisation, 1884–1910

		Mobilisation	
		High	**Low**
Formal Incorporation	**High**	Borders (C) Borders (B)	Aberdeen East (C) East (B)
	Average	Highland (B)	Central (B)
	Low	Dundee Edinburgh Glasgow Clydeside (C) Clydeside (B)	Highland (C)

B=Burghs C=Counties.
Central Counties occupy a median position respecting both the level of formal incorporation and the degree of mobilisation.

Democratisation brought a dramatic increase in the number of voters, almost doubling from December 1910 to 1.1m in 1918, to 1.66m in 1924, to 2.1m in 1929. At the same time, however, it was accompanied by a sharp drop in turnout, which was in contrast to what had followed previous franchise extensions. Excluding the peculiar case of 1918, the average constituency turnout, 1922–1929, was only 71 per cent, about the same as 1832–1865, but around nine per cent lower than between 1868 and December 1910. There was not, however, a close association between regions with greatly increased electorates and those with greatly lowered turnouts. The highest levels of participation, 1922–1929, came in Dundee (80 per cent), the West (75 per cent), Glasgow (75 per cent), Central (75 per cent) and the Borders (76 per cent), and, as previously, was at its lowest in the Highlands (51 per cent), Aberdeen (61 per cent), and the East (67 per cent). In Edinburgh/Leith it was a modest 70 per cent.

Activation. The maintenance of high turnouts following the Third Reform Act indicated that the new classes of voters, particularly in urban/industrial regions, where agitation for an expanded franchise had been considerable, were quickly absorbed into the electoral process, and although turnout dropped after 1918 there is no evidence that the newly enfranchised in class terms were less likely to participate than those previously enrolled. Such high levels of incorporation were clearly assisted by the emergence of political parties across the spectrum. Nor should the role played by trade unions and trades councils, the Orange Order, and the United Irish League, be ignored in the provision of fora for stimulating political participation by working class electors.

After 1884, the socialist parties and miners' unions had increasing success in getting candidates elected to local authorities and school boards. The full impact of working class enfranchisement, however, was not realised until 1922, when skilled manual workers were returned to parliament in large numbers, the Fourth Reform Act having more immediate impact on changing the social characteristics of MPs than any of its predecessors.

In rural constituencies after 1884, the Highland Crofters were sufficiently well-organised to wrest parliamentary representation from the landlords, and elected MPs who were associated with their movement. On the other hand, no crofter became an MP, and crofter participation in county government waned after the first set of elections. By 1895 the Crofters Party had been absorbed into mainstream Gladstonian Liberalism. Similarly, in other rural areas, while tenant farmers and small townsmen formed the backbone of the new Liberal associations, they were content to leave parliamentary representation mostly to London-based outsiders suggested by the whips, and tenant farmers showed almost no interest in contesting seats on the new county councils. Unionist associations, particularly when it came to candidate selection, were dominated by the landed gentry. The main extra-party organisation was the National Farmers' Union, which played an important role in consolidating the agricultural community as a whole behind the Unionists in the decade after 1918. Apart from voting, the rural working class was politically inactive, and weakly aligned to the political system.

The 'class' of electors least activated were women, who made a breakthrough neither in terms of local government nor parliamentary representation, and one suspects were a contributory factor to the drop in turnout. Their inability to realise a fuller emancipation following enfranchisement invites at least a volume of explanation, but three short points might be mentioned here. First: the 1918 Labour Party Constitution and the particularly close association in Scotland between Labour and the trade unions biased candidate selection towards active trade unionists, who were almost exclusively male; second: a general presumption (shared by many women) across the political spectrum that political leadership should be a male preserve; and third: females had no party to promote their distinctive interests as the Liberals had done for the new middle class electors in the nineteenth century and Labour had done for the working class after 1918.[2]

Politicization. The degree of intrusion by national parties into local politics in

Scotland has been historically low. Before the 1960s the Liberals and Unionists did not intervene in local government elections. The major exceptions were the socialist parties, who began presenting candidates from the middle 1880s, and systematically after 1918. The weakness of Labour in rural/small town areas, however, meant that its local government impact was limited to urban/ industrial regions.

The variable impact of Labour in local government elections sharpened the contrast between urban/industrial and rural/small town political culture. In the former, anti-socialist candidate-based alliances of Independents, Progressives etc., consisting of Unionists, Liberals and non-partisans outside the orbit of the national parties, were established to resist the challenge on the left; whilst in the latter, candidates drawn from traditional elites stood without party labels whatsoever. In the former, local elections were routinely fought across virtually all wards, but in the latter contested elections were the exception. Thus, while urban/industrial local elections were a somewhat distorted version of the national battle, in the rural counties the introduction of the elective principle had a minimal impact.

Regional Levels of Integration, 1918–1929. In 1918 most adults were registered to vote, though the realisation of enfranchisement was regionally varied. The active core of the system was formed by industrial Scotland (Dundee, Glasgow, Central and West), centred on the coalfields, and areas dominated by shipbuilding and heavy engineering, characterised by high levels of politicisation, shading away to the rural peripheries of Highland and the East, characterised by low levels of politicisation (see Table 9.2). The exceptions were Aberdeen and Edinburgh,[3] where, despite relatively high levels of politicisation turnout in general elections was low, and Borders,[4] where general election turnout was high despite a non-partisan culture in local politics. With the exception of Edinburgh, this replicated the pattern established between 1885 and December 1910, although it must be stressed that in some industrial areas in that earlier period a high turnout was offset by low levels of registration.

Table 9.2: Politicisation and Mobilisation, 1918–1929

		Mobilisation	
		High	**Low**
Politicisation	**High**	Dundee Glasgow Central West	Aberdeen Edinburgh
	Low	Borders	East Highland

In many respects democratisation increased the differences between the centre and the peripheries because it was associated with the break-up of the Liberal

Party, whose functional-economic alliance between rural and urban radicalism could not be replicated by the Labour Party. Consequently, the increasingly class-oriented conflict of the industrial centre was not paralleled in the agricultural counties. Indeed, rural politics became less socially polarised because the electoral marginalisation of the primary producing periphery following redistribution increased the need for a cross-partisan communal defence against a polity dominated by urban interests. The assumption of that role by the Unionists and National Liberals was assisted by the resolution of the conflict between landlord and tenant farmer, coupled with their mutual fear of land nationalisation and a common interest in agricultural protection. A virtual monopoly of rural representation, allied in urban areas to the working class Orange vote and middle class fear of socialism, was to secure Unionist rule for some 30 years after 1931.

Democratisation, Scotland and the United Kingdom. The various extensions of the franchise weakened the political distinctiveness of Scotland as a whole not simply because the formal arrangements were standardised with those of England and Wales, but because urbanisation and industrialisation mobilised the new electorate on class and religious lines which transcended both the English and Irish borders. Consequently, parties with a peculiarly Scottish focus failed to develop. In some measure the Liberals and Labour gestured to territorial sentiment with their espousal of Scottish home rule, but there was little evidence it resonated with their voters. Indeed, Irish nationalism was more important in Scotland than Scottish nationalism, and Roman Catholics supporting the Liberals and Labour were fearful that Scottish home rule would pose a threat to their communal interests. Rather it was the Unionists, with their defence of traditional Presbyterian institutions and cultural values, who emerged to defend Scottishness, as defined by the Treaty of Union, against the secularism and Roman associations of Labour. The refusal of the Scottish Unionists to rename themselves Conservatives, as the English party had done following Irish independence, represented a greater concession to the Scottish political dimension than had the uncompromisingly centrist Labour constitution of 1918.

The major exception to the general pattern was the Crofters' Party, whose clientele, like the Irish Roman Catholic peasantry, were divided by class, language, religion[5] and general culture from their indifferent or hostile landlords. Had they been more numerous they might well have become the focus of a more general Scottish-based Parnellite political movement, but being confined to only six constituencies they lacked the critical mass not only to extend their influence but to survive as an independent political party.

Despite the failure of Crofters to sustain a national or local movement of peripheral non-elites, the rural regions remained imperfectly integrated within the polity, as indicated by their low level of politicisation. Attempts to complete the process were delayed until the 1970s, when, following local government reorganisation, the Scottish National Party began to mobilise low status Eastern rural/small town electors into a credible independent political force for the first time, challenging the non-partisan culture of local politics and the Conservative monopoly of parliamentary representation. In this context, therefore, the SNP is a function of the 50-year time lag between the enfranchisement and politicisation of rural non-elites, who have provided the party a 'natural' (perhaps only natural) constituency. The politicisation of the Borders and Highland, where the independent tradition in local politics has been particularly strong, has proved more difficult for the SNP and other parties to crack. The process of political integration, therefore, has yet to be completed.

The Constituency System. The major inhibition to the modernisation of the electoral system was the retention of single member constituencies, which, with the odd exception, had been a basic feature of the Scottish electoral process since 1707. Had some form of proportional representation been introduced in 1918 it would have hastened the integration of rural politics into the national system by making it possible for Labour to establish a credible presence outside the industrial areas, arresting their drift towards a-politicism. Proportional representation, with its emphasis on the maximisation of votes rather than on discrete relative majorities, might also have stimulated a greater development of party electoral organisation and increased mobilisation.

More generally, the survival of the traditional constituency system raises the question as to whether its maintenance was not fundamentally at odds with a democratised electoral system, because its principle of representation assumed a plethora of homogeneous corporate interests integrated at the local level (geographically-based constituencies), whereas franchise reform, born out of liberalism, was premised on individual electors possessing views and interests which divided and transcended locality (nationally-based constituencies). Before 1885, the weakness of national political parties (the practical expression of nationally-based constituencies), meant that the maintenance of single member seats was compatible with reform because politics remained locally-based; and the slow movement towards constituencies based on equal numerical size effectively responded to the increasing claims of national constituencies at least until 1918. Whether the maintenance of more or less equal-size electoral districts since 1918 has continued to satisfy democratic aspirations is more difficult to sustain because it continues to discount national support in favour of discrete concentrations. In the twentieth century context, equal electoral districts as an expression of the democratic principle of one vote: one value is less than self-evident.

Finally, the ambiguities of the principles behind the reforms of 1918–28 were part of the wider constitutional incoherence which has always run through British constitutional theory and practice, in which contemporary notions of reform have been tempered by the accumulation of tradition and naked self-interest. With respect to the electoral system, the extensions of the franchise and the realisation of adult suffrage indicated a triumph for reform, whereas preservation of single member constituencies and first past the post represented the influence of traditional values and interests. Thus, while democrats might celebrate the universal adult franchise, they might also ponder the observation of Sir Stafford Northcote that: ‘It is upon the redistribution of seats that power, and the characteristics of our legislation, are to be founded’ (*Hansard*, 285: 459).

Notes

1. In the two Highland Burghs, however, turnout averaged 86 per cent.
2. See Gordon for a discussion of the problems faced by female trade unionists in assuming a prominent place in the labour movement in Scotland before the Great War.
3. An important difference between Aberdeen and Edinburgh and other urban/industrial regions is that they lacked the large-scale industries which were associated with the higher levels of working class mobilisation and politicisation.
4. The distinctively high turnouts in the Borders reflect a region of high political mobilisation over a lengthy period stimulated by historically small constituencies, a political active landlord class, and the geographical proximity of this 'Inner Periphery' to the centre.
5. Of course, the crofters themselves were also divided by religion, principally between Roman Catholics and the staunchly anti-Papist Free Presbyterians.

References:

Gordon, E, *Women and the Labour Movement in Scotland, 1850-1914,* Oxford, 1991.

Bibliography

A: Government Publications

Statutes

An Act to Amend the Law relating to the Representation of the People of the United Kingdom, 48 & 49 Victoria, Cap. 3.

An Act to amend the Law regulating the Registration of Voters in Scotland, 48 & 49 Victoria, Cap 16.

Glasgow Parliamentary Divisions Act, 59 & 60 Victoria, Ch. 17.

Redistribution of Seats Act, 48 & 49 Victoria, Ch. 23.

Representation of the People Act, 7 & 8 Geo. 5, Ch. 64.

Representation of the People (Equal Franchise) Act, 18 & 19 Geo. 5, Ch. 12.

Parliamentary Papers

Boundary Commission (Scotland) Appointment of Commissioners, 1917–18, XXV, cmnd. 8585.

Commission of Inquiry into the Industrial Unrest, 1917–18, XIV, cmnd. 8669,

Hansard, *Parliamentary Debates.*

Letter from Mr. Speaker to the Prime Minister, 1917–18, XXV, cmnd. 8463.

Parliamentary and Local Government Electors (United Kingdom), 1917–18, XIV, cmnd. 8759,

Parliamentary Constituencies (Electors) (Scotland), 1944–45, (313), X, 109.

Return showing the distance of each contributing burgh in Scotland from the other contributing burghs in the same district of burghs, &c. 1866, (314), LVII, 791.

Return showing with respect to each Parliamentary Burgh, Division of Burgh, and District of Burgh, in Scotland, the number of Parliamentary Electors on the Register for 1895, distinguishing them as to their Qualifications, 1895, (389), LXXXIX, 315

Return showing with respect to each County or Division of County in Scotland, the number of Parliamentary Electors on the Register for 1895, distinguishing them as to their Qualifications, 1895, (389), LXXXIX, 319.

Return of the number of Rated Inhabitants in each Parish in Scotland whose names were omitted from the Parliamentary Register in 1898, in respect of Non-Payment of Rates, 1898, (376), LXXX, 755.

Return showing with regard to each Parliamentary Constituency in the United Kingdom, the Total Number, as far as possible, the Number in each class of Electors on the Register now in force. 1901, (85), LIX. 115.

Report on the Housing of the Industrial Population of Scotland, Rural and Urban, 1917–18, XIV, cmnd. 8760, 345.

Report of the Boundary Commission (Scotland), 1918, IIX, (925).

Scottish Census, 1881, 1891, 1901, 1911, 1921, 1931.

B: Commentaries

Blewett, N, 'The Franchise of the United Kingdom, 1885–1918', *Past and Present, Vol. 32*, Dec. 1965.

Butler, DE, *The Electoral System in Britain Since 1918*, Oxford, 1963.

Cay, J, *An Analysis of the Scottish Reform Act with the Decisions of the Courts of Appeal*, Edinburgh, 1850.

Dyer, M, *Men of Property and Intelligence*: *The Scottish Electoral System prior to 1884*, Aberdeen, 1996.

Nicolson, JB, *Analysis of Recent Statutes Affecting Parliamentary Elections in Scotland*, Edinburgh, 1885.

C: Elections

Ball, SR, 'Asquith's Decline and the General Election of 1918,' *Scottish Historical Review*, LXI, 1982.

Brash, JI, *Papers on Scottish Electoral Politics, 1832–1854*, Edinburgh, 1974.
Cook, AB, 'Gladstone's election for the Leith district of burghs, July 1886', *Scottish Historical Review*, Vol. 49, 1970.
Donald, J, *Past Elections in Greenock*, Greenock, 1933.
Kellas, JG, 'The Mid-Lanark By-Election (1888), and the Scottish Labour Party (1888–1894),' *Parliamentary Affairs*, Vol. 18, 1965.
Shedden, Sir Lewis, *The Parliamentary History of Kilmarnock*, Kilmarnock, 1929.
Walker, W, 'Dundee's Disenchantment with Churchill,' *Scottish Historical Review*, Vol. 49, 1970.

D: Members of Parliament

Forster, J, *Members of Parliament: Scotland*, London, 1892.
Knox, W, *Scottish Labour Leaders, 1918–39: A Biographical Dictionary*, Edinburgh, 1984.
Stenton, M, & Lees, S, *Who's Who of British Members of Parliament, Vol. II, 1886–1918*, Sussex, 1978.
Stenton, M, & Lees, S, *Who's Who of British Members of Parliament, Vol. III, 1919–1945*, Sussex, 1979.
Stenton, M, & Lees, S, *Who's Who of British Members of Parliament, Vol. IV, 1946–1979*, Sussex, 1981.
Stephen, Sir L, & Lee, Sir S, *The Dictionary of National Biography, Vol. XVII*, London, 1917.

E: Miscellaneous (Scotland)

Aberdeen Daily Free Press.
Aberdeen Journal.
Arnot, RP, *A History of the Scottish Miners, from the earliest times*, London, 1955.
Buckley, KD, *Trade Unionism in Aberdeen, 1878–1900*, Edinburgh, 1955.
The Catholic Directory and Clergy and Laity, 1923, Edinburgh, 1923.
Crapster, BL, 'Scotland and the Conservative Party in 1876,' *Journal of Modern History*, Vol. XXXIX, 355-60.
Crowley, DW, 'The Crofters Party, 1885–92,' *Scottish Historical Review*, Vol. 35, 1956.
Donnachie, I, (ed) et.al., *Forward! Labour Politics in Scotland, 1888–1988*, Edinburgh, 1989.
Dyer, M, *The Politics of Kincardineshire*, (unpublished Ph.D.) Aberdeen, 1974.
Farquharson, R, *The House of Commons from Within*, London, 1912.
Forward.
The [Glasgow] Herald.
Gordon, E, *Women and the Labour Movement in Scotland, 1850–1914*, Oxford, 1991.
De Groot, GJ, *Liberal Crusader: The Life of Sir Archibald Sinclair*, London, 1993.
Hetherington, S, *Katharine Atholl, 1874–1960: Against the Tide*, Aberdeen, 1989.
Horne, A, *Macmillan, 1891–1945*, London, 1988.
Hunter, J, 'The Politics of Highland Reform, 1873–1895,' *Scottish Historical Review*, Vol. 44, 1965.
Hutchison, ICG, *A Political History of Scotland*, Edinburgh, 1986.
James, RR, *Bob Boothby: A Portrait*, London, 1991.
Kellas, JG, 'The Liberal Party and the Scottish Church Disestablishment Crisis,' *English Historical Review*, Vol. 79, 1964.
Kellas, JG, 'The Liberal Party in Scotland, 1876–95,' *Scottish Historical Review*, Vol. 45, 1965.
Kellas, JG, *Modern Scotland: The Nation Since 1880*, London, 1968.
Mackie, JB, *The Life and Work of Duncan McLaren*, 2 Vols, London, 1888.
McCaffrey, JF, 'The Origins of Liberal Unionism in the West of Scotland,' *Scottish Historical Review*, Vol. 50, 1971.
McGhee, S, 'Carfin and the Roman Catholic Relief Act of 1926,' *Innes Review*, Vol. XVI, 1965.
McLean, I, *The Legend of Red Clydeside*, Edinburgh, 1983.
Middlemas, RKO, *The Clydesiders*, London, 1965.
Perthshire Advertiser.
Savage, DC, 'Scottish Politics, 1885–6,' *Scottish Historical Review*, Vol. 40, 1961.
Scotsman.
Stewart, W, *J. Keir Hardie*, London, 1921.
STUC, *27th Annual Report of the Scottish Trades Union Congress*, Glasgow, 1924.

Urwin, DW, 'The Development of the Unionist Party Organisation in Scotland until 1912,' *Scottish Historical Review*, Vol. 44, 1965.
Walker, W, *Juteopolis*, Edinburgh, 1979.
Warner, G, *The Scottish Tory Party*, London, 1988.
Young, JH, *A History of the Cathcart Conservative and Unionist Association, 1918–1993*, Glasgow, 1994.

F: General

Bealey, F, & Pelling, H, *Labour and Politics, 1900–1906*, London, 1958.
Blewett, N, *Peers, Parties and the People*, London, 1972.
Butler. DE, & Rose, R, *The British General Election, 1966*, London, 1966.
Cole, GDH (edit.), *Beatrice Webb Diaries, 1912–1924*, London, 1952.
Cook, C, *The Age of Alignment, Electoral Politics in Britain, 1922–1929*, London, 1975.
Cornford, J, 'The Transformation of Conservatism in the Late Nineteenth Century, *Victorian Studies*, Vol. 7, 1963.
Craig, FWS, *British Parliamentary Election Results, 1918–1949*, Glasgow, 1969.
Craig, FWS, *British Parliamentary Election Results, 1885–1918*, London, 1974.
Craig, FWS, *British Electoral Facts, 1832–1987*, Aldershot, 1989.
Dunbabin, JPD, 'Parliamentary Elections in Great Britain, 1869–1900: A Psephological Note,' *English Historical Review*, Vol. 86, 1966.
Gregory, R, *The Miners in British Politics, 1906–1914*, London, 1968.
Jones, A, *The Politics of Reform, 1884*, Cambridge, 1972.
Kinnear, M, *The British Voter, An Atlas and Survey Since 1885*, London, 1968.
Morgan, KC, *Wales in British Politics*, Cardiff, 1963.
Pelling, H, *Short History of the Labour Party*, London, 1961.
Pelling, H, *Social Geography of British Elections, 1885–1910*, London, 1967.
Pugh, M, *Electoral Reform in War and Peace, 1906–18*, London, 1978.
Rokkan, S, *Citizens, Elections, Parties*, Oslo, 1970.
Seymour, C, *Electoral Reform in England and Wales*, New Haven, 1916.
Walker, W, *Juteopolis*, Edinburgh, 1979.
Whitaker's Almanac.

Key to Appendices

L – Liberal
Lab – Labour
C – Conservative
Croft – Crofter
LU – Liberal Unionist
IndL – Independent Liberal
Co.U – Co.Unionist
U – Unionist
Co.L – Co.Liberal
NL – National Liberal
Co.Lab – Co.Labour
Ind.Lab – Independent Labour
Com – Communist
Prohib – Prohibitionist

APPENDIX A

Party Support in Scottish Burgh Constituencies, 1832–1880

	1832	1835	1837	1841	1847	1852	1857	1859	1865	1868	1874	1880
Major Cities												
Aberdeen	L	L	L	L	L	L	L	L	L	L	L	L
Dundee	L	L	L	L	L	L	L	L	L	2L	2L	2L
Edinburgh	2L	2L	2L	2L	2L	2L	2L	2L	2L	2L	2L	2L
Glasgow	2L	2L	2L	2L	2L	2L	2L	2L	2L	3L	2L/C	3L
Single Burghs												
Greenock	L	L	L	L	L	L	L	L	L	L	L	L
Paisley	L	L	L	L	L	L	L	L	L	L	L	L
Perth	L	L	L	L	L	L	L	L	L	L	L	L
Burgh Districts												
Ayr	L	L	L	L	L	L	L	L	L	L	C	L
Dumfries	L	L	L	L	L	L	L	L	L	L	L	L
Elgin	L	L	L	L	L	L	L	L	L	L	L	L
Falkirk	L	L	L	C	C	C	L	L	L	L	L	L
Haddington	L	L	L	C	L	L	L	L	L	L	L	L
Hawick										L	L	L
Inverness	C	C	L	L	L	L	L	L	L	L	L	L
Kilmarnock	L	L	C	L	L	L	L	L	L	L	L	L
Kirkcaldy	L	L	L	L	L	L	L	L	L	L	L	L
Leith	L	L	L	L	L	L	L	L	L	L	L	L
Montrose	L	L	L	L	L	L	L	L	L	L	L	L
St Andrews	L	L	L	L	L	L	L	L	L	L	L	L
Stirling	L	L	L	L	L	L	L	L	L	L	L	L
Wick	L	L	L	L	L	L	L	L	L	L	L	L
Wigtown	L	L	L	L	L	L	L	L	L	L	L	L

APPENDIX B

Party Support in Scottish County Constituencies, 1832–1880

	1832	1835	1837	1841	1847	1852	1857	1859	1865	1868	1874	1880
Highland												
Orkney/Shetland	L	C	L	L	L	L	L	L	L	L	L	L
Caithness	L	L	C	L	L	L	L	L	L	L	L	L
Sutherland	L	L	C	L	L	L	L	L	L	L	L	L
Ross & Cromarty	L	L	C	C	L	L	L	L	L	L	L	L
Inverness	L	L	C	C	C	C	C	C	L	C	C	C
Argyll	L	L	L	C	C	C	L	L	L	L	L	L
East												
Elgin & Nairn	C	C	C	C	C	C	C	C	C	C	L	L
Banff	C	C	L	L	L	L	L	L	L	L	L	L
Aberdeen	C	C	C	C	C	C	L	L	C			
Aberdeen East										L	L	L
Aberdeen West										L	L	L
Kincardine	C	C	C	C	C	C	C	C	L	L	L	L
Forfar	L	L	L	L	L	L	L	L	L	L	L	L
Perth	L	L	C	C	C	C	C	C	C	L	C	L
Fife	L	L	L	L	L	L	L	L	L	L	L	L
Central												
Ayr	L	L	L	C	C	C	L	L	C			
Ayr North										L	C	C
Ayr South										L	C	C
Bute	C	C	C	C	C	C	L	C	L	C	C	L
Stirling	L	C	C	C	C	C	C	C	L	L	C	L
Clackmannan & Kinross	L	L	L	L	L	L	L	L	L	L	L	L
Linlithgow	C	C	C	C	C	C	C	L	L	L	L	L
Edinburghshire	L	C	L	C	C	C	C	C	C	L	C	L
Haddington	C	L	C	C	C	C	C	C	C	C	C	C

APPENDIX B (cont)

Party Support in Scottish County Constituencies, 1832–1880

	1832	1835	1837	1841	1847	1852	1857	1859	1865	1868	1874	1880
Clydeside												
Dunbarton	L	L	L	C	C	C	C	C	C	C	C	C
Renfrew	L	L	C	L	C	C	C	C	L	L	L	L
Lanark	L	L	C	C	C	C	L	L	L			
Lanark North										L	L	L
Lanark South										L	C	L
Borders												
Berwick	L	C	C	C	C	C	C	L	L	L	C	L
Roxburgh	L	C	L	C	L	L	L	L	L	L	C	L
Selkirk	L	C	C	C	C	C	C	C	C			
Peebles	C	C	C	C	C	C	C	C	C			
Peebles & Selkirk										C	C	L
Dumfries	C	C	C	C	C	C	C	C	C	L	C	L
Kirkcudbright	L	L	L	L	L	L	L	L	L	L	L	L
Wigtown	L	L	C	L	L	L	L	L	C	C	C	C

Appendix C

Party Support in Scottish Constituencies, 1885–December 1910

BURGHS	1885	1886	1892	1895	1900	1906	Jan 1910	Dec 1910
Aberdeen								
North	L	L	L	L	L	L	L	L
South	L	L	L	L	L	L	L	L
Dundee	2L	2L	2L	2L	2L	1L+1Lab	1L+1Lab	1L+1Lab
Edinburgh/Leith								
Central	IndL	L	L	L	L	L	L	L
East	IndL	L	L	L	L	L	L	L
South	IndL	L	L	LU	LU	L	L	L
West	L	LU	LU	LU	LU	LU	LU	LU
Leith B	L	L	L	L	L	L	L	L
Glasgow								
Blackfriars & Hutchesontown	L	L	L	L	C	Lab	Lab	Lab
Bridgeton	L	L	L	L	C	L	L	L
Camlachie	L	L	LU	LU	LU	LU	LU	LU
Central	L	C	C	C	C	L	C	C
College	L	L	L	C	C	L	L	L
St Rollox	L	LU	L	C	LU	L	L	L
Tradeston	L	LU	LU	LU	LU	LU	IndL	L
West								
Ayr	L	LU	L	C	C	C	C	C
Falkirk	L	LU	L	LU	LU	L	L	L
Greenock	L	LU	LU	LU	C	L	L	L
Kilmarnock	C	L	L	C	C	L	L	L
Paisley	L	L	L	L	L	L	L	L
Borders/Central								
Dumfries	L	L	L	L	L	L	L	L
Hawick	L	L	L	L	L	L	L	L
Kirkcaldy	IndL	L	L	L	L	L	L	L
Stirling	L	L	L	L	L	L	L	L
East								
Elgin	L	L	L	L	L	L	L	L
Montrose	L	L	L	L	L	L	L	L
Perth	IndL	L	C	L	L	L	L	L
St Andrews	IndL	LU	LU	LU	LU	LU	L	LU
Highland								
Inverness	L	LU	L	LU	LU	L	L	L
Wick	IndL	L	LU	LU	C	C	L	L
ALL BURGHS								
% Liberal	74	71	74	55	48	74	77	77
% LU/C	3	29	26	45	52	19	13	16

APPENDIX C (cont)

COUNTIES	1885	1886	1892	1895	1900	1906	Jan 1910	Dec 1910
Highland								
Orkney/Shetland	L	L	L	L	LU	L	L	L
Caithness	Croft	Croft	Croft	L	L	L	L	L
Sutherland	L	Croft	Croft	L	LU	L	L	L
Ross/Cromarty	Croft	Croft	Croft	L	L	L	L	L
Inverness	Croft	Croft	Croft	C	L	L	L	L
Argyll	Croft	C	Croft	C	C	L	L	L
East								
Elgin/Nairn	L	L	L	C	C	L	L	L
Banff	L	L	L	L	L	L	L	L
Aberdeen East	L	L	L	L	LU	L	L	L
Aberdeen West	L	L	L	L	L	L	L	L
Kincardine	L	L	L	L	L	L	L	L
Forfar	L	LU	L	L	L	L	L	L
Perth East	L	L	L	L	L	L	L	L
Perth West	L	LU	LU	LU	LU	L	C	C
Fife East	L	L	L	L	L	L	L	L
Central (+Berwick)								
Fife West	L	L	L	L	L	L	L	Lab
Clackmn/Kinross	L	L	L	L	L	L	L	L
Stirling	L	L	L	C	C	L	L	L
Linlithgow	L	L	L	L	L	L	L	L
Edinburgh	L	L	L	L	L	L	L	L
Haddington	L	L	L	L	L	L	L	L
Berwick	L	L	L	L	L	L	L	L
West								
Ayr North	L	LU	LU	LU	LU	LU	L	L
Ayr South	L	LU	L	LU	LU	L	L	L
Bute	C	C	C	C	C	L	C	C
Dunbarton	C	C	L	C	C	L	L	L
Renfrew East	L	C	C	C	C	L	C	C
Renfrew West	C	C	C	C	C	L	L	L
Lanark Govan	C	C	L	L	L	C	L	L
Mid	L	L	L	L	L	L	L	L
North East	L	L	L	L	L	L	L	L
North West	C	L	C	L	L	C	L	L
Partick	L	LU	LU	LU	LU	L	L	L
Southern	L	C	C	C	C	L	L	L
Borders (–Berwick)								
Roxburgh	L	LU	L	C	C	L	L	L
Peebles/Selkirk	L	LU	LU	LU	LU	L	L	L
Dumfries	L	LU	LU	L	LU	L	L	L
Kirkcudbright	C	C	C	C	C	L	C	L
Wigtown	C	C	C	C	C	C	C	C
ALL COUNTIES								
% Liberal	72	46	56	56	49	90	87	87
% LU/C	18	44	31	44	51	10	13	10

APPENDIX D

Party Support in Scottish Constituencies, 1918–1929

	1918	1922	1923	1924	1929
Aberdeen					
North	Ind.Lab	Lab	Lab	Lab	Lab
South	Co.U	U	U	U	U
Dundee	Co.Lab	Lab	Lab	Lab	Lab
	Co.Lib	Prohib	Prohib	Probib	Prohib
Edinburgh/Leith					
Central	Lab	Lab	Lab	Lab	Lab
East	L	L	L	Lab	Lab
North	Co.U	U	L	U	U
South	Co.U	U	U	U	U
West	Co.U	L	L	U	Lab
Leith	L	L	L	L	L
Glasgow					
Bridgeton	Co.L	Lab	Lab	Lab	Lab
Camlachie	Co.U	Lab	Lab	Lab	Lab
Cathcart	Co.L	Lab	U	U	U
Central	Co.U	U	U	U	U
Gorbals	Co.Lab	Lab	Lab	Lab	Lab
Govan	Lab	Lab	Lab	Lab	Ind.Lab
Hillhead	Co.U	U	U	U	U
Kelvingrove	Co.U	U	U	U	U
Maryhill	Co.U	Lab	Lab	U	Lab
Partick	Co.L	NL	Lab	U	Lab
Pollok	Co.U	U	U	U	U
St Rollox	Co.U	Lab	Lab	Lab	Lab
Shettleston	Co.U	Lab	Lab	Lab	Lab
Springburn	Co.U	Lab	Lab	Lab	Lab
Tradeston	Co.U	Lab	Lab	Lab	Lab
Highland					
Orkney & Shetland	Co.L	L	L	L	L
Caithness & Sutherland	Co.L	NL	L	L	L
Western Isles	L	NL	L	L	L
Ross & Cromarty	Co.L	NL	L	L	L
Inverness	Co.L	NL	L	L	L
Argyll	Co.L	NL	L	U	U
East					
Moray & Nairn	Co.L	NL	U	U	U
Banff	Co.L	L	L	U	L
Aberdeen Central	Co.U	L	L	U	U
Aberdeen East	Co.L	L	L	U	U
Kincardine & West Aberdeen	Co.L	L	U	U	L
Forfar	U	L	L	U	U
Perth Perth	Co.L	U	L	U	U
Kinross & West Perth	L	NL	U	U	U
Fife East	U	L	L	U	L
Montrose Burghs	Co.L	NL	L	L	L

APPENDIX D (cont)

	1918	1922	1923	1924	1929
Central					
West Fife	Lab	Lab	Lab	Lab	Lab
Dunfermline Burghs	Co.L	Lab	Lab	Lab	Lab
Kirkcaldy Burghs	Co.L	NL	Lab	Lab	Lab
Berwick & Haddington	Co.L	NL	Lab	U	Lab
North Midlothian	Co.U	U	Lab	U	U
South Midlothian & Peebles	L	Lab	Lab	Lab	Lab
Linlithgow	Co.U	Lab	Lab	U	Lab
East Stirling & Clackmannan	Co.U	Lab	Lab	Lab	Lab
West Stirling	Co.U	Lab	Lab	U	Lab
Stirling & Falkirk Burghs	L	Lab	L	Lab	Lab
West					
Bute & North Ayrshire	Co.U	U	U	U	U
Ayrshire, Kilmarnock	Co.L	L	Lab	U	Lab
South Ayrshire	Lab	Lab	Lab	Lab	Lab
Ayr Burghs	Co.U	U	U	U	U
Dunbartonshire	Co.U	U	Lab	U	Lab
Dumbarton Burghs	Co.L	Lab	Lab	Lab	Lab
Renfrew East	Co.L	Lab	Lab	U	U
Renfrew West	Co.L	Lab	Lab	U	Lab
Greenock	L	L	L	L	L
Paisley	L	L	L	Lab	Lab
Lanarkshire:					
Bothwell	Co.U	Lab	Lab	Lab	Lab
Coatbridge	Co.U	Lab	Lab	Lab	Lab
Hamilton	Lab	Lab	Lab	Lab	Lab
Lanark	Co.U	U	Lab	U	Lab
Motherwell	Co.U	Com	U	Lab	Lab
Northern	Co.U	Lab	Lab	U	Lab
Rutherglen	Co.L	Lab	Lab	Lab	Lab
Borders					
Roxburgh & Selkirk	Co.L	NL	U	U	U
Dumfries	Co.U	L	L	U	L
Galloway	Co.L	L	L	U	L
TOTAL SEATS PER PARTY					
Co.Unionist	28	-	-	-	-
Unionist	2	13	14	36	20
Co.Liberal	25	-	-	-	-
National Liberal	-	12	-	-	-
Liberal	8	15	22	8	13
Co.Labour	2	-	-	-	-
Labour	5	29	34	26	36
Independent Labour	1	-	-	-	1
Communist	-	1	-	-	-
Prohibitionist	-	1	1	1	1
Total	**71**	**71**	**71**	**71**	**71**

APPENDIX E

List of Tables appearing in

MEN OF PROPERTY AND INTELLIGENCE
The Scottish Electoral System prior to 1884

APPENDIX E (cont)

List of Tables appearing in

MEN OF PROPERTY AND INTELLIGENCE
The Scottish Electoral System prior to 1884

Index